The Power of Populism

This book discusses the Party for Freedom (PVV), a political party in the Netherlands, founded and led by Geert Wilders. Attaining between 10 and 18% of the votes, the PVV has become one of the largest parties in the Netherlands and is the only political party worldwide without members. Between 2010 and 2012 the party supported a minority coalition of liberals and Christian Democrats in exchange for influence on governmental policy. The PVV can be viewed as the Dutch version of an ideological family of nationalist parties linked by their opposition to immigration and to the political and cultural elites. Within this family, Geert Wilders has played an important role as pioneer of a new master frame, in which Islam is portrayed as the historical arch-enemy of the West. As the main figurehead of European Islamophobia, Wilders has inspired political parties and organisations in Europe, North America, Israel and even Australia.

Examining data collected on various aspects of the party (for example, voters, activists, organisation and ideology) and employing theoretical insights from sociology, electoral geography and political science, this book analyses this controversial phenomenon and seeks to obtain a clearer picture of the functioning of the PVV. This book will be of interest to students and scholars interested in European politics and current affairs more generally.

Koen Vossen is a political historian, journalist and lecturer at the Political Science Department of the Radboud Universiteit Nijmegen, the Netherlands.

Routledge Studies in Extremism and Democracy
Series editors: Roger Eatwell
University of Bath
and
Matthew Goodwin
University of Kent.
Founding series editors: Roger Eatwell
University of Bath
and
Cas Mudde
University of Antwerp (UFSIA).

This new series encompasses academic studies within the broad fields of 'extremism' and 'democracy'. These topics have traditionally been considered largely in isolation by academics. A key focus of the series, therefore, is the (inter-)*relation* between extremism and democracy. Works will seek to answer questions such as to what extent 'extremist' groups pose a major threat to democratic parties, or how democracy can respond to extremism without undermining its own democratic credentials.

The books encompass two strands:

Routledge Studies in Extremism and Democracy includes books with an introductory and broad focus which are aimed at students and teachers. These books will be available in hardback and paperback. Titles include:

Understanding Terrorism in America
From the Klan to al Qaeda
Christopher Hewitt

Fascism and the Extreme Right
Roger Eatwell

Racist Extremism in Central and Eastern Europe
Edited by Cas Mudde

Political Parties and Terrorist Groups (2nd Edition)
Leonard Weinberg, Ami Pedahzur and Arie Perliger

The New Extremism in 21st Century Britain
Edited by Roger Eatwell and Matthew Goodwin

New British Fascism
Rise of the British National Party
Matthew Goodwin

The End of Terrorism?
Leonard Weinberg

Mapping the xtreme Right in Contemporary Europe
From local to transnational
Edited by Andrea Mammone, Emmanuel Godin and Brian Jenkins

Varieties of Right-Wing Extremism in Europe
Edited by Andrea Mammone, Emmanuel Godin and Brian Jenkins

Right-Wing Radicalism Today
Perspectives from Europe and the US
Edited by Sabine von Mering and Timothy Wyman McCarty

Revolt on the Right
Explaining support for the radical right in Britain
Robert Ford and Matthew Goodwin

Routledge Research in Extremism and Democracy offers a forum for innovative new research intended for a more specialist readership. These books will be in hardback only. Titles include:

1 **Uncivil Society?**
   Contentious politics in
   post-Communist Europe
   *Edited by Petr Kopecky and
   Cas Mudde*

2 **Political Parties and Terrorist Groups**
   *Leonard Weinberg and
   Ami Pedahzur*

3 **Western Democracies and the New Extreme Right Challenge**
   *Edited by Roger Eatwell and
   Cas Mudde*

4 **Confronting Right Wing Extremism and Terrorism in the USA**
   George Michael

5 **Anti-Political Establishment Parties**
   A comparative analysis
   Amir Abedi

6 **American Extremism**
   History, politics and the militia
   D. J. Mulloy

7 **The Scope of Tolerance**
   Studies on the costs of free expression and freedom of the press
   Raphael Cohen-Almagor

8 **Extreme Right Activists in Europe**
   Through the magnifying glass
   *Bert Klandermans and
   Nonna Mayer*

9 **Ecological Politics and Democratic Theory**
   Mathew Humphrey

10 **Reinventing the Italian Right**
   Territorial politics, populism and 'post-Fascism'
   Carlo Ruzza and Stefano Fella

11 **Political Extremes**
   An investigation into the history of terms and concepts from antiquity to the present
   Uwe Backes

12 **The Populist Radical Right in Poland**
   The patriots
   Rafal Pankowski

13 **Social and Political Thought of Julius Evola**
   Paul Furlong

14 **Radical Left Parties in Europe**
   Luke March

15 **Counterterrorism in Turkey**
   Policy choices and policy effects toward the Kurdistan Workers' Party (PKK)
   Mustafa Coşar Ünal

16 **Class Politics and the Radical Right**
   Edited by Jens Rydgren

17 **Rethinking the French New Right**
   Alternatives to modernity
   Tamir Bar-On

18 **Ending Terrorism in Italy**
   Anna Bull and Philip Cooke

19 **Politics of Eugenics**
   Productionism, population, and national welfare
   *Alberto Spektorowski and
   Liza Saban*

20 **Democratic Extremism in Theory and Practice**
   Power to the people
   Paul Lucardie

21 **Populism in Western Europe**
Comparing Belgium, Germany and the Netherlands
Teun Pauwels

22 **Extreme Right Parties in Scandinavia**
Anders Widfeldt

23 **Catholicism and Nationalism**
Changing nature of party politics
Madalena Meyer Resende

24 **Populists in Power**
Daniele Albertazzi and Duncan McDonnell

25 **The Politicisation of Migration**
Edited by Wouter van der Brug, Gianni D'Amato, Joost Berkhout and Didier Ruedin

26 **Transforming the Transformation?**
The East European radical right in the political process
Edited by Michael Minkenberg

27 **The Populist Radical Right in Central and Eastern Europe**
Ideology, impact and electoral performance
Andrea L. P. Pirro

28 **Radical Right Parties in Central and Eastern Europe**
Mainstream party competition and electoral fortune
Bartek Pytlas

29 **Ideocracies in Comparison**
Legitimation – co-optation – repression
Edited by Uwe Backes and Steffen Kailitz

30 **The Making of Anti-Muslim Protest**
Grassroots activism in the English Defence League
Joel Busher

31 **Radical Religion and Violence**
Theory and case studies
Jeffrey Kaplan

32 **Radical Right-Wing Populist Parties in Western Europe**
Into the mainstream?
Edited by Tjitske Akkerman, Sarah L. de Lange and Matthijs Rooduijn

33 **The Politics of Migration in Italy**
Perspectives on local debates and party competition
Pietro Castelli Gattinara

34 **On Extremism and Democracy in Europe**
Cas Mudde

35 **German Perspectives on Right-Wing Extremism**
Challenges for comparative analysis
Johannes Kiess, Oliver Decker and Elmar Brähler

36 **ETA's Terrorist Campaign**
From violence to politics, 1968–2015
Edited by Rafael Leonisio, Fernando Molina and Diego Muro

37 **The Power of Populism**
Geert Wilders and the Party for Freedom in the Netherlands
Koen Vossen

The Power of Populism
Geert Wilders and the Party for Freedom in the Netherlands

Koen Vossen

LONDON AND NEW YORK

First published 2017
by Routledge
2 Park Square, Milton Park, Abingdon, Oxon OX14 4RN

and by Routledge
711 Third Avenue, New York, NY 10017

Routledge is an imprint of the Taylor & Francis Group, an informa business

© 2017 Koen Vossen

The right of Koen Vossen to be identified as author of this work has been asserted by him in accordance with sections 77 and 78 of the Copyright, Designs and Patents Act 1988.

All rights reserved. No part of this book may be reprinted or reproduced or utilised in any form or by any electronic, mechanical, or other means, now known or hereafter invented, including photocopying and recording, or in any information storage or retrieval system, without permission in writing from the publishers.

Trademark notice: Product or corporate names may be trademarks or registered trademarks, and are used only for identification and explanation without intent to infringe.

British Library Cataloguing in Publication Data
A catalogue record for this book is available from the British Library

Library of Congress Cataloging in Publication Data
Names: Vossen, Koen, author.
Title: The power of populism : Geert Wilders and the Party for Freedom in the Netherlands / Koen Vossen.
Description: New York, NY : Routledge, 2017. | Series: Routledge studies in extremism and democracy | Includes bibliographical references.
Identifiers: LCCN 2016009922| ISBN 9781138123366 (hardback) | ISBN 9781315645735 (e-book)
Subjects: LCSH: Partij voor de Vrijheid (Netherlands) | Wilders, Geert | Populism–Netherlands. | Netherlands–Politics and government–21st century.
Classification: LCC JN5985.P35 V67 2017 | DDC 324.492/03–dc23
LC record available at https://lccn.loc.gov/2016009922

ISBN: 978-1-138-12336-6 (hbk)
ISBN: 978-1-315-64573-5 (ebk)

Typeset in Times New Roman
by Wearset Ltd, Boldon, Tyne and Wear

Printed and bound in Great Britain by
TJ International Ltd, Padstow, Cornwall

Contents

List of illustrations		ix
Preface		x
Acknowledgements		xiii

1 The making of Geert Wilders 1963–2006 1
A Catholic childhood 1963–1980 1
Formative experiences 1980–1990 3
In Dutch politics 1990–2000 6
A tale of two murders 11
Wilders' watershed years 2001–2004 15
The Wilders Group 2004–2006 19
The electoral breakthrough 2006 23

2 The four pillars of the PVV: the PVV's ideology 29
*First pillar: the struggle against Eurabia. The PVV's
    anti-Islamic alarmism 29*
*Second pillar: the common man, aka Henk and Ingrid.
    The PVV's populism 36*
*Third pillar: loyalty to the home country. On the PVV's
    nationalism 40*
*Fourth pillar: for the safety of the country. The argument
    for more law and order 48*
A closer examination of the ideology 50
National populism as strategy or ideology? 56

3 The PVV in action: national and international activities 62
*Representatives of the people: the PVV in the House of
    Representatives 62*
At the centre of power 70
In search of allies in Europe 76

The flying Dutchman 79
Parliamentarian, whistle-blower and media strategist 83

4   A unique party: the PVV as a party organisation   87
The memberless party: making a virtue of necessity 88
Behind the scenes 90
The PVV staff 96
A poverty-stricken party? PVV finances 101
The party model of the future? 105

5   The many guises of Henk and Ingrid: on PVV voters   110
Elections and polls 110
From left and right: PVV voters' parties of origin 112
On the periphery and in the major cities: where PVV voters live 113
Socio-cultural characteristics: non-religious, a 'troubled past', low level of education 116
Why PVV voters vote PVV 118
Driven by fear and resentment? Henk and Ingrid's rationality or lack thereof 126
Signal received? The established parties and the PVV 129
A marriage crisis and the longing for a new cocoon 131

Conclusion   139

Appendix   143
Bibliography   147
Index   159

Illustrations

Figure

5.1	Percentage of the votes for the PVV in parliamentary elections, 2010	114

Tables

3.1	LexisNexis newspaper research results, 1 January 2007–31 December 2009	85
3.2	Institute for Vision and Sound research results, 1 September 2006–1 March 2012	85
5.1	Electoral analysis, 2006–2015	111
5.2	Political views by party choice, DPES 2010 (as presented in CBS report)	119
A1.1	Second Chamber election results, 1989–2012	143

Preface

It was a rainy Friday evening in August when I first saw Geert Wilders speak in person. In a small conference room at the back of the otherwise deserted Ahoy Complex in Rotterdam, his Party for Freedom (Partij Voor de Vrijheid, PVV) proudly presented its list of candidates for the upcoming House of Representatives election on 12 September 2012. His tall figure and bottle-blond Mozart hairstyle placed Wilders firmly at the centre of attention.

'September 12th will be Liberation Day', Wilders declared, at which his following clapped their hands and waved little Dutch flags with abandon. How many of them were there? Two hundred, two hundred and fifty at most? Once some technical hitches were ironed out, the party screened a specially commissioned election film which showed the European Union and Islam to be at the root of all the country's problems. Afterwards, some of the party leader's young assistants handed out election posters. Would we please put them up somewhere?

A casual observer might easily have taken this for the election meeting of some marginal newcomer party. I recognised the atmosphere, having attended similar meetings before – and read about many more – as part of my doctoral research into minor political parties in the Netherlands. The blend of wishful thinking, naïve amateurism, blinkered sectarianism and a pioneering spirit fascinated me. What made people cling to a dream that was so patently an illusion?

Gathered at Ahoy Rotterdam was not some ineffectual party supported by a handful of voters, however, but the third largest political party in the Netherlands; a party with 24 seats in the House of Representatives and the backing of 1.5 million voters. And far from being some failed would-be statesman or a charlatan with a messiah complex, their leader was the most famous Dutch politician in the world at the time. A man who had become, as a columnist put it as early as 2009, a 'national obsession', and whose conspicuous statements and conduct had dominated the Dutch media for over five years. Geert Wilders was the most tweeted-about person in the Netherlands, according to a specialist agency. On 21 April 2012, Wilders single-handedly toppled the minority government his party supported, by walking out of budget negotiations. This led to a general election being called and polling stations opening for almost 13 million registered voters on 12 September. Abroad, Wilders had become synonymous with the political trouble brewing in the – formerly so tranquil – Netherlands since the turn of the century. The Economist considered Wilders, together with Nigel Farage and Marine Le Pen, representatives of the European Tea Party. Especially in the two years in which Wilders and the PVV kept the minority government in power, Dutch diplomats had to work overtime to limit the damage done to the Netherlands' image.

There were more indications that the PVV was not a 'normal' party that evening. Before being admitted to the meeting, attendees were subjected to a range of safety measures that would not have been out of place in a departure terminal for transatlantic flights. Various personal details had to be submitted to the organisation for screening, far in advance. The visitors formed a long queue in the Ahoy foyer, under the grim stare of security agents who scrupulously checked each visitor's name against a list before letting them proceed to the metal detector gates and frisking sessions. Inside, I was ushered to the crowded journalists' section, packed with Dutch, Flemish, German, English and Spanish journalists. Wilders came over to the journalists immediately after his speech, patiently answering all their questions.

What kind of strange party would do things this way? What was the meaning of this bewildering blend of political amateurism, stringent safety measures and high media coverage? How could I find words for this seemingly new phenomenon?

In recent years, finding the right words to describe Wilders and his party has become a popular Dutch pastime in the media, in politics, on web forums and in pubs. Is he a hatemonger or a whistleblower, a racist or a realist, the people's advocate or a con man? Is he the voice of the marginalised, or a power-hungry opportunist? Does he create problems or expose them? Is he an authoritarian despot or a decisive, dyed-in-the-wool democrat? Does he protect Dutch culture or tarnish the country's image? Is Wilders a brave new freedom fighter in the war against Islamic fascism, or does his party actually represent a new kind of fascism?

Questions like this have been hanging over the Dutch polder landscape like a dark cloud for at least six years. Even outside their own country, Dutch people are often asked who on earth that man with the funny hair is who so frequently makes the news. In the Netherlands, the terms people use to talk about Wilders often serve as a kind of litmus test, a way of gauging where they stand politically and whether or not they are fit to be associated with. A negative opinion of the PVV can mark you out as a civilised kindred spirit to some and an arrogant pinko leftist to others. Wilders seems to have split the Netherlands into two camps. Such a highly polarised debate leaves little room for nuance; any attempt at an objective view of the party is often interpreted as too positive – in which case you are seen as a secret sympathiser – or else too negative, making you a politically correct pseudo-academic.

An important aim of this book was to study the party with detachment and dedication. Difficult though it was, I have attempted to present the PVV as a historical phenomenon, something from another age that needs to be explained to people today. To that end, I have made use of insights and theories from sociology, electoral geography and political science, as well as 'erklärendes

Verstehen' (explanatory understanding), a method widely used in historical research to explain opinions and behaviours by exploring them from the inside. I have thus endeavoured to sketch a portrait of the PVV in all its different guises. Why did Wilders found the PVV? What are the party's ideas and how does it try to put them into practice? What has it contributed to the various parliaments in which it has been represented? What is its organisational structure? How many active members does it have? And finally, who are its supporters and why do they vote PVV?

The book reads like a journey from the centre to the periphery, starting in the first chapters with a description of Geert Wilders' political formation against a background of rapid change taking place in the Netherlands. From the party's founder and undisputed leader, I go on to explore its different groups, contacts abroad, organisational structure and its voters. An image emerges of various circles that have formed around Wilders, each with a different relationship to, and expectations of, their centre. Besides close confidantes like Martin Bosma and Fleur Agema, and loyal party officials in several parliaments, there are also the silent backbenchers and candidates making up the election lists. There are the financial backers in the Netherlands and the United States, the foreign sympathisers and the volunteers putting up posters and running pro-Wilders blogs. And there are many voters – a million and a half at least – who all vote PVV with certain expectations. Finally, there are all those observing the PVV from the outside, often shaking their heads in incomprehension, who worry about the impact of the party's success on Dutch society and the country's image.

I have obtained information on the PVV through various channels. My main source was media coverage. Using the newspaper database LexisNexis, I was able to search different national and local media for reports, portraits, reconstructions, news items, and interviews with people I considered relevant. I also referred to primary sources such as Proceedings of the House of Representatives and electoral programmes published by the PVV. Naturally, I consulted the autobiographies of Geert Wilders and Martin Bosma as well as the published memoirs of former PVV parliamentarians, and made grateful use of the few scientific studies there are on the PVV and its voters. On top of that, I interviewed various people for this book (18 in total) who worked for the party at one stage but, for whatever reason, left it. For convenience's sake, I call them 'dissidents' here. While interviewing dissidents does of course raise all kinds of methodological issues – are they objective? – they were a particularly rich source of information. Four of the interviewees insisted on remaining anonymous. I would have liked to have interviewed active party members too, but all those I approached, including Wilders, Agema and Bosma, were unwilling to participate – at least, that is my conclusion from the fact that none of them has ever answered my emails. It is a fate I share with all researchers who have attempted to get in touch with the PVV so far – another distinguishing feature of the party.

Acknowledgements

The present volume is the English edition of a work that I first wrote in Dutch (*Rondom Wilders: Portret van de PVV*). In some respects, the English edition differs from the Dutch edition. First, I have added a special paragraph on the international activities of the PVV and skipped paragraphs on the PVV in provincial and local councils, which I thought were too specific for a non-Dutch audience. Second, I have incorporated information which I derived from six new interviews with insiders, who left the party after 2013. Of course, I also made use of some new publications on the PVV. Third, I have also added a description and analysis of some important new developments since 2013. Whereas in 2013 many commentators anticipated a rapid demise, the PVV seems now, in the winter of 2016, to be alive and kicking again, scoring around 25% of the vote in the polls.

The Dutch Foundation for Literature, the Documentation Center for Dutch Political Parties and the Political Science Department of the Radboud University Nijmegen granted me a subsidy for the translation, for which I am grateful. Anna Asbury and Vivien D. Glass have taken care of the translation from Dutch to English. Furthermore, I wish to thank the various 'dissidents' who were prepared to give me inside information. Thanks are also due to my Dutch publisher, Geert van der Meulen of Boom Publishing House, and to Emma Chappell, Senior Editorial Assistant of Routledge. I am also grateful to the following people for reading parts of the project as it evolved: Bart-Jan Heine, Babette Langbroek, Paul Lucardie, Bram Serrée, Henk te Velde, Gerrit Voerman and Andrej Zaslove.

Last but not least, I want to thank Maaike van Teeseling for her love and patience.

The publisher gratefully acknowledges the support of the Dutch Foundation for Literature.

Translated by Anna Asbury and Vivien D. Glass

Subsidies

Nederlands LetterenFonds/Dutch Foundation for Literature

Documentation Center for Dutch Political Parties (University of Groningen)

Department of Political Science (Radboud University of Nijmegen)

N ederlands
letterenfonds
dutch foundation
for literature

1 The making of Geert Wilders 1963–2006

There have always been political parties dominated to a large degree by their leader. Examples include Charles de Gaulle's Rassemblement du Peuple Français, Henry Ross Perot's Reform Party and Silvio Berlusconi's Forza Italia. But there is probably no other party so intrinsically linked with its leader as Geert Wilders' Party for Freedom. Not only is Wilders the founder, chairman, leading candidate and figurehead of the party, he is officially its only member. In a legal and literal sense, this makes the PVV a one-man party. It follows that any history of the PVV necessarily begins with a sketch of Geert Wilders' background and personality. Who is he? What drives him? Where did he come from? Why did he go into politics? What made him found the PVV?

Wilders' background has been the subject of thorough research through the years. There are two biographies of him, as well as various documentaries and numerous profiles in newspapers and magazines, and the PVV leader has spoken openly about his childhood, youth and inspirations in several interviews. On top of that, Wilders published two autobiographical books while still in his forties, *Kies voor Vrijheid* (Choose Freedom, 2005) and *Marked for Death* (2012).

Questions about his personality and motivations are not easy to answer at a distance without running a real risk of resorting to amateur psychology. I was, however, able to draw on various published statements and interviews given by acquaintances of Wilders to get an idea of the impression he made on his environment, and find recurring patterns. I gained an even clearer image of Wilders by incorporating specific historical and social contexts into the story.

A Catholic childhood 1963–1980

Geert Wilders was born on 6 September 1963. A late arrival, he had an older brother and two older sisters. His father held an executive position at a company that manufactured photocopiers; his mother, originally from the Dutch East Indies, was a housewife. The family lived in Venlo, a medium-sized town in the southern province of Limburg. With its own traditions, culinary culture and a dialect that is often the subject of ridicule and parody in the rest of the country, Limburg has always been something of an outlier in the Dutch nation.[1] At the time Geert Wilders was born, Limburg was, above all, a profoundly Catholic province. Families were large, schools and sports clubs were Catholic, and there was a chapel or crucifix on every corner. There was hardly another region in Europe whose inhabitants visited Sunday Mass so unfailingly, and which sent out so many missionaries. It was a given that a large majority of the electorate voted for the Catholic People's Party (KVP). In the 1963 general election, the KVP won a staggering 77.5% of the votes in Limburg. With 31.9% of the national vote, the KVP was again the largest party.[2]

Wilders' childhood in this Catholic environment was not much different from that of his contemporaries. His own memories, as well as the number of reports that have been published about his youth, sketch a portrait of a wilful, difficult boy with no remarkable talents or special interests. 'I must have driven my parents crazy', he writes in his English autobiography *Marked for Death*.[3] In his teens, he turned his back on the Catholic faith his parents had instilled in him – an easy decision for Wilders, who had never been a fanatical believer. In an interview in the Dutch national newspaper, *Trouw*, Wilders said,[4]

> I attended a Roman Catholic primary school and a Roman Catholic secondary school, and went to church at Christmas. That just about sums it up. I grew up surrounded by the Catholic faith, but it left no impression on me.

His apostasy from Catholicism fitted seamlessly into a general trend of secularisation in the Netherlands. Young adults with a Catholic or Protestant upbringing were leaving the Church in droves, embracing the new, progressive way of life spreading through the Netherlands. Seeing their support shrink dramatically, the KVP and Protestant parties decided to merge into the Christian Democratic Appeal (CDA) in 1980. The Netherlands was rapidly changing from the pious and unassuming country it had been in the 50s, into one of the West's most progressive nations, stunning the world with its libertarian policies on soft drugs, prostitution, homosexuality, squatting and law and order.[5] It was also known for what the American historian Walter Laqueur derisively called 'Hollanditis', the wave of protests against the arms race and nuclear weapons.

But while he initially seemed to fit in with the predominantly left-wing subculture of those years – with his hair in long, as yet unbleached curls, his leather jacket and a taste for what he called 'left-wing anarchist bands' like the Dead Kennedys – there is no evidence Wilders ever sympathised with left-wing politics. According to statements made by himself and others, he was hardly interested in politics at all in his late teens. The question of what eventually sparked his political interest and formed his opinions is the subject of widespread speculation in the Netherlands. The most remarkable explanation is probably that provided by cultural anthropologist Lizzy van Leeuwen, who puts Geert Wilders' political orientation down to his East Indian roots and the 'identity estrangement', caused by post-colonial trauma, which is common in that ethnic group. She even claims he bleached his hair out of shame for his origins.[6] Van Leeuwen underpins her theory chiefly with references to the conservative–nationalist attitude of many Dutch people of East Indian descent in the past and present.

However, there is little evidence that Mrs Wilders' background had any significant influence on the tastes and choices of her children, particularly as three of them would go on to develop left-wing political views. A more plausible explanation seems to lie in what Wilders himself has consistently called his 'formative experiences' in interviews over the years: visiting Israel between the ages of 18 and 19; living in the Utrecht district of Kanaleneiland; and his years working for the Health Care Insurance Board and the Social Security Supervisory Board from 1985 until 1990.

Formative experiences 1980–1990

His stay in Israel in the early 80s has also given rise to countless questions and speculations. One thing we know for certain is that after his final exam, Wilders wanted so see the world. In what was something of a rite of passage, thousands of young people in the Netherlands embarked on long, adventurous journeys abroad, the *Lonely Planet* safely stowed away in their backpacks, between leaving school and getting a job or starting at university. Wilders had initially wanted to go to Australia, but ended up in Israel because of his limited means. He worked in a bread factory for a time, stayed in a kibbutz near Jericho for six months and spent several months travelling the Middle East with a friend. Syria, like Israel, left a deep impression on him. 'Syria is full of adventure. Some places there are completely deserted. Bad roads, no street lights. In such a setting, being invited home to drink tea with twenty people is quite an experience for a hitch-hiker.'[7] There is a well-known photograph of Wilders from this period, showing a young man with long, brown curls, a downy beard and baggy clothes, facing the camera with confidence. The Middle East first sparked his interest in political issues, which seemed so much more exciting and urgent there than in Limburg. Though he did not come from a Jewish background, he has identified strongly with the State of Israel since that trip, to the point of considering it his second home country. By his own account, he has visited Israel over 50 times since 1982, building an extensive network there.[8]

Though there are probably few other Dutch politicians with such strong ties with the country, a sense of kinship with the State of Israel was by no means uncommon in the Netherlands. Few other European countries sympathised so much with the struggle that little Israel put up against its Arab neighbouring countries in the Six Day War of 1967 and the Yom Kippur War of 1973. A popular explanation for the broad sympathy Israel enjoys in the Netherlands is that it stems from feelings of guilt about the huge number of Dutch Jews murdered in the Second World War.[9] Around 1980, anti-fascism and pro-Israel sentiments went hand-in-hand – there was as yet little sympathy for the Palestinian cause.

What influence did Wilders' time in the Middle East have on his political thinking? Was it the seed of his aversion to Islam in later life? In his autobiography *Marked for Death*, Wilders reveals that his aversion to Islam did in fact originate in that period. As a young man, he had an important epiphany while backpacking in Cairo, where he contracted diarrhoea by drinking water from a tap. The epiphany was not so much that some of the warnings in guidebooks are actually true – never drink tap water in developing countries – but that Islam has a destructive effect on a civilisation. Why else was Egypt, a nation that had once been so powerful, not able to provide such basic facilities as clean water? Islam had led to deterioration, apathy and inertia, resulting in an inadequate water supply system and many sick travellers, among other things.[10]

How plausible an explanation is this anecdote? Probably not very, though this kind of story crops up in autobiographies of political leaders remarkably often. In any case, if Wilders really gained this insight in the early 80s, he kept it to himself for a long time. No one close to him seems to have noticed a sudden change in his thinking after returning from the Middle East. It is probably more likely that being in Israel and the Middle East at that stage of his life opened his eyes in a more general sense, to a world outside Limburg; a world in which politics was often a matter of life and death.

After returning to the Netherlands, Wilders completed his military service and moved to Utrecht, the fourth largest city in the Netherlands and a popular university town. By his own account, living in Utrecht provided Wilders with another important experience that formed his political vision. He witnessed the metamorphosis of the Kanaleneiland district, where he moved into a flat in 1985, from a respectable, white middle-class neighbourhood into, in his words, a small Casablanca or Istanbul 'with the streets full of Arabic or Turkish shop signs and women wearing headscarves'. Non-Muslims were intimidated, mugged and harassed into leaving. 'I have been robbed. On several occasions I had to run for safety', Wilders said in a 2013 speech in Australia.[11]

It is true that the Utrecht district, with its many poorly educated immigrants, high unemployment and rampant crime, has been considered a problem neighbourhood for years. In September 2007, a temporary ban on meetings was introduced in an effort to prevent gangs of young Moroccans from causing trouble. Even so, the memory seems a flimsy premise; Wilders' brother, who also lived in Utrecht at the time, does not remember him complaining about immigrants in particular. Nor was there any sign yet of a pronounced dislike of Islam, as he and a number of other sources testify.[12]

In Kanaleneiland, Wilders did witness the impact of a huge influx of non-Western immigrants at first hand. Many Dutch cities in the 80s and 90s saw the emergence of so-called 'black districts', i.e. neighbourhoods with a high concentration of non-Western immigrants. Many of them hailed from Morocco or Turkey, where Dutch companies had actively recruited employees in the 60s and 70s. There were also large groups of refugees from Islamic countries such as Iran, Iraq, Afghanistan and Somalia who were granted asylum in the 90s, as well as immigrants coming to the Netherlands from colonies and former colonies such as Indonesia, Surinam and the Netherlands Antilles. While the Netherlands counted 200,000 non-Western immigrants in 1970 (1.5% of the population), that number had reached 1.6 million (9.7% of the population) by the year 2000. With almost a million adherents, Islam had become the second largest religion in the country. The change in the Randstad, the urban conglomeration in the West of the Netherlands, was particularly striking; its population had gone from milk-white to a multi-ethnic society in one generation. Unfortunately, this coincided with a period in which many industries went out of business, reducing the demand for unskilled labour. Large numbers of immigrants with insufficient qualifications and command of the language ended up on welfare, losing touch with the labour market, and in many cases also with Dutch society. In 2002, unemployment among Turks, Moroccans, Surinamese and Antilleans was three times as high as among the indigenous population. A subclass of unskilled and often poorly integrated foreigners had started developing in the 80s, concentrated in tower block districts on the outskirts of the large cities.[13]

A final formative experience Wilders has often mentioned in interviews is working for the government organisation that supervises the running of the Netherlands' convoluted social security system. He quickly managed to absorb the complex matter of social security law, an achievement in itself given the difficulty of the subject. After his epic, exciting adventures in the Middle East, he was now faced with the slow-paced and somewhat boring Dutch culture of compromise. In the extensive and bureaucratic corporate Dutch administrative machine, reaching consensus and gaining public support were seen as the highest aims, even at the cost of efficiency and justice. In early interviews and in his first autobiography *Kies voor Vrijheid* (Choose Freedom, published in 2005), Wilders underlines the strong aversion to the sluggishness and bureaucracy of the Dutch welfare state that working at those two government organisations instilled in him. He discovered that employers and trade unions used the Disability Insurance Act (WAO) as an easy way of getting rid of superfluous employees. Dutch employees were declared unable to work on the flimsiest medical grounds, because for both employee and employer, this was more advantageous than dismissal. When he flagged up the abuse, however, his predominantly left-wing colleagues tended to draw a veil over it. As he writes in *Kies voor Vrijheid*, 'The public interest was sacrificed to the interest of certain groups'.[14]

In contrast to his stay in the Middle East and living in Kanaleneiland, his stint as a legal adviser did have immediate political consequences. First, it acted as an important incentive to join the People's Party for Freedom and Democracy (VVD) in 1988, the third largest party at the time and coalition partner of the CDA. For a right-wing young atheist, the conservative–liberal VVD was an obvious choice, and thanks to the considerable knowledge he had acquired of the Dutch social security system, a golden opportunity fell into his lap. By a whim of fate, the parliamentary group of the VVD was looking for a social security policy adviser in 1990. Wilders decided to apply for the position and impressed his interviewers with his extensive and detailed knowledge of a complex subject that few liberals knew much about. It was ample compensation for his lack of an academic degree or a past as an active member of either the VVD or its youth division, the JOVD.

And so his political life began with a paid job in the House of Representatives, though there was as yet little to suggest that a great political future awaited him. Unlike many of his later political rivals, the 26-year-old Wilders had not completed any graduate degrees, nor did his curriculum vitae boast a string of advisory activities. Wilders was a boy from the province, a 'practical man' in his mid-twenties, who was given the unique opportunity to prove himself in an environment where there was power and status to be earned. He was to seize the opportunity with both hands. From that moment on, politics became his vocation and Parliament his natural habitat.

In Dutch politics 1990–2000

Political life in the Netherlands takes place in The Hague, or more precisely, in and around the Binnenhof. The complex, which dates back in part to the seventeenth century, houses parliamentary as well as government buildings, and most Dutch ministries are located around the Binnenhof. The Netherlands has had a bicameral system since 1814. Of the two chambers of Parliament, the second chamber (House of Representatives) has the more power. Its 150 members are chosen by a system of proportional representation.[15] In the 1989 House of Representatives elections, the CDA and the social democrat Labour Party (PvdA) won 35.3% and 31.9% of the vote respectively. As usual, the VVD, the party Wilders had joined, trailed slightly behind with 14.5% of the vote. The low electoral threshold allowed for a series of smaller parties in the House of Representatives, such as the left-wing liberal Democrats '66 (D66), GreenLeft, a number of orthodox Protestant parties and the Centre Democrats (CD), a one-man party fiercely opposed to immigration. The CD, which had only just exceeded the electoral threshold with 0.7% of the vote, was generally considered a pseudo-fascist party and existed in complete isolation.

Generally speaking, politics in the Netherlands was neither a very spectacular nor exciting affair, and Dutch politicians tended to be capable and modest. Compared to many other countries, there was little corruption and clientelism, and people generally trusted their government – though there was also dissatisfaction, especially in intellectual circles, about the lack of profile and roots of many politicians, especially since they did not win their Parliamentary seats by being elected in a district but due to their place on the party's list of candidates.

This environment allowed Wilders to work his way up – without having to mount a campaign – from a job on the party staff to full member of the VVD parliamentary group. In the space of a few years, he went from being a rather insignificant office clerk to a fully fledged, professional politician; a Hague insider. According to former colleagues, Wilders was practically always holed up in his tiny, confined Binnenhof room in those years, working as if he was possessed: devouring files and parliamentary papers, writing speeches and parliamentary questions, organising working visits and educational trips, making appointments with various interested people and reading books and articles on a wide range of subjects. Weekends and recesses did not exist to him; Wilders was always at work. The time he did take off, he invested in placements or working visits to foreign organisations that were active in the Middle East and Israel – still his great passion in those years. Hungary and Central Europe also interested him, which was doubtless linked to his marriage in 1992 to the Hungarian, Krisztina Marfai.[16]

Otherwise, his social network consisted mainly of fellow party members, who, in the many portraits of Wilders that have been published, speak of his friendly manner, but also call him a perfectionist and a loner who no one really understood. He avoided party gatherings and contact with grassroots members as much as possible. To become a member of the House of Representatives he was required to raise his profile in his native Venlo, but was too much of a Hague politician to become a true local representative. 'He would turn up whenever there was a meeting of the local branch on a Saturday morning', a former party member from Limburg recalls, 'but as for staying on for an hour or so to chat with the members – forget it. He preferred going home to his computer, to read a report on some Catholic minority in Syria or something.'[17]

Politically speaking, Wilders had cast his lot with VVD leader, Frits Bolkestein. Bolkestein, who would go on to become an EU commissioner, won the VVD leadership in 1990, at a time when the liberals' popularity was at a low point. In the preceding years, the VVD had almost exclusively followed the lead of its coalition partner, the CDA. When the CDA of Prime Minister Ruud Lubbers decided to form a coalition with Wim Kok's PvdA in 1989, the VVD did not have a political agenda to speak of. Bolkestein would go on to develop the VVD's political agenda in the years to come. Bolkestein's political–ideological views were a mixture of neoliberal economic ideas, foreign policy realism and socio-cultural conservatism. His economic neoliberalism manifested itself in his preference for small government, fewer corporatist institutions and less negotiation with unions. His foreign policy realism was heavily tinted by his general scepticism towards lofty ideals and exaggerated ambition, a lesson he learnt from the Second World War. Unsurprisingly, he was critical of the advancing European integration and the extension of NATO, because they were happening too fast with too optimistic a view of their outcome. His socio-cultural conservatism came to the fore in his repeated call for reinstating community values supplanted by the progressive spirit of the 60s. He viewed these community values, which included a civilised nationalism, greater awareness of history, classical notions about high and low culture, a preference for traditional educational systems and an emphasis on the moral and intellectual leadership of the political and cultural elite, as the moral foundations of society.[18]

But Bolkestein was undoubtedly most notorious for being one of the first politicians to denounce the multiculturalism of Dutch minority policy. He argued that the political elite let itself be guided by a principle he described as 'cultural relativism', an idea that had become prevalent since the 60s which states that all cultures are fundamentally equal. According to Bolkestein, minority policies should be based on the assumption of the superiority of Western values and culture; newcomers from other cultures should eventually assimilate into the dominant Western *Leitkultur*. Bolkestein was referring to Islamic culture in particular – an ever more conspicuous presence in Dutch streets, especially those of large cities, since the 90s – which he said increasingly caused feelings of insecurity and uneasiness in the native population.

On the political stage, Bolkestein stood out for his aggressive debating style, untypical by Dutch standards, in that he was aiming for conflict rather than compromise. In concise sentences delivered with an almost brusque conviction, he forced his opponents onto the defensive. He also enjoyed drawing attention to taboos, before making a show of breaking them, in sometimes rambling essays and interviews on subjects ranging from the education system to the effectiveness of development aid, from European integration to the lack of remorse shown by many former communists, and from the necessity of nationalism to the failure of cultural relativism. In an analysis of the debate on multicultural society, the philosopher Baukje Prins aptly described Bolkestein's debating style as 'new realism', a genre that according to her is typified by its author presenting himself as someone with the courage to face painful facts the population at large has always been aware of, but which the predominantly left-wing elite denies out of political correctness.[19]

The press was soon captivated by this politician, so fascinating and unfathomable by Dutch standards, who was always good for an interesting quote. His opponents found refuting his arguments by no means a simple task – too much criticism could easily be construed as an attempt to nip the debate in the bud and carry on denying the truth. Moreover, various polls showed that a growing proportion of the population was increasingly worried about immigration and integration and considered them important political subjects. It follows that Bolkestein's statements on immigration, integration and Islam were a key reason, albeit not the only one, for the VVD's electoral success at the House of Representatives elections of 1994 and provincial elections of 1995; after the latter, it was even the largest party for the first time in its history.

A remarkable result, given it was also the first time the VVD had cooperated with its former sworn enemy, the PvdA, in the so-called 'Purple Coalition', which included the left-wing liberal D66 party and was formed in 1994 after the CDA's crushing defeat at the House of Representatives elections of the same year. For the first time since 1918, a coalition government was formed without the Christian Democrats. The purple coalition, led by the Social Democrat Wim Kok, turned out to be an unexpected success, helped among other things by the economic boom that gave it the financial means to soothe quite a few potential tensions. After their strong election victories in the House of Representatives elections of 1998, both parties stayed in the purple coalition.

The VVD won so many seats at that election that even the member lowest on the party list, Geert Wilders in forty-sixth place, gained a seat in the House of Representatives. In August 1998, exactly eight years after starting work for the party, he was sworn in as one of its 150 members. He soon attracted attention to himself, following Bolkestein's example, by denouncing the 'lethargic culture of compromise' and the 'progressive nonsense'. He stated boldly in an interview that,

> When something isn't right, you need to have the courage to point it out. The lethargic culture of compromise in this country means it often takes a

decade until a good idea or workable plan is realised. I dare to stick my neck out and broach subjects that are actually relevant to people. Politics takes courage.[20]

In those years, Wilders showed such 'courage' chiefly during debates about abuse of social security and the reform of the welfare state. To the horror of D66 and the PvdA, he unearthed a number of alarming facts about large-scale abuse of the Sickness Benefits Act, and argued that lenient regulations with regard to mental disability in particular were a widely-used means for getting rid of difficult or superfluous employees. In no other European country were there so many employees on sickness benefit. With his gift for striking one-liners, Wilders called the Netherlands, 'Europe's village idiot', the Disability Insurance Act a 'rudderless supertanker irrevocably heading for a sand bank' and the House of Representatives a 'Socialist social security fest'.[21] He would have liked to see the minimum wage scrapped and social services made available only to the most destitute. Increasingly, he accompanied his suggestions for drastic reform of the welfare state with a general attack on the Dutch consensus-based 'polder model' of government, which in his view was too centralised and in which trade unions wielded too much power despite being hardly representative anymore. In a controversial article published in the progressive Dutch daily newspaper *De Volkskrant*, titled 'Curb the Unions' Power', he argued that 'everything is discussed to death in this country'.[22] 'The excessive pursuit of social consensus sucks the dynamics out of socio-economic activities, which is something the Netherlands can no longer afford.' Wilders envisaged a leaner, less centralised government, guided by the needs of the individual citizen ('made-to-measure') instead of the largely unrepresentative social organisations. The Netherlands needed a neoliberal revolution such as Ronald Reagan and Margaret Thatcher had unleashed in the United States and the United Kingdom respectively.

Wilders emulated his role model, Bolkestein, in another respect: while his bark was loud, he never actually bit. At the end of the day, both Wilders and Bolkestein always adhered to the coalition agreement entered into with the PvdA and D66. In his role as a VVD parliamentarian, Wilders gave his blessing to various proposals he would later condemn, such as the introduction of the euro, the expansion of the European Union with Eastern European countries, the launch of negotiations with Turkey about joining the EU, and countless others he was to dismiss as multicultural nonsense. Working for the party, he even helped draw up a private member's bill for equal opportunities for foreigners on the labour market. There was as yet little sign of the criticism he would later voice on subjects like European integration, fighting crime, and the government's environmental and minority policies.

So did Wilders' later aversion to immigration and Islam come completely out of the blue? Not quite, though in those years, he focused his attention on Islamic fundamentalism and terrorism in the Middle East. His many travels in the region, his close ties with the Israeli embassy and countless conversations with experts about the situation in the Middle East provided him with an in-depth knowledge of emerging Islamic extremism. In the 90s, this political Islam manifested itself in various places, such as Algeria, where a bloody civil war was raging between Islamists and the secular regime; Afghanistan, after the Taliban seized power; Israel, where Hamas perpetrated terrorist attacks; and of course Iran, which had been an Islamic republic since 1979. His preoccupation with the subject became clear when, in December 1999 and over a year after being sworn in as a member of the House of Representatives, he handed in a bulky report on the dangers of Muslim extremism and weapons of mass destruction in the Middle East. In preparation for the report, he had held extensive conversations with people from counterterrorist organisations and many experts including Donald Rumsfeld, who would later become the US Secretary of Defence. Asked by a journalist whether the subject was not too remote for Dutch citizens, Wilders countered,

> On the contrary – extremism in those countries is threatening the stability of Europe and the Netherlands. It is set to become the greatest problem of the coming decade, as migration will bring extremism to the Netherlands. It is happening already, though no one seems to talk about it.[23]

But neither the House of Representatives nor the press had much interest in Muslim extremism in December 1999. The country was engrossed in the soaring stock market and Máxima Zorreguieta, Crown Prince Willem Alexander's new girlfriend. 'It is almost frightening how cheerfully the Netherlands is ringing in the next thousand years', a journalist wrote shortly before the turn of the millennium.[24] According to the polls, the Prime Minister Wim Kok's second purple cabinet did seem to rule the country to the complete satisfaction of a large majority of the population. The gross domestic product had again risen by 4% in 1999, unemployment was at a historically low level, the budget was balanced and the far-right Centre Democrats had all but vanished from the stage since their election defeat in 1998. Wim Kok enjoyed international esteem as one of the founders of the Third Way, the reconciliation of social democracy and economic liberalism. 'You were first, Wim!' Bill Clinton complimented the Dutch prime minister during a meeting of Third Way leaders in 1999.[25] The only dissenting voice was that of the Socialist Party (SP). Founded in 1972, the SP had only gained a parliamentary seat in 1994 after the Maoist sect had reinvented itself as a populist, left-wing protest party. They opposed the purple coalition's 'neoliberalism' and 'free-market fundamentalism', as well as the growing chasm between the ordinary people and the professional technocratic politicians in The Hague. In the House of Representatives and during interviews, its leader Jan Marijnissen presented himself as an authentic spokesman for these 'ordinary people', whom he felt were being left in the lurch by politics in general and the PvdA in particular.[26] The party put itself squarely on the map with a sophisticated publicity campaign, extra-parliamentary activism and very active and fierce opposition in the House of Representatives, gradually increasing its support to 3.5% in 1998, while other opposition parties – the CDA, GreenLeft – were taking a far more cautious approach. Hoping one day to become a governing party, possibly with the purple parties, they only delivered constructive criticism couched in mild terms. As a result, the Binnenhof of the year 2000 was smothered under a blanket of dullness and predictability. Who would be able to shake things up?

Not Geert Wilders, in any case. His strong but carefully dosed comments on the welfare state and his eccentric hairstyle may have made him stand out a little more than the average backbencher, and those in the know probably recognised his political talent, but he was completely unknown to the public at large. At the beginning of the new millennium, he seemed destined for a good position as a mayor, junior minister or high-ranking bureaucrat. No one then would have predicted that Wilders would be an MP five years later, under constant police protection and frantically trying to get his own political party off the ground. By that time, the optimism of the year 2000 had all but evaporated. According to many commentators, the Dutch were no longer cheerful, but 'angry' and 'confused', fearfully hiding behind their dykes.[27] What had gone wrong in the Netherlands?

A tale of two murders

The beginning of the unrest can be dated fairly accurately to 11 September 2001, the day the terrorist organisation Al Qaeda carried out a series of attacks in the United States, claiming thousands of lives. In one blow, the period of peace, harmony and prosperity that had begun with the fall of the Berlin Wall in 1989 seemed to come to an end. The 9/11 attacks caused an acute feeling of threat and insecurity worldwide. President George W. Bush called for a war on what he dubbed the 'Axis of Evil', a group of rogue states including Afghanistan, Iraq, Iran and North Korea who were threatening the West. Many in the Netherlands feared a new world war, or at least fresh terrorist attacks at home. Opinion polls were published that showed that many Muslims living in the Netherlands sympathised with the attacks to some extent, while half of the Dutch population stated that the attacks had negatively affected their personal opinions of Islam and Muslims.[28] This placed Islam, now the country's third largest religious denomination, at the centre of attention.

One of Islam's fiercest critics was Pim Fortuyn, a former sociology professor who had made a name for himself as a columnist and the author of several books. A month after the attacks, Fortuyn said in an interview that a 'cold war against Islam' was needed, which he called a 'backward, agrarian desert ideology' that clashed with Western values. Just like Frits Bolkestein and his pupil Geert Wilders, Fortuyn wanted nothing to do with the 'cultural relativism' of the progressive parties (which he called 'the Left Church') and called for a fundamental reform of the welfare state. Though he aspired to a political career, Fortuyn was not admitted to the VVD or any other party; his high-pitched, shrill voice, foppish appearance, often blunt columns and flamboyantly expressed homosexuality seemed to doom Fortuyn to an existence as a mediagenic outsider. When Bolkestein announced that he was happy to continue cooperating with the PvdA, Fortuyn decided to enter the political stage independently of the established parties – unlike many others in the Netherlands, he found the continuation of the purple coalition a 'chilling prospect'. He believed it had made Dutch politics a stultifying, technocratic affair, while the Netherlands actually yearned for a government with vision, élan and leadership. Even before securing the formal backing of a party, he immediately announced he was running for the highest post. In an interview in *Elsevier* he emphasised,

> My ambition to become prime minister is not a joke. I would never joke about that. It is not a fantasy. Every human being needs a purpose, and since my childhood, my purpose has been to rule the country. Don't ask me how, but I feel it is going to happen.[29]

Fortuyn was initially roped in to become the political leader of Liveable Netherlands (LN). This new political movement, a conflation of a number of local parties, wanted to lead the attack on the established parties. To that end, they employed an American-trained spin doctor and media expert, whose first advice was to appoint a well-known and charismatic leader. Though Fortuyn seemed the perfect candidate at first, he soon clashed with the party leaders over some of the strong statements he made about Islam and integration. In February 2002, he left LN to found his own party with a couple of business friends of his, and called it after himself, the 'Pim Fortuyn List' (LPF). As the general elections were to be held in May 2002, Fortuyn had very little time to put together a list of candidates, raise funds for the campaign and write an election programme. The latter proved to be the easiest part, thanks to his ten years' experience shining his light on a whole range of subjects as a columnist. The resulting programme turned out to be an elaboration on Fortuyn's analysis of the Dutch consensus economy, whose bureaucratic structure and entrenched agreements he claimed were out of touch with the age of globalisation and the Internet – only a drastic reform of the public sector and liberalisation of the consensus economy could bring the Netherlands into the twenty-first century. According to Fortuyn, this had not happened yet because it was not in the interest of the Dutch elite, the party members who passed each other all the plum jobs created by bureaucracy and the many management tiers.[30]

Fortuyn had another reason for thinking that the Netherlands needed a change of politics. He endorsed Samuel Huntington's vision of a future in which different civilisations would clash with each other and the strongest and most vigorous would eventually win. This meant it was the role of politics to not only cherish and nurture its culture, but to protect it from decadence and nihilism. Fortuyn argued that Dutch culture and identity had been sidelined, leaving much of the Dutch population feeling 'orphaned'. Consequently, it was essential for a new political elite to actively strengthen the Dutch identity and propagate Dutch standards and values, which according to him included such progressive achievements as the emancipation of women and homosexuals that immigrants from other cultures, such as Islam, had to accept. 'I don't feel like doing the emancipation of women and homosexuals all over again', Fortuyn declared repeatedly. In his view, a restrictive immigration policy was necessary because all the energy was needed for the assimilation of already-present immigrants into Dutch culture.[31]

Neither the media nor the other parties knew what to make of Fortuyn's candidacy, or his barely organised little party. Due to the voting system and low electoral threshold, political fortune-hunters and small protest parties had always been part of Dutch electoral folklore, but Fortuyn appeared to be of a different calibre. He dominated the election debates, partly because of his liberal and social democrat rivals' weak opposition, and the ratings soared whenever he appeared on television. Attempts by his opponents to dismiss him as a far-right extremist backfired when Fortuyn accused them of trying to 'demonise' him, and even stated that they would be responsible if anyone attempted to harm him.

His words turned out to be prophetic when, on 6 May 2002, Fortuyn was shot dead in the Hilversum Media Park by a 33-year-old animal rights activist who believed he was acting in the interest of vulnerable members of society. The murder sparked strong reactions throughout the country. In Rotterdam, thousands of people left flowers outside Fortuyn's house, while in The Hague, an angry mob marching to the Binnenhof had to be restrained by riot police. 'The bullet came from the left', a close colleague of Fortuyn's said, and many agreed with him. His followers declared on television and in the papers that Pim had been someone who had finally 'dared to say what so many thought', and had paid for it with his life. His funeral escalated into an almost pseudo religious display of affection and public emotion that reminded British journalists of the funeral of Princess Diana.[32]

Despite the commotion, the House of Representatives elections of 15 May 2002 took place as planned, though the campaign was discontinued. Pim Fortuyn won almost 1.5 million votes – 17% – posthumously. With 26 seats in parliament, the LPF shot up to being the second largest party in the country. The emotions of the preceding days did not even seem to have distorted the result: on the day of the murder, the polls had predicted the same outcome. What did come as a surprise, was the CDA ending up as the largest party; after a leadership crisis, the Christian Democrats had put forward the completely unknown and not very prepossessing Jan Peter Balkenende as a candidate. Many voters who did not want to vote purple saw Balkenende as the alternative to Fortuyn. The purple parties were hit particularly hard, the PvdA losing almost half and the VVD over a third of their voters.

As a result of the election, Jan Peter Balkenende was to form a coalition, and the inexperienced Christian Democrat found willing coalition partners in both the LPF and the VVD. In concession to the LPF, the new government presented a whole new set of proposals on asylum law, integration and immigration – they did not come to anything, however, as the LPF soon proved unequal to the responsibility. Not altogether surprising, given the chaos and anarchy that had broken out in the LPF after Fortuyn's murder: in the absence of a leader and a shared past, the LPF soon descended into internal squabbles, culminating in a flaming row between two of the party's ministers. On 16 October 2002, after only 86 days, the cabinet collapsed and fresh elections were called.

Superficially, the result of these elections in January 2003 looked like a shift to normality. The LPF lost two-thirds of its following and would face even greater losses in the years that followed. Under its young new leader, Wouter Bos, the PvdA regained much of its lost ground, winning 27% of the vote. The VVD, too, recovered a little, though less than it had hoped. The CDA was still the largest party, and Jan Peter Balkenende continued as prime minister. This time, Balkenende formed a coalition with the liberal right-wing VVD and left-wing D66, bringing two of the three purple parties back to the centre of power.

With the CDA, PvdA and VVD once again the largest parties and the smaller D66 facing an uncertain future, the old order seemed to be restored. Nevertheless, the whole episode – often called 'the long year of 2002' in the Netherlands – caused major repercussions in a variety of fields. For one thing, it showed more clearly than ever that a large part of the Dutch electorate felt alienated by the established parties. Each vote was a struggle, and new parties were now in with a chance. Fortuyn also proved that it was possible to get voters on board without much in the way of party organisation – ready access to the media and regular airplay turned out to be of at least as much value. What was more, the Dutch media had become more willing than ever to offer political newcomers a platform since Fortuyn's arrival. Not only did eccentric and opinionated outsiders like Fortuyn boost viewing figures, journalists were also afraid of missing out on certain political and social trends. After the events of 2002, they swarmed out to get the opinion of the 'man in the street', and subjects like integration, immigration and Islam shot up the political agenda thereafter. A widely held view was that Dutch integration policy had failed because criticism of immigrants was a taboo subject. Previously seen as a time of prosperity and contentment, in hindsight the 90s came to be viewed as a period of political correctness and evasion of the real issues.[33] The question whether freedom of speech was more important than the right of freedom from discrimination and insult would become a hot topic, while Fortuyn's murder had given the debate on these subjects a whole new dimension. The Netherlands, too, had to learn to live with the possibility of political violence.

The impact of Fortuyn's murder was compounded by a second murder of another extremely outspoken Dutch celebrity, the filmmaker Theo van Gogh on 2 November 2004. Van Gogh was better known in the Netherlands for his provocative remarks and black humour than his films. He called Muslims 'goat fuckers' and Jesus 'that rotting fish of Nazareth', and he ridiculed the Holocaust by joking that 'cremated Jewish diabetics smelled of toffee'. Ian Buruma accurately characterised him as someone who, out of a typically Dutch type of offensive libertarianism, pushed the boundaries of freedom of speech and progressive decency in the conviction that 'words normally were without consequences'.[34]

The murderer was a young Islamic fundamentalist of Moroccan descent who had grown up in Amsterdam. He left a note on Van Gogh's body, declaring that his primary target was actually Ayaan Hirsi Ali. In August 2004, Van Gogh and Hirsi Ali had made a film together, titled *Submission*, with the aim of exposing Islam's oppression of women. In it they projected various verses from the Koran, which appeared to justify violence against women, onto naked women's bodies. Van Gogh was not the only one captivated by this mediagenic and attractive Somali refugee who had renounced her Islamic faith; various well-known Dutch intellectuals worshipped Ayaan Hirsi Ali for her courage to criticise Islam and alert the Dutch to the dangers of too much naïvety. According to Hirsi Ali, Muslims who wanted to be part of Dutch society should follow her example and take a 'shortcut to the Enlightenment'. Though she had started out as an active member of the PvdA, she switched to the VVD in late 2002, where she was immediately put forward as a candidate for the January 2003 elections. She soon caused controversy in the VVD by saying in an interview that 'by Western standards' the Prophet Muhammad was a 'pervert' and a 'tyrant'. Her strong opinions generated a flood of hate mail which, after Fortuyn's murder, was taken very seriously, and the security measures implemented ensured that not she, but the unprotected Van Gogh, was targeted.[35]

A year and a half after Fortuyn's assassination, therefore, the previously so peaceful Netherlands was again shaken up by a political murder. The weeks after the murder saw several incidents, including arson at an Islamic school. The Dutch police also arrested a group of Islamic fundamentalists who had drawn up plans for various terrorist attacks. Naturally, the two murders were linked in the public mind – Fortuyn and Van Gogh were not only both very outspoken and mediagenic personalities, they were also equally critical of Islam and the progressive consensus. After Van Gogh's murder, the debate on freedom of speech and political correctness on the one hand and the nature and position of Islam on the other flared up as never before. Van Gogh's friends, including various authors and columnists, led the way, assisted by a number of new blogs, such as the widely read and much-discussed *GeenStijl* (literally 'No Class') which openly prided itself on its 'biased, unfounded and needlessly offensive' content.

Comparing the impact of the two murders in the Netherlands with that of previous political murders in the United States (the Kennedys and Martin Luther King) and Sweden (Olof Palme and Anna Lindh), the American sociologist Ron Eyerman concluded that the impact on Dutch society was severe enough to cause cultural trauma, that is to say a widely shared feeling of having reached a turning point. The two murders were generally viewed as a watershed, a rift in the nation's history and 'a jolt to the self-image of a nation that saw itself as more sensible, better organised and less violent than others. All the taboos about political and social correctness, at least in public behaviour, seemed to vanish.' This was replaced by an extremely dominant narrative surrounding the two murders, 'which blames the Left for creating an atmosphere in which the violent attack on political opponents was tolerated, if not condoned'. In Eyerman's words, the murders represented 'an open wound, which will remain present in the collective consciousness and continue to be available for exploitation and mobilization'.[36]

Wilders' watershed years 2001–2004

The 38 months between 11 September 2001 and 2 November 2004 were of crucial importance to Geert Wilders' political career. In that time, he went from being a little-known backbencher to one of the most talked-about politicians in the Netherlands. First of all, 9/11 allowed Wilders to present himself as a wrongfully ignored whistle-blower. Had he not been one of the few people warning of the dangers of terrorism and Muslim extremism? His in-depth knowledge of Muslim extremism made him a sought-after expert on the subject, and he made many media appearances in the months after 11 September 2001. He built a reputation as a very loyal supporter of the American War on Terror and all accompanying measures, such as military interventions in Afghanistan and later Iraq. As far as he was concerned, he declared roundly, Syria, Saudi Arabia and especially Iran should also be 'dealt with' to eliminate the threat of Islamic terrorism. When Bush started talking about the Axis of Evil in his State of the Union speech, the excitement 'literally' gave him 'goose bumps'. 'Fantastic! Just my way of thinking!' He believed 'immediate, substantial action' was needed, the VVD should 'act decisively' without budging 'a millimetre', because it was 'the eleventh hour' and the country needed some 'hard-nosed realism' to avert the new danger.

Compared to later statements, however, his views on Islam were still relatively moderate. For instance, in a popular talk show on 24 September 2001, he criticised Fortuyn's call to a 'cold war on Islam'. 'I find the remark reprehensible because it lumps all Muslims together', Wilders said. 'There is nothing wrong with Islam, it is a respectable religion. Most Muslims in the world, and in the Netherlands, are good citizens that have done nothing wrong. The problem lies with a handful of Muslim extremists.'[37]

Wilders was one of the few of his party to recognise early the electoral danger Fortuyn presented to the VVD. After Bolkestein had left for Brussels to become an EU Commissioner, the VVD made a major shift to the centre under the leadership of Hans Dijkstal, giving up the initiative Bolkestein had seized in debates on integration, immigration, the reform of the welfare state, European integration and the polder model. Just like Bolkestein had done a decade earlier, Fortuyn identified himself as the man who dared to break the taboos of the 'Left Church'. It soon became clear that a large proportion of VVD voters were highly receptive to Fortuyn's programme, and with this in mind, Wilders tried to convince Dijkstal to launch a more active, right-wing campaign à la Bolkestein, and led by example by demanding stringent measures in the media against the many Turks and Moroccans he claimed were committing benefit fraud. The conciliatory Dijkstal had no intention of changing course, however, and as Wilders had feared, the VVD paid dearly for it. No other party lost so many votes to the LPF as the VVD did: over a third of Fortuyn's voters had supported the VVD in 1998. The many analyses conducted afterwards showed that Fortuyn's position on immigration and integration was a decisive factor for many voters.

Fortuyn's victory also had personal consequences for Wilders. In thirtieth place on the list of VVD candidates, he was not re-elected to the House of Representatives, and despite having twice proven his keen political instincts, he saw his political career come to an abrupt halt. Many sources confirm it was a hard blow for him. Party members close to him remember that he looked glum for weeks. 'He has no life outside of politics. Politics is his life and his life is politics. It was more than he knew how to handle; it left him in a black hole.'[38] In his memoirs, the former minister Gerrit Zalm even suspects that the trauma of his forced departure in May 2002 was the prelude to his eventually leaving the VVD in September 2004. He did not want his political fate to depend on the party's internal squabbling about the order of the list of candidates – only the electorate should have a say in his future.[39] That seems far-fetched, especially considering Wilders was able to return to his beloved place in the House of Representatives after only two months. What does seem likely is that from the moment of his return to parliament, Wilders was more convinced than ever that the electoral future of the VVD lay on the right. The LPF may have had its day, but this did not mean that 1.5 million Fortuyn voters had happily returned to the established parties. Various opinion polls showed that there was a demand for a new, Fortuynesque party that called for more stringent integration and immigration policies.

In addition, Wilders started becoming ever more critical of Islam in general in 2003. An important cause of this shift was a new fellow party member who kept reiterating her view that movements like Al Qaeda were at the heart of Islam: Ayaan Hirsi Ali. Wilders was fascinated by this striking new party member, who even managed to attract international media attention, and another party member claims Hirsi Ali 'cast a spell on Wilders'. 'She was the catalyst that caused Wilders' behaviour to get more and more extreme, too.' On 12 April 2003, Hirsi Ali and Wilders published a sensational article in *NRC Handelsblad*, significantly titled 'It is Time for a Liberal Jihad'. 'The Islamic community inside and outside Europe is rapidly radicalising', they warned. They believed that all kinds of extremist organisations, financed by Saudi Arabia, were poisoning the minds of Islamic youth and recruiting hundreds of Islamic fighters to carry out acts of terror. The 'much-praised Dutch consensus model and quasi politically correct conduct' no longer sufficed, as 'a procrastinating and deliberating government makes a weak rather than a strong impression'. They concluded that,

> [I]n order to preserve a tolerant and liberal country, we must set aside even elemental rights and laws when dealing with the people who abuse them and intend to remove them as foundation of our society. The only solution is a liberal Jihad.[40]

In the months that followed, Wilders and Hirsi Ali cooperated on several articles about the struggle they considered necessary against political Islam, which they viewed as 'a nihilist, anti-Semitic, violent religious ideology whose contempt for humanity equals that of National Socialism'. Not only did they display an increasing aversion to the wishy-washy consensus culture of Dutch politics, they also shared the neoconservative American administration's optimism about democratising the Middle East, and believed the American invasion of Iraq deserved more support from the Netherlands. 'Bush is a president with balls', Wilders declared his unconditional support for the American president. 'Bush has taken the right geopolitical decisions. It is rubbish that he has deceived the world.'[41]

While Hirsi Ali limited herself to voicing largely abstract views on freedom and Islam, Wilders presented a whole set of concrete measures to protect the rule of law, such as deporting potential terrorists and radical imams, declaring a state of emergency and preventively arresting and detaining suspicious individuals. Drawing up these resolute proposals he made good use of his knowledge of Israel's security policies, and they gained him a lot of publicity – ever since Fortuyn, journalists had been only too keen to offer a platform to political mavericks. 'A quick visit to Wilders' office at the Binnenhof yields a torrent of blunt, not to say crass, statements', two journalists of the *De Volkskrant* noted in November 2003. Journalists elicited all kinds of statements about dubious imams ('Deport them!'), headscarves ('I can't stand them!') and left-wing politics ('Whether they call themselves social liberals, social democrats or I don't know what else, they are all socialists; birds of a feather, all with the same strange ideas').[42]

Inside the VVD, Wilders' proposals and statements met with little support. Though Wilders presented his measures as a protection of the rule of law, he increasingly exceeded the boundaries of constitutional liberalism, whose main core values have traditionally been equality before the law, the protection of individual citizens and judicial precision. Moreover, to the horror of many of his fellow party members, Wilders increasingly started associating Islam with a wide range of problems, such as crime by young Moroccans, honour killings and the high percentage of benefits claimants and drop-outs among non-Western immigrants. He asserted that minority policy should aim at the complete assimilation of Muslims into Western society, and at the same time hinted at a temporary immigration ban for Muslims. Many Dutch politicians, including members of the VVD, completely 'lacked a sense of urgency', he declared time and again. No one within the VVD seemed to understand that the age of 'cloying harmony' and of 'singing songs, holding hands and wearing yellow bracelets' was over. This unprecedented political juncture, which he believed had emerged with the 9/11 attacks and the rise of Pim Fortuyn, called for a different programme, and a different type of politician than the 'grey mice' that manned the VVD.[43]

When Wilders presented a ten-step plan to shift the VVD to the right in July 2004, it was the last straw for many of his fellow party members. They believed Wilders had become a publicity-crazed troublemaker who was out of control, especially since he categorically refused to agree with the VVD's viewpoint on Turkey's possible entry into the EU. An Islamic country like Turkey should never be allowed to become a member of the European Union, Wilders asserted. As far as he was concerned, the time of compromise was over; the VVD could not force him to agree to something that went against his conscience.

After several attempts at reconciliation, Wilders finally resigned from the VVD on 2 September 2004. Though he had won few preference votes and owed his seat solely to the VVD's election results in 2003, he decided to stay in the House of Representatives as an independent candidate. From there, he intended to found a new party, an unadulterated conservative voice in the progressive Netherlands.

The Wilders Group 2004–2006

In autumn 2004, Wilders' chances of successfully establishing a new party seemed slim. A large majority of new parties in the Netherlands ended in failure – even those that managed to get into the House of Representatives usually only made headlines for internal rows and misconduct. The choice of the word *conservative* did not seem auspicious, either, as the term did not have positive connotations in the Netherlands, where to most people it was almost synonymous with backwardness, small-mindedness and parochialism. This had been true even in the highly traditional, 'pillarized' Dutch society before the war, when a well-known Catholic politician remarked that a Dutchman would rather be called a thief or arsonist than a conservative.[44] Since the 60s especially, the seemingly opposite term *progressive* had become a mode of life and guiding principle to many. Whether it was on the subject of the legalisation of euthanasia, abortion or same-sex marriage, reform of the education system, European integration or the welfare state, the same progressive mantras were repeated about the Netherlands 'moving forward' and 'going with the times' – or preferably slightly ahead of them – as a 'model country'. 'A culturally progressive discourse is more deeply entrenched in the Netherlands than anywhere else', the sociologist J.W. Duyvendak concluded.[45]

However, Wilders' perspective had changed radically after Theo Van Gogh's murder. As one of the best-known critics of Islam, he found himself squarely in the spotlight, which suddenly made his new movement extremely relevant despite its conservative label. The 'Wilders Group', as his party was tentatively called, soared to Fortuynesque heights in the polls. Even more importantly, Wilders, like Hirsi Ali, was forced to go into hiding for a short time after Van Gogh's murder, as his name also turned up on the Islamic fundamentalists' hit list, and the Dutch security forces were not prepared to take any risks. Two days after Van Gogh's murder, Wilders and his wife were picked up by security guards and taken to a safe address in the woods near the Belgian border. Some time later, he was moved to a prison cell at Camp Zeist, a former US Air Force Base, where a few years earlier the suspects of the Lockerbie bombing had been held before and during their trial, between 1999 and 2001. Later, Wilders moved to a heavily protected, secret apartment in or near The Hague. From November 2004 until today, he has been under the highest level of protection, which means he is permanently guarded by armed members of the Royal and Diplomatic Corps Protection Department (DKDB). A night out at a restaurant or the cinema with his wife, a walk in the park, shopping at the supermarket, going for a spin in his beloved Audi TT or a meeting with kindred souls are all pastimes he has not been able to take for granted since 2004.

The impact of such a sudden change of lifestyle is hard to imagine; we will return to the subject later in the book. One thing is certain, however: the events of autumn 2004 have only heightened Wilders' combativeness and missionary zeal. Van Gogh's murder had again proved that far from being a panic monger, Wilders had on the contrary accurately assessed the dangers. The fact that his life had been made more difficult was no reason for him to end his crusade against the Islamic threat. 'It helps that I have always been a loner. I was never a regular at social gatherings like VVD get-togethers – a waste of time, I prefer working', he tried to play down the situation.[46]

The Wilders Group existed for 18 months, until it changed its name to Party for Freedom (PVV) on 22 February 2006, to prove it was not a personality cult around Wilders. It was still far from being a properly organised party, however; the Wilders Group and the PVV consisted de facto of just three people: Geert Wilders, Martin Bosma and Bart Jan Spruyt. The latter two played an important role in the history of the PVV and merit a brief introduction.

Bart Jan Spruyt was managing director of the Edmund Burke Foundation, a think tank established in the year 2000 with the aim of spreading conservatism in the Netherlands. A member of the orthodox Restored Reformed Church with a PhD in history, Spruyt came from a very different background than Wilders. He was dissatisfied with the lack of influence and ambition of the small Christian parties and had familiarised himself with conservatism, an ideology that, in his view, recognised 'the crucial value of tradition and decency' without automatically being linked with the Christian faith. The September 11 attacks and Fortuyn's popularity convinced Spruyt that now more than ever, the Dutch political landscape was in urgent need of drastic reform. 'I believed we should stop standing on the sidelines. It had become abundantly clear that the existing parties had no answers to the large problems the Netherlands would face in the future. Conservatism did have the answers', Spruyt says.[47] He envisaged the Edmund Burke Foundation playing a pivotal role in leading the way to the establishment of a conservative people's party that would absorb parts of the CDA, VVD and LPF, and the small Christian parties. His goal was one large party, comparable to the US Republican party, which would accommodate different kinds of conservatives – neoconservatives, evangelicals, libertarians and more classic conservatives. In September 2004, after being rejected by the existing parties, Spruyt finally turned to Wilders, who had, after all, also voiced his intention to found a conservative party.

In the same month, the 40-year-old journalist Martin Bosma also offered his services. Bosma would eventually become – and remain – Wilders' most important ally. In his 2010 autobiography, Bosma is vague about his reasons for giving up his career as a journalist in favour of an uncertain future alongside a dissenting Member of Parliament. Money certainly was not one of them, as a monthly allowance of 300 euros was all the party could afford at first. Was it idealism? In any case, Bosma and Wilders had a lot in common. Like Wilders, Bosma felt a strong connection with Israel and hated left-wing politics with a passion. Bosma's strong aversion to the left is somewhat understandable, given that he studied political science at the University of Amsterdam at a time when the university was dominated by far-left students. These were the latter years of a tumultuous period of rioting squatters, extra-parliamentary protests against nuclear weapons and manifestos against the 'rising racism and fascism'. Left-wing rebellion had been the norm in Amsterdam for years – anyone with differing opinions was better off elsewhere. So Bosma left for New York in 1990, to study at the famous New School for Social Research, and to work as a journalist. He became fascinated by the way political campaigns were run in America – the strong focus on the leader's personality, use of powerful one-liners and sometimes merciless discrediting of opponents. In his autobiography, he writes that in those years, he 'devoured everything he could lay his hands on by authors like Bob Shrum, Karl Rove and Lee Atwater' and was 'very familiar with the history of American speechwriting, in particular the work of Peggy Noonan, Pat Buchanan and Peter Robinson'. He also became fascinated by neo-conservative thinkers like Leo Strauss, Norman Podhoretz, Allan Bloom and Irving Kristoll, and retrospectively admired Ronald Reagan, who was generally reviled in the Netherlands. Back in the Netherlands, Bosma entered the Amsterdam journalism scene, helped to found a multicultural radio station and for a long time steered clear of politics. As a vegetarian, member of a car-sharing scheme, hands-on father and inhabitant of the libertarian city of Amsterdam, he did not exactly fit the description of someone aspiring to convert people to conservatism. He did enjoy rubbing people up the wrong way with his deadpan, archaically phrased remarks, though that fits into an Amsterdam tradition of provocative irony which had also been Van Gogh's trademark. His feeling for language, quirky sense of humour and knowledge of American campaign techniques made him an exceedingly useful ally for Wilders and Spruyt.[48]

For the time being, however, Spruyt was still the movement's leading ideologist. In January 2005, Spruyt took Wilders on a three-week educational trip to the United States. Besides fundraising in Spruyt's American network, the aim of the trip was to deepen Wilders' knowledge of conservatism – sorely needed in Spruyt's opinion, as Wilders knew little about conservatism as a political philosophy. Says Spruyt,

> Wilders gains his knowledge from reading reports; he is a practical political man, not an intellectual who occasionally delves into political philosophy. The conservative canon, including authors like Thomas Hobbes, Edmund Burke and Leo Strauss, was virtually unknown to him.

The trip to the US was meant to reduce this intellectual deficit. In New York and Philadelphia, Wilders and Spruyt visited the editors of the renowned *Commentary* magazine, as well as think tanks such as the Heritage Foundation, Foreign Policy Research Institute and the American Enterprise Institute. In Washington, they spoke with Republican politicians including Richard Perle – a former adviser to Ronald Reagan – and Grover Norquist, chairman of an anti-tax lobby and author of *Leave Us Alone. Getting the Government's Hands Off Our Money, Our Guns, Our Lives*. 'In the Netherlands, we don't have a party dedicated to lowering taxes. That opens up possibilities', Wilders thought out loud in the presence of a Dutch journalist.[49]

What impressed Wilders most, however, was his visit to the Investigative Project on Terrorism, a heavily guarded Institute in Washington. The Institute's founder was Steve Emerson, an investigative journalist known in the United States for his documentary, *Jihad in America*. To some, it made him an important authority in the field of Islamic terrorism, to others he was above all a charlatan who lined his pockets by spreading fear. 'The Institute had an enormous intelligence archive at its disposal on radical Islamic factions worldwide', says Spruyt. 'Their message to us was that the Netherlands was still gravely underestimating the threat and could be subjected to an attack at any moment. It made a huge impression on Wilders.'[50]

Shortly after returning from the United States, the Wilders Group published its first political manifesto, '*Onafhankelijkheidsverklaring*' (Declaration of Independence), largely written by Spruyt. The title of the manifesto was meant as a clear signal that Wilders would distance himself from the Dutch political elite from now on. He had declared his 'independence' and, with great dramatic flair, called on the rest of the Dutch population to do the same. He viewed the Dutch elite as an all but homogeneous caste of 'scared, cowardly people' who scratched each other's backs and did everything in their power to evade problems. In contrast, Wilders presented himself as someone with the courage to tell the truth. In his simultaneously published autobiography, *Choose Freedom*, Wilders provides an extensive insight into his new life in hiding and under constant supervision, complete with photos of his plainly furnished and heavily guarded safe address at Camp Zeist. These photographs, as well as the texts, lend both publications a strong sense of impending crisis, a feeling that the world has reached a critical juncture and that choosing the wrong direction could be fatal. The country had to be made defensible to face a world full of conflict and danger. The wording of many of the proposals in the *Declaration of Independence* was quite rigorous and blunt by Dutch standards. Where security was concerned, Wilders called for a 'series of concrete measures' such as introducing a minimum penalty and reform camps, putting five detainees in one cell, preventive frisking and, if necessary, deploying the army to maintain law and order. Islamic radicals threatening Dutch security should be deported without pardon, as should 'street terrorists' with dual nationality. The borders should be shut to non-Western immigrants for five years, and wearing headscarves banned in the public sector. The Wilders Group's socio-economic agenda had an American ring to it: drastic tax reductions, a smaller government, fewer rules, less power to the unions and cuts in social security were the name of the game. They argued that the welfare state had made many citizens lazy, dependent and inert, and that the stringent dismissal laws, the minimum wage, the progressive tax system, and endless consultations between social partners put the economy at risk of stagnation.[51]

The phrasing may have been more radical, but the ideas were unmistakably the same as Wilders had put forward in his latter years in the VVD. The only new part was a focus on education, care for the elderly and political reform. Perfectly in line with conservative thinking, education was attributed an important role in character forming. Every self-aware citizen should possess an in-depth knowledge of their country's history and national culture, which would strengthen their sense of national pride. 'Students who create disturbance and are in need of a firm hand' were to attend re-established reform schools. This disciplining of young and working people was offset by generous care for those Wilders called the 'genuinely vulnerable' – the elderly, who had literally 'earned' the country's support – in contrast to the 'pseudo-vulnerable', those 'made' vulnerable by the paternalism of the welfare state.

His suggestions for political reform were clearly Spruyt's contribution. Before leaving the VVD, Wilders had been an avowed opponent of political reform. In his ten-step plan of June 2004, he declared roundly that 'there's no point in changing the electoral system, what we need are courageous and decisive politicians'. Now, however, Wilders was arguing for a new electoral system in which 'the electorate has a closer relationship with their representative, and those elected are answerable to their voters'. As a way of narrowing the gap between citizens and politicians, the Wilders Group called for binding referenda on important issues as well as directly elected mayors and, in large cities, police chiefs. Another remarkable point of view, given that in his VVD years, Wilders was against a referendum, on principle. As a liberal Member of Parliament he voted against the planned referendum about the 'Treaty establishing a Constitution for Europe'.

Fortunately for him, a majority in the House of Representatives disagreed, and the referendum on 1 June 2005 presented a good opportunity for Wilders to take the spotlight again. He managed to make logical connections between three of his arguments: his opposition against Turkey entering the European Union; the struggle to preserve a national identity; and the fight against a political elite in The Hague that was out of touch with the people. Or, as he stated in *Trouw*, 'If the Brussels clique get their way and make Islamic Turkey a member of the Union, I fear the worst for such vital issues as immigration.'[52] His campaign earned a lot of publicity because he was one of the few people openly opposing the constitution, but also because it was the first time the general public became aware of the stringent security measures he was subjected to. It revealed a paradox that would haunt Wilders for the rest of his career. On the one hand, the security measures made it difficult for him to campaign on the street, handing out pamphlets and speaking in public. On the other hand it generated a huge amount of extra publicity, which went a long way towards compensating for his confined circumstances. In short, the setback also turned out to be a huge advantage.

The electoral breakthrough 2006

By opposing the treaty Wilders once again proved the acuteness of his political instinct. No less than 61.6% of the turnout (which was small) voted against the treaty. The established parties who had all supported the treaty had again failed to convince a large proportion of their voters. Three years after the Fortuyn elections, there still seemed to be room for something different. In the months following the referendum, however, it became increasingly clear to Wilders that Spruyt's neoconservative programme was not the best way of getting the voters behind him. In early 2006, Spruyt had written an extensive ideological manifesto called *A New-Realistic Vision*, in which he refers to the work of numerous philosophers like Alexis de Tocqueville, Peter Sloterdijk and Leo Strauss to emphasise the importance of citizenship and such traditional institutions as the family, the church, the neighbourhood association and the school. He wanted to call a halt to the spreading spirit of slackness, lawlessness and cultural and moral decline by launching a conservative civilising offensive through reform of the education system and an increased focus on family and upbringing. However, the manifesto was hardly noticed by the press, just as Wilders generally attracted less and less media attention in 2006. The lack of media interest went hand in hand with a steep decline in the polls from February 2006 onwards. By the summer of 2006, the PVV barely won 1% of the vote in some polls. Publications like *A New-Realistic Vision* were probably too academic to appeal to a wider public, and unlike Ayaan Hirsi Ali, Wilders never managed to gain the support of the small group of neoconservative intellectuals in the Netherlands, either. On top of that, American neoconservatism could hardly be held up as an inspiring example anymore – in the summer of 2006 it was becoming evident that the democratisation of Iraq and Afghanistan propagated by the neoconservatives was turning into a disaster. In the US and the world over, George W. Bush's popularity had plummeted to an all-time low. Who would want to be associated with that?

In anticipation of the early elections about to be held in November 2006, Wilders decided to change tack that summer. 'He wanted to focus on immigration and Islam, completely ignoring such conservative issues as education and the importance of a cultural foundation for society. Those things didn't really interest him', says Spruyt. According to him, Wilders increasingly allowed electoral considerations to determine his point of view. For instance, he suddenly argued for a blanket ban on Polish workers in the labour market, even though this contradicted the neoconservative belief in a free market and removing obstacles for trade and industry. 'Brandishing *De Telegraaf*, which predicted a tidal wave of Polish workers, Wilders and Bosma pointed to opinion polls – if the voters they were hoping to reach were against this, then so were they', says Spruyt, who handed in his resignation in August 2006.

The shift in content that Spruyt flags up also emerges in the 2006 electoral programme, and in interviews Wilders gave in the summer and autumn of the same year. The somewhat reflective, elitist conservatism had given way to a much simpler rhetoric on the dangers of immigration and Islam. This also called for a different kind of candidate. Wilders replaced the candidates put forward by Spruyt – mainly conservatives with a Christian background – with individuals outside the political world, such as the Amsterdam police inspector Hero Brinkman, the Rotterdam real estate agent Barry Madlener and a television producer from Limburg, Dion Graus. Wilders needed publicity – lots of publicity, as there was no budget for a large-scale campaign – and he knew he would not get it by publishing conservative newspaper essays. His savage one-liners, evocative doom scenarios and vicious personal attacks on his opponents were more successful. In an interview with *De Volkskrant*, for instance, he warned that the country was in danger of being flooded by a 'tsunami of Islamisation'. 'If we do nothing to prevent it, the other points of my programme will be redundant', he said ominously, arguing that the high crime rate among Moroccans could not be treated as a separate issue from Islam. 'Their behaviour arises from their culture and religion', Wilders said; he no longer believed in the existence of a moderate, liberal Islam. During the campaign, he made no mention of the necessity of a moral bond, changes and improvements to the education system or a more decent society – the conservative educator of the people had made way for an anti-Islamic crusader.

The new direction soon bore fruit. Though the PVV had slowly started creeping up the polls, the result of the House of Representatives election in November 2006 exceeded all expectations. According to Geert Tomlow, in twelfth place on the list of candidates, even the most optimistic of party members had not counted on more than six seats, or 3% of the vote. 'Martin Bosma and Dion Graus were in fifth and sixth place, and Bosma especially felt uneasy about it. Madlener, Van Dijck and Fritsma, numbers seven, eight and nine, didn't even get their hopes up.' Not an overly pessimistic reaction, given that the polls predicted the PVV would get four or five seats. But the PVV won 579,490 votes, 5.9% of the vote, which gained the party nine seats in the House of Representatives.

Though the result did not come close to Pim Fortuyn's posthumous victory in 2002, it was certainly an encouraging debut. In one blow, the PVV had become the country's fifth largest party, larger than D66 and GreenLeft. What was more, none of the other small parties that had emerged from the LPF passed the electoral threshold, allowing Wilders to appoint himself as Fortuyn's definitive political successor – and there were various signs that the PVV was still far from having peaked. First, the PVV did remarkably well at mock elections held at secondary schools immediately before the House of Representatives election; of the roughly 150,000 participating, 12% voted for Wilders' party. A second sign was the huge number of preference votes won by Rita Verdonk, the second candidate on the VVD's list. With 620,555 votes, she single-handedly trumped not just the PVV, but also the VVD's leading candidate, Mark Rutte. The staggering number of preference votes could largely be seen as an expression of support for the firm stance Verdonk had taken in her role as Minister for Integration and Immigration, and to the horror of many VVD members, it was reason enough for Verdonk to claim leadership of the party. Though the attempt failed, it was yet more proof that the liberals had still not recovered from the blow Fortuyn had dealt them. To Wilders, Verdonk's popularity was above all a sign that immigration and integration were issues that would be able to win the PVV many more seats in the future.

And so the year 2006, which had started off so badly for Wilders, ended on a high note after all. With nine seats in parliament, the PVV had made its parliamentary breakthrough and would now be able to think seriously about building an organisation and devising a strategy. Without Bart Jan Spruyt acting as the party's conservative conscience, the PVV also set a new ideological course. In the next chapter I will discuss this new ideological direction in more detail.

Notes

1. H. Knippenberg, 'The Incorporation of Limburg in the Dutch State', in *Nationalising and Denationalising European Border Regions, 1800–2000. Views from Geography and History*, J.D. Markusse and H. Knippenberg, eds, 153–172. Dordrecht: Kluwer Academic Publishers, 1999.
2. H. Bakvis, *Catholic Power in the Netherlands*, Kingston, Ontario: McGill-Queen's University Press, 1981.
3. G. Wilders, *Marked for Death. Islam's War against the West and Me*, 31, New York: Regnery Publishing, 2012.
4. A. Visser, 'De tien geboden van Geert Wilders', *Trouw*, 16 October 2004.
5. J.C. Kennedy, *Building New Babylon: Cultural Change in the Netherlands During the 1960s*, University of Iowa, 1995; P. de Rooy, *A Tiny Spot on the Earth: The Political Culture of the Netherlands in the Nineteenth and Twentieth Century*, Amsterdam: Amsterdam University Press, 2015.
6. L. van Leeuwen, 'Wreker van zijn Indische grootouders. De politieke roots van Geert Wilders', *Groene Amsterdammer*, 2 September 2009.
7. 'De vakantieplek van Geert Wilders', *Elsevier*, 6 July 2005.
8. T. de Hoog, 'De sterke wil van Wilders', *Nieuw Israelitisch Weekblad*, 3 October 2005;. T. Koelé and M. Kruyt, 'Verliefd op Israel', *De Volkskrant*, 10 April 2007; M. de Vries, 'De wilde haren en jonge jaren van Geert Wilders', *HP De Tijd*, 2 September 2009.
9. I. Buruma, *Murder in Amsterdam. Liberal Europe, Islam and the Limits of Tolerance*, London: Penguin, 2007.
10. Wilders, *Marked for Death*, 53–54.
11. G. Wilders, 'Islamification of Western Societies Threatens Everyone's Freedoms', *The Australian*, 18 February 2013.
12. J. Mat, 'Één man, zeven gezichten', *NRC Handelsblad*, 19 June 2010.
13. F.J. Lechner, *The Netherlands. Globalization and National Identity*, London: Routledge, 2007; H. Wansink, *Het land van Beatrix. De eerste geschiedenis van hedendaags Nederland 1980–2015*, Amsterdam, 2013; L. Lucassen and J. Lucassen, *Winnaars en verliezers. Een nuchtere balans van vijfhonderd jaar immigratie*, Amsterdam, 2011. Trans, in German, *Gewinner und Verlierer. Fünf Jahrhunderte Immigration. Eine nüchterne Bilanz*, Münster; New York: Waxmann, 2014.
14. G. Wilders, *Kies voor vrijheid. Een eerlijk antwoord* [n.p.] 2005, 26.
15. R.B. Andeweg and G.A. Irwin, *Governance and Politics in the Netherlands*, 2nd ed., New York: Palgrave Macmillan, 2005.
16. M. Fennema, *Geert Wilders. Tovenaarsleerling*, 9–36, Amsterdam, 2010; L. Wytzes, 'Een politiek roofdier', *Elsevier*, 18 August 2007; H.E. Botje and Th. Niemantsverdriet, 'De draai van Geert', *Vrij Nederland*, 10 April 2010.
17. Mat, 'Één man, zeven gezichten'.
18. M. van Weezel and L. Ornstein, *Frits Bolkestein. Portret van een liberale vrijbuiter*, Amsterdam, 1999; A. Maas, G. Marlet and R. Zwart, *Het brein van Bolkestein*, Nijmegen, 1997.
19. B. Prins, 'The Nerve to Break Taboos: New Realism in the Dutch Discourse on Multiculturalism', *Journal of International Migration and Integration*, 3 (2007): 363–379.
20. E. Vrijsen, 'Wij worden de grootste', *Elsevier*, 2 October, 1999.
21. E. Lammers, 'Het is leuk, die heftige reacties', *Trouw*, 17 December 1999; H. van Soest, 'VVD'er Wilders schopt iedereen naar zich toe', *Rotterdams Dagblad*, 21 June 2001; A. de Jong, 'De blonde engel kiest de aanval', *De Telegraaf*, 13 March 1999; E. de Boer and J. Hoedeman, 'Hard blaffen en niet bijten', *De Volkskrant*, 22 October 1999; Botje and Niemantsverdriet 'De draai van Geert'.
22. G. Wilders, 'Stop de vakbondsmacht', *De Volkskrant*, 15 February 2001.

23 Lammers, 'Het is leuk, die heftige reacties'; B. Soetenhorst, 'Een roepende in de woestijn op het Binnenhof', *Het Parool*, 22 September 2001.
24 G.J. van Schoonhoven, *De nieuwe kaaskop. Nederland en de Nederlanders in de jaren negentig*, Amsterdam: Prometheus, 1999.
25 Th. Niemantsverdriet, *De vechtpartij. De PvdA van Kok tot Samsom*, Amsterdam: Atlas Contact, 2014.
26 On the SP: T. Pauwels, *Populism in Western Europe. Comparing Belgium, Germany and the Netherlands*, 128–141, Routledge, 2015; K. Vossen, 'The Different Flavours of Populism in the Netherlands', in *The Changing Faces of Populism. Systemic Challengers in Europe and the US*, H. Giusto, D. Kitching and S. Rizzo, eds, Brussels; Rome: Foundation for European Progressive Studies, University of Rome, 2013; S. van Kessel, 'Explaining the Electoral Performance of Populist Parties: The Netherlands as a Case Study', *Perspectives on European Politics and Society* 12 (1) (2011): 68–88.
27 J. Lucassen and L. Lucassen, 'The Strange Death of Dutch Tolerance: The Timing and Nature of the Pessimist Turn in the Dutch Migration Debate', *The Journal of Modern History* 87 (1) (1 April 2015): 72–101.
28 H. Wansink, *Land van Beatrix: Moslim in Nederland. Rapport Sociaal Cultureel Planbureau*, Den Haag, 2004.
29 *Elsevier*, 1 September 2001.
30 Ph. Van Praag, 'Winners and Losers in a Turbulent Political Year', *Acta Politica* 38 (2003): 5–22; P. Lucardie and G. Voerman, 'Rootless Populists? The Dutch Pim Fortuyn List, the Freedom Party and Others', in *Rural Protest Groups and Populist Political Parties*, D. Strijker, G. Voerman and I. Terluin, eds, 265–290. Wageningen: Wageningen Academic Publishers, 2015.
31 T. Akkerman, 'Anti-Immigration Parties and the Defence of Liberal Values: The Exceptional Case of the Pim Fortuyn List', *Journal of Political Ideologies*, 10 (2005): 337–354; J. Vellenga, 'Huntington in Holland. The Public Debate on Muslim Immigrants in the Netherlands', *Nordic Journal of Religion and Society*, 21 (1) (2008): 21–41; D. Pels, *De geest van Pim. Het gedachtegoed van een politieke dandy*, Amsterdam: Anthos, 2003.
32 P.J. Margry, 'The Murder of Pim Fortuyn and Collective Emotions. Hype, Hysteria and Holiness in the Netherlands?' *Etnofoor* 16 (2003): 102–127.
33 Lucassen and Lucassen 'The Strange Death of Dutch Tolerance'.
34 Buruma, *Murder in Amsterdam*.
35 D. Scroggins, *Wanted Women. Faith, Lies and the War on Terror: The Lives of Ayaan Hirsi Ali and Aafia Siddiqui*, New York: Harper, 2012.
36 R. Eyerman, *The Cultural Sociology of Political Assassination. From MLK and RFK to Fortuyn and Van Gogh*, New York: Palgrave Macmillan, 2011.
37 Talkshow 'Barend en Van Dorp', RTL, 22 September 2001; Robin de Wever, 'Wilders in citaten', *Trouw*, 20 March 2014. On Wilders' ideological development: K. Vossen, 'Classifying Wilders. The Ideological Development of Geert Wilders and his Party for Freedom', *Politics* 31 (3) (2011): 179–190; K. Vossen, 'Populism in the Netherlands after Fortuyn: Rita Verdonk and Geert Wilders Compared', *Perspectives on European Politics and Society* 11 (2010): 22–39.
38 Remark by Frans Weekers, VVD MP, 1998–2010 and a close friend of Wilders. A. Blok and J. van Melle, *Veel gekker kan het niet worden. Het eerste boek over Geert Wilders* 95, Hilversum, 2008.
39 G. Zalm, *De romantische boekhouder*, 279–281, Amsterdam: Balans, 2009.
40 Articles by Hirsi Ali and G. Wilders, 'Democratiseer het Midden Oosten', *Trouw*, 27 April 2004; 'Steniging laat moslims koud', *Trouw*, 20 March 2003; 'Het is tijd voor een liberale jihad', *NRC Handelsblad*, 12 April 2003.
41 *Trouw*, 20 October 2004. Wilders was one of the seven MPs in the Second Chamber who preferred Bush Jr over John Kerry in the American presidential elections in 2004.

28 The making of Geert Wilders 1963–2006

42 E. de Boer and T. Koele, 'Een rechtse directe', *De Volkskrant*, 20 November 2003; N. Marbe, 'Ik ben van nature recalcitrant', *Vrij Nederland*, 31 July 2004; F. van Deijl, 'Ik lust ze rauw', *HP De Tijd*, 6 February 2004.
43 Vossen 'Classifying Wilders'.
44 H. von der Dunk, 'Conservatism in the Netherlands', *Journal of Contemporary History*, Vol. 13, 4 (1978):741–763.
45 J.W. Duyvendak, *Een eensgezinde, vooruitstrevende natie. Over de mythe van dé individualisering en de toekomst van de sociologie* [A United, Progressive Nation: On the Myth of 'the' Individualization and the Future of Sociology], Amsterdam: Vossius Press, 2004; *The Politics of Home. Belonging and Nostalgia in Western Europe and the United States*, 84–105, Houndmills; New York: Palgrave Macmillan, 2011.
46 B. Soetenhorst, 'Geert Wilders: Ik ben geen extremist', *Het Parool*, 31 December 2004.
47 Interview, Bart Jan Spruyt.
48 Information on Bosma is derived from: M. Bosma, *De schijnélite van de valse munters. Drees, extreem rechts, de sixties, nuttige idioten, Groep Wilders en ik*, Amsterdam, 2010; and from interviews and biographical articles in the Dutch media. S. Derkzen, 'Jekyll and Hide', *Vrij Nederland*, 27 June 2009; 'Motor achter Wilders', *De Telegraaf*, 24 September 2010; R. Meijer, 'Gedreven door ideeën en complotten', *De Volkskrant*, 16 June 2008; Interviews in *De Volkskrant*, 25 September 2010; *NRC Handelsblad*, 25 September 2010; *Het Parool*, 25 September 2010, and *Financieel Dagblad*, 25 September 2010.
49 M. Chavannes, 'Wilders snuift in de Verenigde Staten conservatieve thema's op', *NRC Handelsblad*, 15 January 2005.
50 Interview, Spruyt.
51 G. Wilders, *Kies voor vrijheid* (incl. *Onafhankelijkheidsverklaring*).
52 *Trouw*, 14 May 2005.

2 The four pillars of the PVV
The PVV's ideology

As we saw in the last chapter, the PVV's parliamentary breakthrough in 2006 was preceded by a change of course and the resignation of the conservative ideologist, Bart Jan Spruyt. Geert Wilders and his adjutant, Martin Bosma, had chosen a new ideological direction without putting any clearly defined outlines in writing. That would not happen until the publication of the new election programmes, *De Agenda van Hoop en Optimisme* (The Agenda of Hope and Optimism) and *Hún Brussel, óns Nederland* (Their Brussels, Our Netherlands) in 2010 and 2012 respectively, as well as Bosma and Wilders' other works. The new policies adopted by the PVV in 2006 are based on four key principles, namely the fight against Islam, the struggle against the elite on behalf of the people, national pride and sovereignty, and heavy penalties for crime and the disruption of the natural order. Metaphorically speaking, the PVV's ideology from that moment on can be compared to a square whose corners represent anti-Islamic alarmism, populism, nationalism, and a belief in discipline. All of the PVV's views and strategies lie somewhere between these four extremes, sometimes closer to one corner and sometimes to another, depending on context and political constellations.

None of the themes were new in 2006, though they changed in tone and content afterwards. We will examine each of them separately below, before answering the question of which label is appropriate to describe the new programme, and whether it should be seen as an ideology or a strategy.

First pillar: the struggle against Eurabia. The PVV's anti-Islamic alarmism

If there is one theme that becomes dominant in the PVV's electoral programme after 2006, it is the conviction that Islam has historically been the West's arch enemy and is now trying to conquer Europe for the third time in history. Where does this conviction come from? As we saw earlier, Wilders developed a deep fascination with Israel and the Middle East when first visiting the region in 1982. As a result, he was one of the first in the Netherlands to come into contact with the emerging Islamic extremism, which gained support in the 80s and 90s and had important bases in countries such as Iran and Saudi Arabia. He did initially discriminate clearly between Islam as a religion and the politicised Islamic extremism of Hamas, Hezbollah and Al Qaeda, a distinction he even adhered to after the September 11 attacks in the United States and the rise of Pim Fortuyn. In an interview with *De Volkskrant* of 20 November 2003, his tone is still quite moderate: 'I don't agree with Fortuyn that Islam is backward, but the political culture in Arab and Muslim countries *is* backward, mediaeval even, when it comes to human rights, women and homosexuals.'[1]

Only in the years that followed did the distinction between Islam, Islamic fundamentalism and Islamic culture become blurred in Wilders' mind. Could the attacks perpetrated by Islamic terrorists really be separated from the Koran's war rhetoric? Was Islam not intrinsically malicious? Was the 'backward Islamic culture' not synonymous with Islam as a religion? Influenced by Ayaan Hirsi Ali among others, Wilders became convinced that 'pure Islam', i.e. an Islam that follows the Koran to the letter, was a dangerous political ideology that posed a real and urgent threat to the free West and had to be eliminated by any means. By talking about a 'pure Islam', he still implicitly recognised the existence of a less belligerent, 'impure' Islam. He also acknowledged a difference between Islam and Muslims. While Islam was difficult, not to say impossible, to reconcile with democracy, it *was* possible to win over Muslims to democracy – at least, those who were prepared to give up part of their identity. Even after leaving the VVD, Wilders – and Spruyt – continued to stress the necessity of 'investing' in moderate Muslims, who would lead the way in the assimilation of Muslim immigrants into Western society.

When Spruyt left the party in 2006, however, Wilders rapidly lost all nuance and sense of perspective on Islam. He and Bosma developed a more negative view of Islam in general, which has often been categorised as *Islamophobia*. The term, popularised in the 90s as a label for negative and generalising views of Islam and Muslims, was controversial from the start.[2] Not surprising, given that the use of the suffix '-phobia' presumes, at least implicitly, a psychiatric disorder rather than a political vision. As such, the term can be employed to brand criticism of Islam as irrational hogwash from the outset. The British comedian Pat Condell, often accused of Islamophobia, suggested the term should be used as an honorary nickname, since 'Islamophobia is Islamic shorthand for free speech, secular democracy and common sense'.[3]

It is vital to formulate ideological labels in as neutral a language as possible to avoid terms that appear to pass a value judgement. For this reason, I have rejected the term *Islamophobia* in favour of the more neutral term *anti-Islamic alarmism*. Wilders has, after all, based his opinions on the premise that Islam presents a very serious threat that many are unaware of.

At the core of anti-Islamic alarmism lies the essentialist view of Islam as a totalitarian, immutable ideology, regardless of time and location. This means the Islam of Indonesia or suburban Amsterdam is identical to the Islam of the seventeenth century Ottoman Empire, Moorish Andalusia or Muhammad's Medina. The ideology is totalitarian in that, just like communism and fascism, it seeks complete control of the lives and behaviour of its subjects. According to Wilders and Bosma, Islam has been more successful at achieving that than either communism or fascism. They claim the behaviour of Muslims is to a large extent attributable to Islam, brushing aside – or at least declaring of secondary importance – any economic, neurological or socio-cultural influences. The message is that to understand the behaviour of Muslims, one must consult the Koran, Islam's command centre. The Koran's many instructions are considered orders of Allah himself that are to be obeyed unconditionally. In short, something like a 'Homo islamicus' has evolved, citizens of the world who are guided by a religion that can only be interpreted one way. Consequently, Wilders and Bosma consider Islam an active party, a person almost, with a goal and will of its own. They both know this 'person' intimately, for, as they keep emphasising, they practically know the Koran by heart. From its beginning, the Koran's most important instruction has been to conquer the world and subjugate other faiths and peoples. 'That is the crux of Islam: it is an ideology of global war', Wilders writes in *Marked for Death*.[4] Almost anything is permitted to achieve this and Wilders gives a detailed account of the bloodshed, plundering, rape and slavery that accompanied Islamic military campaigns. 'Terrorism, atrocities, betrayal, deception, deceit, assassination and hostage-taking are all halal (permitted) because Muhammad himself set the "good" example', Wilders writes. 'Whenever Islam becomes empowered, the non-Muslim population suffers', as 'Islam is always finding new, creative ways to humiliate non-Muslims'.[5]

Twice, this ideology almost succeeded in conquering Europe. The first Islamic invasion was brought to a halt by Charles Martel at Poitiers in 732. The second Islamic invasion started in the fifteenth century and was only defeated in 1683 at the gates of Vienna by the Polish king, Jan Sobieski. According to anti-Islamic alarmism, the world is currently witnessing a third Islamic invasion, which is to change Europe into 'Eurabia'. This time however, Islam does not deploy armies but uses a devious strategy of immigration, propaganda, misinformation and demographic increase.

Wilders and Bosma list three concrete tactics used by Islam to undermine the Western world. The first is immigration, following the example of the emigration of Muhammad and his followers to the Arabian city of Yathrib, where they were welcomed by the open-minded Jewish inhabitants. Muhammad and his followers showed their gratitude by taking over the city in a short space of time by way of intimidation, violence and plundering. Yathrib was renamed Medina. This strategy of immigration, intimidation, violence and plundering has often been employed by Muslims since, and is being pursued in present-day Europe, where many districts of larger cities have been 'taken over' by Muslims. 'What happened to the native Dutch in Slotervaart, Kanaleneiland and dozens of other boroughs also happened to the Jewish tribes of Yathrib after 622', Wilders writes, recalling his own experience in Kanaleneiland.[6] This perspective views Moroccan repeat offenders not merely as troublemakers, but as street terrorists and soldiers of jihad who are slowly but surely taking possession of the public space. Hence Wilders' remark during a House of Representatives debate in 2009 about Moroccan boys causing riots in the Dutch city of Gouda:

The elite romantically calls these Moroccans, who come here and cause trouble, "new Dutch citizens". I prefer to call them "colonists". Muslim colonists. They haven't come here to integrate, but to take over, to subdue us.[7]

Another method of weakening the West from the inside is by siphoning off as much money as possible to Islamic countries through widespread abuse of the welfare state, since taking money from non-believers is not a sin but, on the contrary, part of the holy war. 'The wealth transfer from Western taxpayers to Islamic immigrants is consistent with Islam's history of raiding', claims Wilders.[8] The relatively high percentage of Muslims claiming benefits is not so much a consequence of their lack of schooling or harsh working conditions, but part of jihad. Or, as Wilders concludes, 'By viewing the world as Islam sees it, we come to understand why some Muslims consider it only natural to extract money from infidels, whether by robbing and raiding them or by making them pay jizya'[9] (a tax for *dhimmis/ethnic minorities*).

To that end, Muslims are also permitted to mislead and cheat non-believers. The concept of *taqiyya* allows Muslims to temporarily mask their true intentions in the interest of the Holy War, presenting themselves to the outside world as perfectly assimilated citizens. In this way, certain Islamic terrorists were able to trick their environment into believing they were well-integrated citizens, while at the same time preparing attacks. '*Taqiyya* allows jihadists to take the shape of the enemy or assume whatever identity is necessary to fool the infidels.'[10] There is also something called *hudna* in Islam, a 'deceptive truce, armistice or peace agreement' for the times the *Umma* (the global Muslim community) is not strong enough.

In short, from 2006 onward the PVV viewed Islam as an inherently malicious ideology with a vast repertoire of means to reach its goal – which is, ultimately, dominion over the world. What were the consequences of this shift from criticism of Islam to anti-Islamic alarmism? First, the sweeping scope of this analysis allows it to serve as a new framework, an overarching theme with which all kinds of phenomena can be explained – from honour killings in Turkish families to suicide attacks in Iraq; from Turkey's bid to join the European Union to the relatively high number of Muslims on benefits; from Somali pirates in the Gulf of Aden to Moroccan repeat offenders; all could be directly attributed to Islam. This made jihad an everyday reality on television and the streets of cities and towns. Or, as it says in the 2010 election manifesto, 'Those who think Islamisation is a single-issue question should learn to count.'[11]

Second, the party gave up on its plan of using liberal Muslims to lead the way in the assimilation of Muslim immigrants. The *taqiyya* doctrine cast doubt on the sincerity of so-called integrated, moderate Muslims – for how could you tell whether a seemingly well-adapted Islamic social democrat was not in reality a jihadi warrior? Furthermore, Wilders and Bosma now dismissed the idea of a moderate Islam as impossible. According to their new conviction there was only one Islam, and that was a malignant, violent ideology. Questioned on the point, they were prepared to concede that there were moderate, responsible citizens even among the Muslim population, but put that down to a lack of knowledge of their own faith. And according to the *taqiyya* concept, even such ignorant, moderate Muslims might actually be dissemblers. Instead of investing in liberal Muslims whose moderate attitude might well be a front, the PVV's policies now aimed at a comprehensive ban of Islam and the marginalisation of Muslims. Many of the proposals the party has made since 2007 move in that direction, such as banning the Koran, closing down Islamic schools, prohibiting the construction of mosques, implementing a general and permanent ban on immigration from Muslim countries, withdrawing subsidies for Islamic media and institutions, banning headscarves for public sector workers and in public buildings, prohibiting Koran lessons in schools and, finally, introducing a tax on headscarves. The proposed deportation of poorly integrated immigrants and criminals with dual nationality would eventually facilitate a large-scale removal of Muslims from the country. But the PVV's wish to marginalise or banish Muslims manifests itself not only in concrete policy proposals, but also in its use of offensive terms like *head rag* for headscarf, or *hate palace* for mosque. The message is clear: practising Muslims do not belong in the Netherlands.

How many poorly integrated Muslims are there? What criteria would the PVV apply? And how exactly would they go about deporting these people? As regards the situation in the Netherlands, Wilders has yet to answer those questions, though he stated in an interview with a Danish television station that at a European level, there were tens of millions of Muslims whose radical stance was a threat to European civilisation.[12]

A third consequence of this view of Islam is that the PVV risked straying even further from the beaten track of Dutch politics. Criticism of Islam was not new in itself – as we have seen, Frits Bolkestein, Pim Fortuyn, Theo van Gogh and Ayaan Hirsi Ali preceded the PVV. In a sense, anti-Islamic alarmism dovetails with a deep-seated European fear that dates back to a time long before fascism or communism were even heard of, though Wilders and Bosma's anti-Islamic alarmism is of a particularly ominous and comprehensive kind. In their view, the world really is at a crossroads, and the end is imminent. This seemed to place the PVV in a different political reality from other parties – the political reality of the established parties was one in which arguments about the division of public spending were resolved peacefully, and policies were devised with the aim of reducing or managing existing tensions. In Wilders and Bosma's political reality, the world was witnessing a new episode in a centuries-old struggle between the forces of good and evil. In other words, while the other parties lived in a time of peace, they lived in a time of war, and therefore considered it their primary duty to alert the world to the great danger it was facing. 'If we fail to understand the nature of evil, we are doomed to become its next victims', Wilders said.[13] Exposing Islam's true nature, they would open people's eyes to the fact that their dream of eternal peace was an illusion. 'Provoking a discussion is at least as important as the number of seats we win. We are missionaries almost as much as we are politicians', Bosma writes in his book.[14] Given that he views this as a global rather than a purely Dutch problem, Wilders has put more effort than any other politician from the Netherlands into propagating his views internationally. To that end, he has brought out a film and a book in English (*Fitna* and *Marked for Death*), founded the Geert Wilders International Freedom Alliance, and held talks in practically every Western European country as well as Australia, the United States, Canada and Israel between 2008 and 2015. We will go into this in more detail in the next chapter.

What is Wilders' specific view of Islam based on? Who inspired it? Several names spring to mind, three of which stand out: the Italian journalist, Oriana Fallaci, who died in 2006; the historian, Bat Ye'or; and the Dutch Arabist, Hans Jansen. Of the three, Fallaci is probably the best known. Her spectacular war reports, social engagement and probing interviews with world leaders such as Henry Kissinger, Willy Brandt and Golda Meir made her the world's most famous journalist for a time in the 60s and 70s. After the 2001 attacks on her home city of New York, Fallaci, ravaged by cancer, decided to put her last strength into warning the world of the rise of Islam. In her books *The Rage and the Pride* (2001) and *The Force of Reason* (2004), she claims that Islam is on an 'inverted crusade' against a decadent Europe, by way of, among other things, mass immigration and the 'politics of the womb'. 'Their goal is to destroy our soul, our ideas, our feelings and our dreams. To subjugate the West again', Fallaci writes in *The Force of Reason*, Wilders' favourite book. She believed that Europe's loss of pride and intellectual capacity had already doomed the continent, which was so thoroughly Islamised as to have changed into Eurabia, an Islamic colony. In Fallaci's words, the continent had 'sold itself to sultans, caliphs, viziers and mercenaries of a new Ottoman Empire like a prostitute'.[15]

Fallaci had borrowed the term *Eurabia* from another of Wilders' heroines, the Swiss British historian Giselle Littman, better known under her pseudonym Bat Ye'or. When she was young, Bat Ye'or (Hebrew for 'daughter of the Nile') and her family were driven out of Egypt because of their Jewish background. She wrote several books about the perilous situation of ethnic minorities, or *dhimmis* in Islamic countries. *Dhimmis* were expected to pay extra taxes and acknowledge the superiority of Islam. This status led some *dhimmis* to develop a genuine submissiveness and respect for Islam – they suffered from what Bat Ye'or called 'dhimmitude'. In her book *Eurabia: The Euro-Arab Axis*, Bat Ye'or expands a theory that was meant to explain why white European politicians had done nothing to resist the Islamisation of Europe: according to her, in the 70s top-secret deals were made on the very highest level between European and Arab leaders, which stated that in exchange for oil and peace, Europe would open its doors to Arab immigrants and the Islam they brought with them. The book, written like an academic thesis, develops the theory with a long list of documents, countless details and numerous anecdotes, though without providing any solid evidence. Nevertheless, in an interview with *HP De Tijd* magazine, Wilders declares that *Eurabia* made a 'big impression' on him when it was published in 2005. 'I believe she is right, it is just very difficult to prove that there have been targeted policies to that end', said Wilders, who peppers his own speech with numerous terms coined by Bat Ye'or such as *Eurabia* and *dhimmitude*.[16] Hardly anyone in the academic world takes Bat Ye'or seriously, and her Eurabia thesis is seen as a classic conspiracy theory, though there are scholars in the Netherlands and beyond, even fairly renowned ones, who refuse to dismiss out of hand Bat Ye'or's theory as nonsense. One of them was the Dutch Arabist, Hans Jansen.

Hans Jansen enjoyed a national and international reputation as a respected Arabist and expert in the field of Arabic manuscripts and Muslim fundamentalism. His remarks – always edged with sarcasm – also made him a sought-after guest on talk shows and current affairs programmes. After Theo van Gogh's murder, Jansen turned out to be one of Islam's fiercest critics, no longer differentiating between its radical and moderate forms. To him, Muslim behaviour was almost entirely shaped by instructions given in the Koran, of which he had an expert knowledge. As Jansen showed in various publications, these instructions were often not particularly peaceable, and clashed with the standards and values of the West.[17] Consequently, he believed Islam and the Western world were actually at war without the West being aware of it, and that the progressive elite had had the wool pulled over its eyes with a lot of sweet-talking about a multicultural society and the common ground between Islam and Christendom.

While Jansen was still widely regarded as the Netherlands' best known Arabist and his popularising books sold well, few Dutch Arabists and Islamologists took his latest insights seriously. His analysis did, however, resonate with a small, international group of publicists and scholars who had taken it upon themselves to warn the world of the threat of Islam. This group of anti-Islamic alarmists constituted an almost sect-like scientific community with its own institutions and organisations (including the Gatestone Institute, the Middle East Forum and the International Free Press Society), websites and conferences, where its members tended to routinely cite each other's work as they did not trust most of the Arabists and Islamologists working at universities. The distrust was mutual.[18]

Many of these anti-Islamic alarmists attended a conference Jansen had organised in cooperation with the scientific committee of the LPF in the building of the House of Representatives in February 2006. It was one of the last activities the LPF organised before being permanently disbanded. The papers contributed to the conference were later collected in a volume with the telling title *Eindstrijd. De finale clash tussen het liberale westen en een traditionele Islam* (Endgame. The Final Clash Between the Liberal West and Traditional Islam).[19] Besides Jansen and Bat Ye'or, one of the speakers at the conference was the American historian Daniel Pipes, founder of the neoconservative think tank the Middle East Forum and rumoured to be an important adviser to the White House. Wilders attended the conference, as did other well-known figures like the American publicists Robert Spencer and Bruce Bawer, Lars Hedegaard from Denmark, Peder Are Nøstvold Jensen, better known as Fjordman, from Norway, the Pakistani ex-Muslim Ibn Warraq, the Flemish Arabist Urbain Vermeulen and his countryman Paul Beliën, managing director of Islamist Watch. In 2010, Beliën became Wilders' personal assistant and helped him in the writing of *Marked for Death*. Wilders would see many of the other attendees again, too – including Robert Spencer and Daniel Pipes – during various international conferences and demonstrations on the dangers of Islam.

Wilders and Bosma's anti-Islamic alarmism was therefore not just a personal vision, but part of a wider theory with a small global following among Arabists and Islamologists – self-appointed or otherwise. Though the views propagated by these 'brave, truth-telling outlaws of Islamic Studies',[20] as Bruce Bawer called them, were controversial to say the least, they did give anti-Islamic alarmism an intellectual and scientific gloss. In several countries their ideas made the mainstream media, albeit sometimes in watered-down form. Their ominous analyses also turned out to be a commercial success, as books by Hans Jansen, Bat Ye'or, Christopher Caldwell, Bruce Bawer, Mark Steyn and Oriana Fallaci made it onto national and international bestseller lists.[21]

Another attractive aspect of anti-Islamic alarmism was that it appointed a second enemy besides Islam, namely the political and cultural elites. While not all anti-Islamic alarmists believed in Bat Ye'or's theory of a conspiracy of the elite, they unanimously agreed that the rise of Islam was caused by the failure of the political and cultural elites. This links anti-Islamic alarmism to the second important pillar of the PVV programme – populism.

Second pillar: the common man, aka Henk and Ingrid. The PVV's populism

Populism is probably the term most widely used in the Netherlands and beyond to typify the PVV's ideas and conduct. Just like Islamophobia, however, it is a somewhat problematic label. In the first place, the PVV itself never uses the term when talking about its own ideas – which is not surprising, given that being labelled populist is not usually a compliment. Second, the term is open to multiple interpretations. For example, some would call the PVV populist because it allows its course to be determined by electoral motives, 'currying favour' with the voters. 'Populism boils down to buttering up the crowd for your own benefit', as the writer Gerrit Komrij defined it, putting populism on a level with opportunism.[22] Others consider the PVV populist because its style and ideas capitalise on people's 'gut feelings'; instead of introducing sensible policies to assuage people's fears, the party rhetoric reinforces them. By this definition, populism is equal to demagogy.

Used by political scientists, philosophers and historians, the term often takes on yet another meaning. But while there is some discussion among them about whether populism is a strategy, an ideology or a style, they widely agree on what constitutes its core: the conviction that there is a gaping chasm between the people and the elite which needs to be bridged. In populism, the people and the elite are typically presented as homogenous, almost personified units with a unique voice, personality and autonomy ('the people have spoken' or 'the elite holds the view'). Exactly who counts as the people or the elite can vary, but no matter what their make-up, the people are inevitably seen as the embodiment of good virtues, while the elite is portrayed as being corrupt and decadent. According to populists, the people do not need to be guided or educated, but given a voice. In fact, their inherent 'common sense' and 'pragmatism' would allow

The four pillars of PVV ideology 37

them to solve most problems. That is the reason populists call for a democracy with a minimum of obstacles and restrictions, in which the people would see their wishes genuinely reflected in politics. This is why populists often put a lot of faith in various forms of direct democracy, such as referenda, citizens' initiatives and directly elected leaders and administrators.[23]

By this more neutral definition of populism, can Wilders still be called a populist? He certainly can, but only once the three main, interlinked elements of populism – idealisation of the people, vilification of the elite and a preference for direct democracy – become apparent from 2007–2008 onwards. There can be no doubt as to his strong aversion to the Dutch political elite. As a young member of the VVD, he had held the view – in imitation of Bolkestein – that the Dutch elite all too often drew a veil over abuse, though at the time he directed his venom not so much at the elite as such but predominantly at left-wing parties – the PvdA, GreenLeft and D66 in particular – whom he said all had 'the same strange ideas'. His criticism of the elite became noticeably more radical and vicious in his 2005 *Declaration of Independence*, in which he depicted the elite, among whom he now counted Bolkestein, as a virtually homogenised caste of politicians who cover each other's backs and are in agreement on most key issues. Wilders claimed to know from experience that they keep up the appearance of a political struggle during campaigns by determining which issues to disagree on beforehand. Basically, however, all political parties – including the VVD he had once been a member of – had subjected themselves to the 'so-called progressive spirit of the age' that in the Netherlands had led to 'political correctness, a megalomaniac government, multiculturalism and submission to Brussels bureaucrats', and which had spread from the left-wing parties to the political elite like a stain that ran deep into the VVD and CDA. The terms *elite* and *left wing* had in fact become all but synonymous: both served as what the political philosopher Ernesto Laclau once called 'empty signifiers'; terms designed to uniform a heterogeneous reality.[24]

By putting their old enemy, the left wing, on a par with the new enemy, the elite, Wilders and his associate Bosma were provided with a whole new arsenal of rhetorical weapons they were to make frequent use of in following years. Using the same kind of rhetoric with which left-wing politicians had lashed out at the 'smug bourgeoisie' and 'cowardly rulers' in the past, the PVV now opened the attack on the 'wealthy left-wing urbanites and their clammy little friends'. The rich urban elite lived in a world of 'left-wing do-gooders' and their 'so-called ideals', who created well-paid 'cushy jobs' for themselves in government bodies, universities, the media, the cultural sector and other institutions on a 'tax drip'. With their good manners, sophisticated tastes and cosmopolitan world views, they had ensconced themselves in posh, exclusively white neighbourhoods, from where they looked down on the stupid, uncultured masses. It was the world of 'left-wing blah shows' on that 'horrible state-owned station', of 'unlimited funds for subsidy-dependent artists who make paintings you wouldn't wish on your worst enemy' and 'freebie subsidies' for 'climate madness' and for 'African dictators' who owed their 'Swiss country houses' to Dutch development aid.

38 The four pillars of PVV ideology

With this fierce, caricatural criticism of the elite, the PVV elaborated on Fortuyn's famous metaphor of the 'Left Church' that had supposedly dominated Dutch politics and society since the 60s. According to Fortuyn, the 'Left Church' did not limit itself to politics but spread its tentacles deep into the media, the civil service and the judiciary. Wilders and Bosma may also have been inspired by American neoconservative views. The 'new class' theory, popular in neoconservative circles, states that in the 70s and 80s a new generation of left-wing politicians seized power in the public sector, the media, the judiciary and politics, thanks to a systematic policy of nepotism, endless subsidy handouts to non-profit organisations and a taboo on any dissenting views. In his book *De schijn-élite van de Valse Munters* (The Sham Elite of Counterfeiters), Martin Bosma shows himself a particularly ardent follower of the new class theory. He interprets the 70s as a 'period of extreme-left takeovers. They capitulated one by one: newspapers, broadcasting stations, universities.' And it is the 'leftists who play first fiddle in key positions of society'. 'They run the civil service, the art world, the media, the unions, the judiciary, universities, and dish out the dough and the jobs in the all-powerful Left-wing Subsidy Network.'[25]

Unlike many American neoconservatives, however, Wilders and Bosma did not consider the undermining of traditional Christian values the greatest sin of the elite, but allowing mass immigration and Islamisation. They believed the left-wing elite converted to multiculturalism in the 60s and 70s, which Bosma sees as a variant of the cultural Marxism that had become dominant in universities. With their 'down-with-us' mentality, they have supposedly given up on the superior Western values and allowed the Islamisation of the West. In *Marked for Death*, Wilders claims that,

> Everyday Europeans have been victimized by a cynical, condescending cultural elite that loathe their own people's supposed illiberalism, intolerance, lack of sophistication, and inexplicable attachment to their traditional values. These ruling cosmopolitans do not see European culture as a tradition worth defending, but as a constantly evolving political project. In this utopian scheme, everyday people are reviled for their cultural conservatism, while immigrants are lionized precisely because they are not attached to those traditions.[26]

In imitation of Bat Ye'or's Eurabia theory, Wilders and Bosma even repeatedly insinuated that the left, blinded by a 'perverse cultural relativism' and possessed by the need to attract new voters, had consciously and deliberately given its blessing to mass immigration of Islamic immigrants.

In short, the PVV had pitted itself against a three-headed monster: the left, the elite and Islam. On the other side, according to Wilders and Bosma, were the 'hard-working Dutch people', who 'never had anything handed to them on a silver platter' but were expected to 'pick up the bill' for the elite's 'left-wing hobbies', and have been repaid for it with mass immigration and street terrorism. Perfectly ordinary, decent people with modest wishes and ideals, who had never asked for mosques, smoke-free pubs, multicultural festivals, wind farms or the euro, got saddled with them anyway thanks to the 'happy-go-lucky elite'; people who were 'seldom heard' in the House of Representatives, because they were 'dismissed as proles and xenophobes, as provincials'. In 2010, the PVV gave them a name: Henk and Ingrid.

But Wilders' tendency to present himself as the protector of the common man did not mean he subscribed to the populist ideal of the people as the embodiment of wisdom and happiness. On the contrary, during his neoconservative period Wilders criticised the modern Dutch citizen for being boorish, rude and undisciplined, complaining too much and 'looking to the state for help' while 'demanding almost unlimited freedom for himself'. While Wilders persisted in blaming the elite's cultural relativism, he nevertheless believed the Dutch could do with some re-education, if his book *Een nieuw-realistische visie* (A New Realistic Vision) is to be believed. But with Spruyt's resignation, this conservative elitism largely disappeared from PVV ideology in favour of a populist view of the people. Bosma even went as far as stating that only 'the goodness and perseverance of the people' would be able to bring about the necessary change.[27] The PVV saw the good qualities of the Dutch people come to the fore in historic periods in particular, such as the Dutch Revolt in the sixteenth century, the Golden Age in the seventeenth century, and the 1950s. Immutable character traits like courage and a love of freedom emerged during the Dutch Revolt, confidence and entrepreneurship in the Golden Age and a strong sense of solidarity and work ethos in the 50s.

By presenting its participation at the elections as a movement of the 'common people' and by introducing a more direct form of democracy, the PVV hopes to reinstall such favourable traits of the Dutch people as guiding principles for running the country. 'Only radical democratisation can break the dominance of the left-wing elite', it claimed in its 2010 election manifesto. Consequently, the party advocates the people's right to demand binding referenda and elect prime ministers and mayors, as well as the abolition of the Senate. 'Let the people have their say – collectively, they know more than the left-wing clique.'[28]

Remarkably, the PVV also argued for a modernisation of the monarchy, in which the king or queen would have a purely ceremonial function and receive a smaller allowance. Up to that point, anti-royalist sentiment in the Netherlands – such as it was – had been associated with the left, but the PVV's relationship with the royal family had suffered a serious blow by remarks made by certain royal figures, which Wilders considered as direct attacks on his party. For example, the then Princess Máxima had said in a speech that there was no such thing as a 'single Dutch identity', and in her Christmas speech, the then Queen Beatrix had called for more tolerance and less 'coarseness in word and action'. From that moment, the royal family seems to have become irreversibly linked in Wilders' mind to the left-wing elite that was trying to cross him. But where criticism of the royal family was once equal to electoral suicide – due to the old myth of an almost mystical bond between the Dutch people and the House of Orange through a shared aversion to the regents – Wilders' attack on the royal family had very little impact on his electoral success, showing that even such enduring myths can evaporate in time.[29]

And it was not just the royals who would see cuts to their funding. The PVV was envisaging a whole set of economic measures designed to break the hegemony of the 'left elite', such as a drastic reduction of the ample salaries and redundancy schemes of many office holders, including those in the House of Representatives, of perks such as trips abroad, official cars and expensive receptions for the elite, and of subsidies for political parties. Subsidies for such left-wing dominated sectors as arts and culture, new social movements and the environment should largely be scrapped, as should those for the broadcasting stations 'who claim to have a broad political spectrum but are all as left-wing as each other'.

The PVV's populism clearly shows in the party's preferred policy of attempting to break down perceived elite privileges, and in proposals to introduce a more direct form of democracy. Stylistically, this manifests itself in the frequently coarse denunciations of the elite as morally corrupt, and an idealisation of the people. This last aspect especially flows seamlessly into another cornerstone of PVV ideology: nationalism.

Third pillar: loyalty to the home country. On the PVV's nationalism

The terms *populism* and *nationalism* are similar in many ways, not least because both of them are mainly used to malign opponents. Ever since the Second World War – or in any case since the 1960s – nationalism has often been associated with war, fascism and racism. At the same time it is no exaggeration to argue that, just like populism, nationalism resonates with widely held popular views, such as a fundamental distrust of politicians and the elites (populism) and feelings of solidarity with compatriots and pride in national achievements (nationalism), which range from widespread celebrations of Dutch sporting victories to a strong empathy with the Dutch victims of large-scale international disasters. Given that both populism and nationalism are based on a powerful attachment to the country of birth, it is sometimes difficult to determine the boundaries between the two. A key difference lies in their respective views of the nature and goal of politics. Populists see politics primarily as a struggle of the people against the elite, with the aim of establishing a political system based on the will of the people. To nationalists, politics is largely about protecting the national interests and autonomy, and promoting the unity and culture of the nation.[30]

The protection and promotion of national interests and autonomy are not difficult concepts to understand. National autonomy is the aim to become, politically at least, a completely self-governing nation. The enemy can vary from an aggressive foreign power (such as the Third Reich) to supranational organisations like the European Union and NATO. Putting national interests first means rejecting more idealistic foreign policies and trade policies: development aid, human rights policies and international rule of law are only promoted if they are in the nation's best interest. But what is meant by promoting and protecting national unity and identity? That is more difficult to define. From a racial point of view, national unity can be interpreted as protecting one's own race against foreign influences, as happened in the *Volksgemeinschaft* (people's community) of the German National Socialists. The decline of racial thinking, however, has led to national unity currently being understood in a cultural sense, as a monocultural community in which everyone shares roughly the same language, history, habits, standards and values. It is the duty of politics to shield this national culture from influences from the outside (foreign cultures) or within (modernist, cosmopolitan views). In this context, the national culture is often presented as a recognisable, indivisible phenomenon that goes back centuries. The true nature of the people can be derived from its history and used as a moral compass for the future.

The PVV itself prefers to refer to its own programme with the more neutral term, *patriotism*. Patriotism, which means love of the homeland, is more an attitude than an ideology. According to the above definition, however, the PVV can unequivocally be considered a nationalist party. The party's programmes focus strongly on national culture, unity and autonomy while it increasingly peppers its rhetoric with nationalist metaphors and symbols. In *Marked for Death*, Wilders considers national pride the best means of protecting Western liberties against Islam. 'The people of the free world can defend their liberties only if they can rally around a flag with which they identify', he writes.[31] In short, being proud of one's nation and community is a necessity of life.

Five policy areas clearly highlight the party's nationalist tendencies:

- an aversion to the European Union
- a strong emphasis on Dutch interests in the party's foreign policies
- active policies promoting and protecting national culture
- an increasingly unambiguous anti-immigration agenda
- maintaining and protecting the national welfare state for its own citizens.

The Dutch referendum on the European Constitution in June 2005 gave Wilders the opportunity to vent his aversion to the European Union at an early stage. This aversion did not hinge solely on the possibility of Turkey becoming a member state – his reason for resigning from the VVD – but also on a lack of transparency, the high cost and the tendency of Brussels to interfere in such matters as Dutch immigration policy. In an article in *De Volkskrant*, he accused 'just about all politicians at The Hague' of 'putting Dutch interests in second place in favour of the interest of a European superstate that should never be established'. 'The Netherlands must continue to exist', was the slogan Bosma penned for Wilders' campaign against the constitution.[32]

Criticism of the European superstate would remain a fixed part of the PVV's programme, albeit largely in connection with the main themes, immigration and Islam, at first. In its 2006 and 2010 electoral programmes, the party proposed limiting European collaboration to economic and monetary cooperation. The

European Commission's power should be reduced as much as possible, while the European Parliament should be abolished. The struggle against the European Union gained prominence again in 2011 with the deepening euro crisis and credit crisis. Europe, rather than Islam, was the main theme of the PVV at the House of Representatives election in September 2012. In its electoral programme, titled *Hún Brussel, óns Nederland* (Their Brussels, our Netherlands), the PVV calls for drastic measures such as leaving the European Union and the euro zone, and immediately withdrawing from the European Stability Mechanism (ESM), the emergency fund that grants loans to impoverished EU countries like Greece, Spain and Ireland. According to the PVV, the European Union is a 'snare' that 'keeps tightening', into which the 'proud people of the Netherlands' have been 'lured by the progressive elite'. Unworldly Brussels technocrats are supposedly bent on 'forcing the country into line within a great European Superstate', in which we would be 'tied to countries with completely different cultures by a rope around our necks'. The programme continues,

> In the Netherlands we believe that 'if you take care of the pennies the pounds will take care of themselves'. People in other cultures are more interested in early pensions, dodging taxes and lazing in the sun with a drink.[33]

Just like Norway and Switzerland, the Netherlands should limit its involvement in the EU to signing trade treaties.

On the whole, the PVV believes that 'Dutch foreign policy should be in the Dutch national interest'. A seemingly watertight argument, except that 'the Dutch national interest' can be interpreted in different ways. To the PVV it means, among other things, that the Netherlands should pull out of expensive military missions abroad. This includes missions targeting Islamic fundamentalism – a remarkable change of tack, given Wilders' earlier neoconservative ambitions. Did his nationalism triumph over his more internationally oriented anti-Islamic alarmism after all? That would be jumping to conclusions, as the PVV regularly puts the international fight against Islam before national interests. For instance, the party argues for freezing relations with, and stopping arms deliveries to, most Islamic countries, regardless of negative economic consequences. And how does its call for protecting threatened Christian minorities in the Middle East, such as the Copts in Egypt or the Armenians in Turkey, serve the national interest? The same is true of the paragraph on Israel in the party programme, which includes such demands as 'political support for the construction of Jewish villages in Judea and Samaria' (the West Bank), 'moving the Dutch embassy from Tel Aviv to Jerusalem', and the recognition of Jordan as the only Palestinian state ('Jordan = Palestine') – radical viewpoints even by Israeli standards.[34]

When it comes to the promotion of national culture and identity, nationalist arguments clash somewhat with those of populism. According to Wilders, decades of progressive 'cultural relativism' and cosmopolitan idealism have dimmed people's awareness of their own culture and history. They are in need of some 're-education'. To achieve this, the PVV warmly advocates a stronger focus on national history in schools and museums, highlighting its positive aspects in particular: 'Our country's heroic history deserves to be put in the spotlight.' The Dutch flag should fly on schools and public buildings, and Wilders is also a supporter of introducing a daily flag ceremony similar to the American Pledge of Allegiance. Probably more than any other Dutch politician, he sprinkles his speeches with references to heroes of national history like William of Orange and the seventeenth century admirals Piet Heyn and Michiel de Ruyter. At a photo shoot for *Veronica Magazine*, Wilders even posed as his great hero, Michiel de Ruyter. To Wilders, such national heroes are the embodiment of timeless national strengths that are in the genes of the Dutch people. 'We are destined for great things. We are still the race of Piet Heyn and Michiel de Ruyter. Our deeds are limited only by our capacity to dream.'[35] The PVV also lash out against groups who, in their view, sully national traditions and history by laying exaggerated emphasis on the Netherlands' slave trade history, or condemning 'Black Pete', Saint Nicholas' helper who traditionally wears black make-up, as racist.

While Wilders wants to foster pride in the nation's history, Bosma in particular has made it his aim to protect the Dutch language. For example, he used his position as chair of the Dutch Language Union to speak up against the Anglicisation of the Dutch education system and academia in the House of Representatives. 'Dutch is in danger of becoming a rural dialect that is apparently no longer good enough for teaching at an academic level', Bosma said.[36] He also tabled a motion to guarantee a minimum of 35% Dutch-language songs broadcast on the Dutch national station, Radio 2. Another of Bosma's ideas is supporting Afrikaans, a language closely related to Dutch spoken in South Africa and Namibia. The position of white South Africans is particularly close to Bosma's heart. The PVV tabled questions in the House of Representatives as well as at the European Parliament on the white population's precarious situation under the new, in its view racist, ANC regime. In May 2015, Martin Bosma published a 500-page book on the fate of the Afrikaners, which he saw as a model of what the Dutch would be facing if mass immigration continued.

> A people is marginalised on its own soil – other peoples are taking over its place. The fate of the Afrikaners seems to be a precursor to our future: building up a country, letting masses of newcomers in and finally being reduced to a powerless minority ourselves.[37]

Though Bosma explicitly declared his opposition to the old apartheid system, Wilders was far from happy with his flirtation with the Afrikaners. A dissident says,

> According to Wilders, this fascination with South Africa could easily be construed as racism. He has blocked parliamentary questions on the subject in the past, but when it comes down to it, Bosma is too important to Wilders to be dismissed for that reason.[38]

44 The four pillars of PVV ideology

Besides the Afrikaner cousins, Bosma sees the Flemish as a kindred people and frequently refers to Flanders as the Southern Netherlands. In an article in *NRC Handelsblad* in July 2008, Bosma and Wilders even suggested strengthening the ties to the country by establishing a Flemish–Dutch union, using the widely expected downfall of the state of Belgium as an opportunity to 'finally rectify historic mistakes'. After all, were Flanders and the Netherlands not united by a single culture and was the national border dividing them not purely artificial? 'The Northern and Southern Netherlands have a shared history', according to Bosma and Wilders. 'We are about to find out that we will also have a shared future. The Netherlands must embrace the Flemish Lion and say, welcome home, we have never forgotten you.'[39] The two PVV members believed a referendum would be the proper way of finding out what the Dutch and Flemish thought about a reunion.

Should this plan be treated seriously? Did it stem from a deep-seated conviction, or was the party putting out feelers? The latter seems to be the case, as the PVV has never returned to the subject in the House of Representatives, while the party's electoral programmes only discuss intensifying the collaboration with Flanders in very broad terms. Yet, premature as they were, the reunion plans dovetail neatly with what is often considered the main aim of nationalism, namely the merging of cultural and political nations. Nor is it a new idea. Even before WWII, the historian Pieter Geyl was an important advocate for a Greater Netherlands, comprising the Netherlands, Belgium and South Africa. To his chagrin, however, the idea was soon taken over by fascist and semi-fascist movements in the Netherlands and Flanders, turning the discussion about a Great Netherlands into a taboo subject for a long time after WWII, even though the Benelux and the Dutch Language Union made efforts to strengthen the bond between the two countries. Judging by the lukewarm reactions the PVV's plan triggered in the Netherlands and in Belgium, the taboo had since been replaced by a lack of interest.[40]

Incidentally, the party's territorial ambitions were not aimed solely towards expansion, but included giving up some of the Kingdom of the Netherlands' territories. As far as the PVV was concerned, the Dutch Antilles were welcome to declare independence 'sooner rather than later'. In PVV rhetoric, the archipelago in the Caribbean Sea was called 'a largely corrupt den of thieves' where the 'piña colada mafia' lined its pockets with Dutch taxpayers' money. Their ties to the Crown also made it easy for Antilleans to settle in the Netherlands. In cities like Den Helder, Dordrecht, Eindhoven and Rotterdam, groups of predominantly unskilled young Antilleans were perceived as causing disorder and contributing to a rise in crime. If the PVV had a say in it, criminal Antilleans would be sent straight back to their islands, something that would be greatly facilitated by breaking off political relations. With his usual tact and diplomacy, Wilders suggested 'selling the Antilles on eBay', or failing that, making a gift of them to President Hugo Chávez of the neighbouring Venezuela.[41]

While the PVV's campaign against the Antilles was less fierce than the one against Islam, it showed the PVV was able to separate the subjects of

The four pillars of PVV ideology 45

immigration and integration from Islam. Its anti-immigration stance was based not only on anti-Islamic alarmism, but also on a broader need to protect the national community against newcomers. Besides the Antilleans, immigrants from Central and Eastern Europe were the target. The criticism was not directed at the refugees or descendants of refugees who had come from Hungary or Czechoslovakia in the 50s and 60s, or the Polish immigrant workers in the 20s – after all, they had all but assimilated into the national community and were often recognisable only by their surname – but at the Eastern Europeans who had started coming to the Netherlands in 2007 to find temporary, or permanent, jobs. With Poland, Romania and Bulgaria joining the EU, the PVV predicted the Dutch labour market would be flooded by new, cheap labour from such countries. Surely it was up to the Dutch government to protect its own hard-working population against this wave of immigrant workers? Besides creating economic competition, many of these Eastern Europeans (generally called Poles in the Netherlands for convenience's sake) supposedly caused trouble and disorder in many places. The party launched a website in late 2011 where people could report complaints about Central and Eastern Europeans as a means of mapping the problems. The party's electoral programmes argued for barring Eastern Europeans from the Dutch labour market before they 'force our people out'.[42] The fact that the Netherlands would probably be in breach of EU regulations by doing so only served as another reason for leaving the European Union, according to the PVV.

Similarly, the Netherlands should ignore all those European treaties on asylum policies, as most asylum seekers from African and Muslim countries were just 'economic fortune seekers' who try to secure a place in the Netherlands with devious tricks like making up stories of persecution, lying about their nationality, starting a family or deliberately delaying asylum procedures. Asylum policy should therefore be based on distrust rather than compassion. Only emergency situations should justify allowing refugees into the country, and then no more than 1000 a year. The refugee crisis of 2015 only served to harden the PVV's stance rather than soften it.

As we have seen, the PVV links the issues of immigration and integration to fairly specific groups such as Muslims, Antilleans, recently arrived immigrants from Central and Eastern Europe and the more diverse group of asylum seekers. The party is not generally opposed to other ethnicities such as the Chinese and Vietnamese minorities in the Netherlands, which it has never agitated against. At the House of Representatives election of 2006, the party even put forward a Chinese-Dutch candidate who also campaigned in the Chinese community.[43] Similarly, people from Suriname and the former Dutch East Indies (Indonesia) have never collectively been the subject of its criticism. Furthermore, the PVV has repeatedly declared itself to be fiercely opposed to anti-Semitism in the Netherlands. The PVV's anti-Islamic alarmism has reportedly found followers in the Hindustani–Surinamese and Moluccan communities, while some Dutch Jews support the party because of its strong identification with Israel. Just how large these groups are is unclear, however.

Be that as it may, the distinction the PVV makes between different ethnic minorities goes to prove that, in the strictest sense of the word, the party cannot be called racist. Skin colour and 'racial purity' are irrelevant to the question of whether or not a minority should be allowed to be part of the national community – arguing otherwise would, after all, be absurd coming from someone with Indonesian ancestry like Wilders. So what does the party see as the deciding factor? National culture is part of it. While the PVV may not think in terms of superior or inferior races, it does distinguish between what it sees as superior and inferior cultures. Newcomers bringing with them a culture that is deemed inferior (explicitly Muslim culture, implicitly also African and Antillean cultures) should be barred, or at least encouraged to return to their home countries, as much as possible. They only have a future if they manage to free themselves from their own cultures and adapt perfectly to Dutch society, thus no longer causing trouble. But why does the party not agitate as much against the Hindu, Indonesian, Chinese or Jewish populations even though they, too, often adhere to many of their habits and traditions? In the party's view, those minorities probably either have overly strong historic ties with Dutch culture (particularly the Jewish and Indonesian populations) or are not considered a threat due to their small numbers and generally positive contribution to the economy (the Chinese and Hindu populations). Over the years, they have become a more or less integral part of the Dutch nation. The inconsistency of the PVV's reasoning also manifests itself in the party's views regarding the recent immigrants from Central and Eastern Europe. The Polish plumber, Bulgarian plasterer and Romanian lorry driver are not so much a cultural as an economic threat to the national community. That reason in particular, and to a much larger degree than their 'culture', makes their presence undesirable.

The PVV's stance on immigration and integration can therefore not be ascribed to racism or xenophobia, but is motivated by a combination of anti-Islamic alarmism (where Muslims are concerned) and a specific type of nationalism. This type – usually called *nativism* – affords the most rights to the people who have lived in a country the longest.[44] It is a world view most succinctly expressed by Flemish Bloc, the right-wing nationalist party, in its slogan, 'Our people first'. The PVV never adopted this motto; in an interview with the Flemish paper *De Standaard* in November 2004, Wilders even called it 'an objectionable slogan' and a 'despicable thought' which made him 'sick to the stomach' because it reminded him of a 'tragic past I wouldn't want to reintroduce to the Netherlands'.[45] In reality, however, the idea that the country's original population have more rights than foreigners increasingly became a guiding principle. The PVV did concede that certain groups of immigrants had become part of the Dutch population over time, as they were completely integrated and had therefore stopped causing trouble. Having adapted perfectly to the point of merging with the native population, they had earned the same rights. They, too, should consider themselves part of what the PVV called 'our people'. Not so the immigrants and their descendants who did supposedly inflict serious damage in the form of unfair competition, crime, abuse of social services, and by contributing to the housing shortage and constituting an irritating religious or cultural presence. According to the PVV, it is an important task of politics to protect 'our people' against such immigrants.

The nativist element is particularly prominent in the party's attitude to social security. 'Our laboriously built-up welfare state is a source of pride, but has also become a magnet for unskilled immigrants in recent decades', the party concludes in its 2010 electoral programme.[46] The PVV has made several proposals to allow only the indigenous Dutch population access to the welfare state as much as possible, demanding that immigrants need to have lived and worked in the Netherlands for ten years to be able to claim benefits. Any immigrants who have not sufficiently mastered the Dutch language or still wear burkas after that period, forfeit that right. Migrant workers should be barred from entering the country as much as possible and made to leave immediately after their contracts expire. The PVV expects such stringent measures to save the government a lot of money, in turn removing the need for many of the welfare reforms that other parties consider necessary, such as raising the pension age, relaxing dismissal regulations, abolishing student grants and raising health insurance co-payments.

This change of attitude to the welfare state has undoubtedly been the biggest substantive U-turn of Wilders' political career. Was Wilders not an out-and-out neoliberal in his VVD years, who argued for drastic social security cuts and wanted to abolish various employee rights? His 2005 *Declaration of Independence* still uncompromisingly states that 'an extensive and detailed system of benefits, subsidies and services has made many citizens dependent on a government that watches over its children and declares them to be "weak" or "needy" at the slightest pretence'.[47] Now, the welfare state has suddenly become 'a source of pride', 'a shield for the poor', and 'a question of civilisation', which 'the Dutch people have willingly funded with part of their salaries for decades'. His role model in this is no longer Ronald Reagan but Willem Drees, the social democrat who was prime minister in the 50s and is generally regarded as the father of the Dutch welfare state. Wilders believes that only the PVV can be trusted with his legacy. However, the welfare state chauvinism that Wilders introduced to the PVV in 2006 does not mean he no longer believes in a free market. In most cases, the PVV still argues for drastically rolling back government intervention, substantial deregulation and large tax cuts. After all, a large government does not fit with the PVV's image of the Netherlands as a country of entrepreneurs.

The nativist, 'our people first' way of thinking is also key to the party's position on safety and combating crime. Its demand for higher penalties for criminals with a different or dual nationality can hardly be interpreted any other way. The party believes such criminals should be deported to their country of origin immediately after serving their sentences, and if it were up to the PVV, criminal Antilleans would share that fate. Does it follow that the party is more lenient towards 'home-grown criminals'? Not exactly. After all, the fourth pillar of PVV ideology constitutes a strong emphasis on law and order.

Fourth pillar: for the safety of the country. The argument for more law and order

Though the law-and-order pillar is quite straightforward compared to the others, this does not make it of less importance to the PVV's programme. In fact, the 2010 electoral programme raises the subject of safety even before discussing Islam and immigration. While the PVV often links its call for law and order to the subjects of immigration and Islam, it is also an expression of a more deeply held view of society which can be defined as the idea that there is a certain natural order everyone should subject themselves to, and that those who violate it should be severely punished. On the one hand, this natural order is based on traditional values such as respect for another's property, care for the elderly, obedience to authority and working hard to make a living, and on the other hand, the PVV has embraced more modern values such as equal rights for men and women and for heterosexuals and homosexuals, respect for animals, a certain degree of freedom of choice regarding abortion and euthanasia, and wide-ranging freedom of speech.

This mixture of traditional and modern values supposedly comprises a normality recognised by all reasonable people as the key to keeping society liveable. The emphasis on normality explains why members of the PVV so often use words like 'mad' (or even 'barking mad'), 'abnormal', 'madness', 'insane' and 'nonsense' to typify situations or measures they disagree with.[48] The ideas of their political rivals are not so much different as abnormal, and have nothing to do with reality. Having said that, opponents of the PVV have also frequently associated the party's opinions with mental illness, as the use of terms like *xenophobia*, *Islamophobia* and *paranoia* show. The PVV itself considers its programme a pinnacle of 'common sense'. With its 'sensible outlook', it proposes 'practical solutions' in 'everyday language' in order to restore the natural order that has been disturbed since the 60s by all kinds of 'crazy hippie ideas' in a whole range of fields such as the 'fun-and-games' culture in education, the 'softly-softly approach' to treating drug addicts and the 'climate madness' of the 'environment freaks'. The PVV argues for restoring the natural order, among other things by focusing the education system on imparting knowledge, forming character and teaching discipline and respect for authority (for instance by forbidding pupils to address teachers informally). Vocational schools and reform schools should be reinstated for the benefit of practically minded and incorrigible children respectively. Drug addicts should be forced into rehabilitation, and if that fails, be 'excluded from freedom of movement in society and put to work in government labour camps'.[49]

According to the PVV, the largest disturbance of the natural order is caused by a huge increase of crime in the Netherlands. 'Our streets are plagued by thugs', it says in the *Agenda of Hope and Optimism* electoral programme. 'Large parts of the Netherlands are very unsafe. Where crime used to be limited to isolated incidents, we are now seeing whole neighbourhoods being taken over. Street terrorists are in control.'[50] If the government is no longer able to guarantee the safety of its citizens, the country has a serious safety and authority crisis on its hands that urgently calls for radical, unorthodox measures, and the PVV has a whole set of them at the ready. The party believes that in order to combat crime, the police need to 'hold sway over the street' again. One way of achieving this is by expanding and reforming the police force on the one hand, so there will be a greater police presence on the street ('Police that take action rather than talk'). Police officers should be selected for their decisiveness rather than social skills, supplied with improved equipment (including American batons) and uniforms that 'stand out'. On the other hand, the PVV wants a zero tolerance policy similar to the one former New York mayor Rudolph Giuliani introduced with some success. The police should take immediate action no matter how slight the offence, 'to leave no doubt about who is in charge in our districts, villages and cities'. The PVV argues for a radical break with the Dutch tradition of tolerance. For instance, the party wants the ban on squatting, which it was partly responsible for implementing, to be strictly enforced, and administrative disobedience (such as a mayor refusing to deport illegal immigrants) to be punished immediately. Though the party initially voiced some very outspoken views on the famous Dutch policy of tolerance regarding soft drugs, demanding in its 2006 election pamphlet that coffee shops (establishments selling cannabis) be closed down and homegrowing dealt with rigorously, that rigid view had been watered down by 2010 and 2012 to only closing coffee shops within a one-kilometre radius of schools. Whether the change of tack was dictated by new insights, the unfeasibility of a general ban or even electoral motives is hard to say.

The party displays greater consistency in its call for much heavier penalties for criminals. According to the PVV, criminal justice has focused too much on offenders' rights, motives and future in the past 40 years. Should it not in fact have been based on retribution on behalf of the victim and on the deterrent effect of severe punishment? In the memorandum *Justitie en Politie met Ambitie* (Judiciary and police with ambition), the PVV bluntly demands that in criminal proceedings, compassion and understanding be shown only to victims, as the perpetrators of a crime have 'violated the trust of society, eroding the citizens' sense of freedom and safety'. 'The consequence of this should be that society cancels its trust in the criminal, in a way that effectively restores a feeling of freedom and safety in our society.' Not only does the PVV want longer sentences for hardened criminals, but also for them to be served in less luxurious prisons. Inmates should fund their own stay by working, not get early release for good behaviour and receive less guidance when returning to society. The PVV wants to build special 'thug villages' in remote corners of every province, where repeat offenders are to live in special container houses. Minors may be accompanied by their families. 'Dump all the trash in one heap', said Wilders, who claimed the idea came from Denmark. Besides isolating them, the PVV simultaneously wants to expose criminals by placing photos of them online and putting them to work publicly in so-called chain gangs. To heighten their humiliation, they should also be made to wear 'cheerful pink outfits' – one of the measures taken from the infamous American sheriff Joe Arpaio's vast arsenal.[51] The PVV did not take over other typically American law-and-order policies, however. For example, the party is opposed to the death penalty on principle and draws the line at the right to bear firearms which many Americans find so important.

The trouble was of course that the PVV could make any number of bold proposals, but that they would in all likelihood be ignored by the Dutch judiciary. Wilders did not place much confidence in the 'left-wing liberal' Dutch judges, who in his eyes handed out far too lenient sentences and did not treat asylum applications with due strictness. The PVV argued for limiting their liberties without, however, abolishing the rule of law, by appointing judges for ten-year periods so it would be possible to dismiss those who had demonstrably failed. Members of the Supreme Court of the Netherlands should even be appointed by direct election. On the other hand, the PVV wanted to implement heavy minimum and maximum penalties and introduce the American principle of 'three strikes and you're out', by which a third conviction automatically leads to life imprisonment.

Wilders' distrust of the judiciary does not seem to have been lessened by his acquittal in 2011. In 2009, the Amsterdam Court of Justice had Wilders prosecuted on several charges of inciting hatred and discrimination. The 'trial of the century', as Wilders called it, started in January 2010 and went on for more than 18 months. It generated a lot of national and international publicity for Wilders, and enabled him to portray himself more than ever as a victim of left-wing political correctness. 'Where the left and Islam come together, freedom will suffer. My friends, make no mistake, my prosecution is a full-fledged attack by the left on freedom of speech in order to please Muslims', he claimed in a speech in New York.[52] However, the trial was also a drain on his strength and nerves, various dissidents report. 'He was terrified of being convicted. Not least because it would make it more difficult for him to enter the United States.'[53] He had also taken the costly step of acquiring the services of famous lawyer Bram Moszkowicz, which set the PVV leader back around half-a-million euros.

But his acquittal in 2011 was not to be the last time Wilders would be involved with the Dutch judiciary. In 2014, the public prosecutor pressed new charges on the grounds of a remark Wilders had made at a post-election party gathering in April 2014. Wilders asked a cheering crowd of followers whether they wanted more or fewer Moroccans. To his followers' chant of 'fewer, fewer', Wilders replied, 'Then we will make sure of that'. Not only did that speech lead to a new trial, it induced several people, including two members of the House of Representatives, to leave the party.

A closer examination of the ideology

Anti-Islamic alarmism, populism, nationalism and law and order form the four pillars on which the PVV project is based. Almost all of the party's views can be derived from these four principles, supplemented with further principles as needed to support particular positions. A popular PVV target, for example, is young Moroccan criminals, since this brings together law and order, alarmism over Islam and the principle of putting 'our people first'. Wilders' 'fewer Moroccans' speech killed several birds with one stone. Some subjects cannot be derived directly from the four pillars, as in the case of animal rights and animal welfare, to which the PVV has devoted considerable attention. These issues were smuggled into the party by animal rights activist Dion Graus, a member of the House of Representatives since 2006. The subject is not particularly well worked out, but we can at least be certain that the PVV, unlike the Party for the Animals, is not led by a radical, environmentally friendly vision of society in which humans and animals are seen as equal. The PVV's emphasis is on fundamental rules of conduct such as 'decency and respect for defenceless living creatures' along with severe punishment for transgressors. The party has also successfully argued for an animal welfare emergency line and special 'animal cops' to provide protection and catch perpetrators of cruelty. The subject is more than a personal hobby for Graus, as shown by the party's support for a bill to prohibit ritual slaughter, which caused internal controversy because it affected Jews as well as Muslims.

The PVV's ideological project raises several questions. First, how should the party's ideology be labelled? Does it fit within an existing ideological trend? What parties, past and present, domestically and internationally, does it resemble? There is also the question of how seriously we should take that ideology. Surely a man like Wilders is first and foremost a practical politician, more of a strategist than an ideologist? Or to put it rather less diplomatically, is the party's ideology anything more than pure opportunism captured in words and guided by the flavour of the month? For some time, 'Stick a label on the PVV' has been something of a nationwide parlour game in which Dutch citizens from all walks of life, from celebrities to the man on the street, journalists, scholars and politicians – whether still active or sidelined – have participated. As is often the case with parlour games, it has descended into misunderstanding, incomprehension and bickering. In an attempt at mediation, an editorial in the newspaper *NRC Handelsblad* called on people to abandon all labels, stating that 'A party with objectionable views should be countered with arguments, not labels.'[54]

It is not surprising that this call fell on deaf ears, as *NRC Handelsblad* is asking the impossible here. Every attempt at interpretation involves some degree of labelling, as the newspaper illustrates by itself attributing objectionable views to the PVV, before calling for an avoidance of such labelling in the very next sentence. The issue is rather whether the terms used are sound and as neutrally grounded as possible, and whether we avoid confirmation bias by also looking for evidence that contradicts our views. The need for labels is perfectly understandable. In order to judge politicians and parties, particularly in the case of newcomers, we must know what compass guides them, what their core values are and what developments we can expect in the future. Placing them in a particular political movement and comparing them with other parties, past and present, is therefore the standard approach.

The labels most often used to characterise the PVV are *populism*, *fascism* and *far right*. Going by commonly held views in political research, populism is certainly one of the pillars of PVV ideology, but it does not cover everything. Do the four PVV pillars combined form an ideology that could be called fascist? To call the term *fascism* emotionally charged would be an understatement. Labelling a party as fascist connects it with the Second World War, the moral benchmark for good and evil since 1945. Nevertheless, the loaded nature of the term is not in itself a reason not to use it about the PVV in concrete cases. Such reasoning, however, must follow from an ideological comparison between fascism and PVV ideology. True, there are certain discernible similarities between the PVV and fascist movements, such as the National Socialist Movement (NSB) in the 30s and 40s in the Netherlands, including strong nationalism, law and order ideology and the denunciation of an elite class characterised as a homogenous block. The ideological cocktail presented to us by the PVV and the NSB, however, contains additional ingredients which constitute significant differences between the parties. In the case of the NSB that ingredient is clearly Italian fascism and from 1934–35 German National Socialism. This means that the NSB was against liberal democracy in principle because it was based on what was seen as the false notion of human equality. The PVV, by contrast, embraces liberal democracy and sees itself as its protector against a new danger comparable to fascism, that of Islam. According to the PVV, Islam threatens another attainment which the fascists regarded as unimportant, namely the right to individual development. With his emphasis on 'the people', the liberal Wilders has become more collectivist over time, but he is still miles from the Nazi adage, '*Du bist nichts, dein Volk ist alles*' (You are nothing, your nation is everything).[55]

What the PVV and NSB have in common is their aversion to a certain community: Muslims in the case of the PVV and Jews in the case of the NSB. Nevertheless, there is a crucial difference between anti-Islamic alarmism and anti-Semitism. The former is directed at a religion (or ideology, as the PVV puts it) which can in principle be renounced. The anti-Semitism of the NSB, however, conforming with that of the German Nazis, was biologically underpinned. Those who no longer felt any affinity for Judaism could still be persecuted as Jews according to racial doctrine. In that respect it might make more sense to compare the PVV's alarmism over Islam with antipapism, the aversion to Roman Catholicism, present in the Netherlands in forms ranging from mild to virulent until the 60s. Many of the arguments now employed by the PVV against Muslims (disloyalty towards the Dutch nation, intolerance, tyrannical tendencies, demographic conquest) appear to come directly from pre-war antipapist papers and pamphlets.[56] Nevertheless, Wilders is on shaky ground here, as shown by the outcry over his 'fewer Moroccans' speech, when many, even within his own party, feel he crossed a line. 'This is no longer a matter of a religion you can renounce; this is a background which you cannot do anything about', says one of those who turned their back on the PVV for this reason.[57]

Still, on detailed comparison, there is little reason to consider the PVV ideology to be fascist, raising the question whether it would not be better to avoid this extremely loaded term as far as possible. Is the PVV an extreme right-wing

The four pillars of PVV ideology 53

party, perhaps? Basing their theory on a study of party documents and interviews, researchers for the Anne Frank Foundation conclude that it is, albeit at the moderate end of extreme right-wing politics (which they term 'new radical right'). They define extreme right-wing as 'a positive orientation towards one's own culture, aversion to what is "foreign" and political opponents, and a tendency towards authoritarianism', a rather broad definition open to multiple interpretations, which made it easy for Bosma and Wilders to dismiss the study in an opinion piece in *De Volkskrant* as yet another attempt by the 'Left Church' to silence the party.[58] What politician was not positively oriented towards their own culture? And in what way was the PVV averse to what is foreign? The PVV was one of the few Dutch parties to build a reputation beyond the borders, Bosma and Wilders pointed out. The fact that the Anne Frank Foundation researchers characterised the PVV as occupying the moderate end of the extreme right did not help matters. How can something be moderately extreme?

It is easy to criticise, but how *should* the PVV be characterised? Is there an existing label which fits the party or have Wilders and Bosma come up with something completely new? If we restrict ourselves to the Netherlands, the most obvious comparison is of course with the LPF. Although Wilders and Bosma never worked for the party, as we will see the PVV counts many former Fortuyn sympathisers among its voters and activists. Wilders himself has on several occasions acknowledged that he is indebted to Professor Pim and his Fortuynesque ideas. Could the PVV be considered a Fortuynesque party?

When we line up the party programmes and documents side by side, we do indeed find a number of similarities. The PVV's criticism of the elite is almost identical to that of the LPF, including use of typical Fortuynesque terms such as 'Left Church', 'cultural relativism', 'subsidy socialists' and 'backroom politics'. Both parties see the cause of the leadership crisis as dating back to the 60s, a decade dominated by progressive cultural relativism, a self-effacing, internationalist view on national identity and a general aversion to authority. In response to the weakened Dutch society Wilders and Fortuyn both present Islam as the advancing enemy at odds with Western culture and achievements such as the emancipation of women and homosexuals.

Nevertheless, despite his call for a 'Cold War on Islam', Fortuyn ultimately paid relatively little attention to the religion in his bestseller *De puinhopen van acht jaar Paars* (The Wreckage of Eight Purple Years) and the election manifesto *Zakelijk met een hart* (Professional with Passion). When it comes down to it, Fortuyn saw the reform of the welfare state and public sector as his most important aim. It was after his death that many of his followers made the battle against Islam a spearhead of Fortuynesque ideology. In March 2004, the LPF proposed a motion to prohibit wearing headscarves in official civil service positions (a motion Wilders, as a VVD MP, voted against at the time). In February 2006, the LPF think tank worked with Hans Jansen to organise the conference on Islam mentioned above. However, the issue of 'Islamisation' was never as dominant for the LPF after Fortuyn as it is for the PVV, with the LPF proposing less far-reaching measures and using milder language. A tax on headscarves, prohibition of the Koran, denaturalisation of Moroccan street criminals with double passports and possible deportation of Muslims with radical ideas are measures which were never proposed by Fortuyn or his disciples.

On various other subjects, such as crime, asylum policy, European integration and environmental policy, we see the same tendencies in both parties, but a difference in the radical nature and tone of the solutions. Despite all its criticism of Europe, the LPF never considered departure from the European Union or the euro, while its proposals on law and order come across as relatively moderate. Fortuyn's arguments for a more positive attitude to the nation did not translate into glorification of national heroes such as Michiel de Ruyter and Piet Heyn, American-style flag waving or elevation of 'the Dutch people' as a unified force unchanged through the ages. A more principled, clear-cut difference between the two parties is in their attitude to the welfare state. Fortuyn, like the young Wilders, was a strong proponent of greater market influence, a less extensive social security system and a substantial reduction in the number of civil servants. Since 2006, however, the PVV's socio-economic programme appears to have become more left wing, and subordinate to their nationalism. The extensive welfare state is no longer presented as a strange Dutch abnormality but as a source of national pride which should be protected against immigrants and Eurocrats.[59]

In comparing the LPF and PVV, we must of course bear in mind that the context in 2002 was different from that in 2012. Fortuyn's early death prevented him from experiencing the murder of Theo van Gogh, the attacks in Madrid, London and Mumbai and the banking and euro crises. Would Fortuyn too have become more radical as a result of these events? It is quite possible. In any case the LPF's tone, which shocked so many Dutch citizens in 2001 and 2002, sounds rather more moderate in retrospect; much as Elvis Presley sounded a good deal more innocent after the Rolling Stones. Due to its more radical proposals, harder tone and more bombastic brand of nationalism, as well as its welfare-state patriotism, the PVV comes closer than the LPF to a family of parties, as political scientists term them, which has emerged in Europe since the 90s.

This family is generally referred to as exhibiting some combination of populist, radical or new-radical, right-wing and nationalist characteristics.[60] Although there is some scholarly debate behind the various terms used, it is sufficient here to note that these parties oppose immigration and supranational collaboration in the name of national unity, while also wanting to bridge the substantial gap between the morally superior people and a corrupt elite. Dutch political scientist Cas Mudde adds authoritarianism as a fundamental characteristic, the belief in a strictly ordered society, in which undermining authority is harshly punished. Other more peripheral characteristics identified by various authors as belonging to this family, which I term *national populist* here, are resistance to economic and cultural globalisation, a preference for traditional family values, a tendency towards conspiracy theories and a certain opportunism when it comes to economic and foreign policy issues, which these parties consider to be of secondary importance. According to Mudde, the economic aspect in particular marks out the sometimes unclear boundary between this family and its ideological neighbours, neoconservatives and liberal populists (among whom Mudde counts Fortuyn), who give the economy top priority.

The best known and largest parties in this family are the French Front National of Jean-Marie Le Pen and his daughter Marine Le Pen; the Schweizerische Volkspartei (Swiss People's Party, SVP); the Freiheitliche Partei Österreichs (Freedom Party of Austria, FPÖ), which was really placed on the map by Jörg Haider and is now led by Heinz-Christian Strache; Pia Kjærsgaard's Danske Folkeparti (Danish People's Party, DFP); the Vlaams Blok/Vlaams Belang (Flemish Bloc/Flemish Interest, VB) led by Filip Dewinter and Gerolf Annemans; and finally the Italian Lega Nord (Northern League, LN).

Based on the literature which has appeared on these parties it is not difficult to see the family resemblance with the PVV; they all exhibit a clear aversion to an elite, generally including the established parties, the media, the judiciary, the civil service and universities, while typically talking of 'the people' as a character whose voice only the party itself is able to hear. When it comes to socioeconomics, many national populist parties have notably exchanged their neoliberal position for a kind of welfare chauvinism directed against the European Union on the one hand and immigrants who abuse the facilities of the welfare state on the other. Here the European Union has few supporters, and the parties appear to compete in coming up with new hard measures to combat crime and punish criminals. Resistance to immigration and mistrust of immigrants is another family trait: some political scientists therefore consider these parties as primarily 'anti-immigrant parties'.[61] For most of these parties the anti-immigration position has been connected since 9/11 with anti-Islamic alarmist views. Bat Ye'or's books fly off the shelves in such circles, though Wilders' and Bosma's crusade mentality is absent in most cases: most parties see Islam as one issue among many.

There are further differences between these parties. The different contexts in which the members of the family operate give each one their own peculiarities. Flemish Bloc/Interest and Lega Nord, for example, focus their nationalism on specific regions within their states, namely Flanders and Northern Italy (dubbed 'Padania' by Lega Nord). In Haider's FPÖ and Jean-Marie Le Pen's Front National the history of national collaboration played an important role (whereas among their successors as party leaders this seems less important). The Danish People's Party is deeply rooted in the Scandinavian tradition of resistance to the pressure of high taxes, while the Swiss SVP started out as a conservative party for farmers and tradesmen.

Besides the PVV's heavy focus on Islam, the PVV differs in its relatively libertarian views on a number of ethical issues. Wilders and his fellow party members stand up for the right to abortion, embryo selection and euthanasia, while also projecting an image as protector of the emancipation of women and homosexuals, who they see as threatened by Islam. For parties such as Flemish Bloc, the Front National and Lega Nord, homosexuality is seen as an aberration and the emancipation of women as a threat. It is difficult to imagine even the rather more libertarian Marine Le Pen supporting the PVV motion which would allow homosexual soldiers to take part in Gay Pride parades in uniform.[62]

Initially, Wilders openly distanced himself from most of his political relatives, seeking allies in Israel and the United States rather than Europe. In Israel he feels closely connected with far-right nationalists such as Avigdor Lieberman and his party, Yisrael Beiteinu, and with Aryeh Eldad and his Hatikva Party, which are particularly popular among settlers.[63] Since his neoconservative phase Wilders has sought inspiration in the United States. The fact that Wilders wrote his latest book in English and had it published by an American publisher shows that he has more than half an eye on the other side of the ocean. Wilders' network is increasingly limited to a fairly isolated, small group of anti-Islamic alarmists who, like the PVV, tend to feel closely connected with Israel. In the next chapter we will look into his American contacts in more depth and see that in 2013 and 2014, Wilders sought contact with the Front National, the FPÖ and Lega Nord. In doing so he acknowledged what had long been clear to many onlookers.

The PVV's pro-American and pro-Israeli bias and libertarian ethical views may well make them an outsider in this family. These peculiarities may have been necessary ingredients to make a national populist programme palatable in the Netherlands. The orientation towards the US and Israel allays possible associations with World War II, which far-right parties otherwise risk triggering in the Netherlands: how can a party which stands up so strongly for Israel be seen as wrong or fascist? By defending libertarian achievements the PVV has also succeeded in elevating its own specific national populism above pure hatred of foreigners, narrow-mindedness and resentment. The emphasis on protection of libertarian ethical achievements against progressive naïvety and Islamic threats dovetails nicely with the Fortuynism which previously proved so successful in the Netherlands.

The final judgement here must be that the PVV has developed a strongly radicalised ideology, a variant of Fortuyn's liberal populism, which has thus taken it into different political territory, namely that of national populism. The strong focus on Islam, orientation towards Israel and the US, and relatively libertarian ethics and politics makes the PVV something of an outsider in its political family; a status all too familiar to Wilders.

National populism as strategy or ideology?

In certain circles the search for the right label for Wilders' ideology may arouse some irritation. Does it really make any difference whether the PVV is described as liberal populist, national populist or radical right? Are we not, in fact, taking the man and his ideas far too seriously, looking for an intellectual consistency and depth which simply are not there? On the first point, yes, it matters that we use the right label, not only because terms such as fascism are used rather lazily but also because the label allows us to understand what guides the PVV and what to expect in the future. This means taking the PVV's ideas seriously, rather than seeing them as interchangeable slogans intended purely to win votes. But what if that is precisely what they are? What if Wilders is a born opportunist who knows from his years of experience in politics in The Hague precisely what he should say to win votes or gain power? Did he not quietly switch emphasis in his 2012 campaign from Islam to resistance to the European Union? Did he not drop his resistance to raising state pension age when power beckoned? Various publicists in recent years have accused Wilders of exploiting fear and conflict purely for his own electoral success. A 'fearmonger', as historian Geert Mak called him, the type of politician who has historically always emerged in times of unease.[64] Other commentators call Wilders a 'political entrepreneur', who like all other entrepreneurs is looking for a 'gap in the market'. In any case, if we are to believe these judgements, then it is not nationalism, populism, anti-Islamic alarmism and law and order that form the pillars of the PVV's political project, but opportunism, demagoguery, hunger for power and opinion polls. If the latest polls showed that many Dutch citizens were afraid of China or wanted more windmills, Wilders would have exploited these points just as enthusiastically.

We are clearly on thin ice with such speculations and apparent certainties. When do we ever know for certain that a person really means what they say? The answer, of course, is never. This applies as much to any politician as it does to Geert Wilders. It is therefore an issue of scholarly integrity that we take people at their word and do not attribute secret agendas to them. At the same time we do not need to be hardened cynics to suspect that strategic rather than ideological motives sometimes lie behind their actions. Anyone who doubts this can find examples in almost any randomly selected political biography. Certainly in the battle for the voters' favour, promises are quickly made and warnings are the order of the day. Hope and fear are powerful human emotions which every politician uses in one way or another. It is part and parcel of the political battle that one man's hope is another's nightmare and that real worries for one (melting ice caps or rising national debt) are dismissed as irrational fears by others (climate hysteria, an obsession with the figures). In this sense all politicians are 'fearmongers', not just Wilders.

Every claim as to Wilders' honesty is at best a calculated bet. We can, however, perform our calculations as scrupulously as possible, for example by looking at the consistency of his ideas over time. We must then observe that he has quite drastically changed several of his views, such as his position on direct democracy (initially opposing and later supporting it), on the welfare state (initially in favour of cuts, later of maintaining the system) and foreign policy (first for active participation in the 'war on terror', later against it). In other areas it is not so much a case of change of principles as a shift in emphasis, such as his view on Israel (effectively transferring support from Likud to Lieberman), on Islam (from criticism to alarmism), on the European Union (from moderate to fierce objector) or crime (from harsh to extremely harsh punishments). Although anyone can honestly change their opinions, the above inconsistencies in direct democracy, the welfare state and foreign policy lead us to suspect that these views are more strategically than ideologically motivated. On these issues the

PVV has also clearly shifted in the direction in which many voters can be found, or to put it another way, these views may well have changed in order to acquire further support for Wilders' core ideology; the conviction that Western culture and Islam are irreconcilable and on a collision course. 'My focus has always been on Islam', he states in an interview in 2015. 'In the Netherlands and abroad, it's an existential problem. That's what I wake up to in the morning and what I take to bed at night; it's what I think about every second.'[65]

This view on Islam clearly became more radical after 2006 but, as stated, the difference is more one of shift in emphasis than a change of principles; Wilders did not 'invent' this enemy in 2001 or 2006, but it has grown larger and more menacing. The fact that his position on Islam is of core importance is also indicated by his career. His adult life is to a large extent dominated by his fascination with the Middle East and love for Israel. How else can we explain his regular visits to Israel (approximately 50 times since 1982), his internships in his spare time with Middle East experts or his weighty report on Muslim extremism in 1999? He has not weakened his views on Islam or kept them hidden as a result of the threats he has received since 2003. From November 2004 he has paid a very high price for these views in the form of permanent security which effectively makes a normal life impossible. Would someone rejecting Islam for purely strategic reasons not have cut his losses at that point?

The constant presence of bodyguards around him also means constant affirmation of his view that Islam forms a serious threat. One does not need to be a psychologist to find an explanation here for the forceful radicalisation of Wilders' view on Islam. Moreover, radicalisation is a symptom that ties in with the effects of constant security on a person's psychological state as observed in psychological reports, which include increased stress, a lack of perspective and an increased sensitivity to conspiracy theories.[66] Wilders himself has never participated in such a study, so of course we do not know if this applies to him too, but it is a reasonable guess.

Another method for investigating which of the PVV's views are closest to his heart is examining the PVV's political practice. This means first looking at the House of Representatives, where the party has been active since 2006, though it has also been represented in the Senate, the European Parliament and all States Provincial as well as the municipalities of The Hague and Almere since 2009 and 2010. The party acted as parliamentary supporter to the first Rutte cabinet and took part in the Provincial Executive in Limburg. The PVV however did not restrict itself to national politics only, as we will see. In the following chapter the focus will be less on the ideas and more on the practicalities.

Notes

1 *De Volkskrant*, 20 November 2003.
2 P. Gottschalk and G. Greenberg, *Islamophobia. Making Muslims the Enemy*, 1–11, Lanham: Rowman & Littlefield, 2008.
3 Pat Condell, 'I'm offended by Islam'. Video, 3 April 2013. On www.patcondell.net/im-offended-by-islam/

4 Wilders, *Marked for Death*, 78.
5 Ibid., 97.
6 Ibid., 145.
7 Speech, Geert Wilders in House of Representatives, 16 September 2009.
8 Wilders, *Marked for Death*; also Bosma, *Schijnélite*, 190–191.
9 Wilders, *Marked for Death*, 153.
10 Wilders, *Marked for Death*, 88; Bosma, *Schijnélite*, 176–177.
11 *De Agenda van Hoop en Optimisme. Een tijd om te kiezen. PVV 2010–2015*.
12 'Wilders wil miljoenen moslims uitzetten', www.nu.nl, accessed 15 June 2009.
13 Wilders, *Marked for Death*, 132.
14 Bosma, *Schijnélite*, 226.
15 O. Fallaci, *Rage and the Pride*, New York: Rizzoli, 2001; and O. Fallaci, *The Force of Reason*, New York: Rizzoli, 2004.
16 J. Niemöller, 'Geert Wilders: ik capituleer niet', *HP De Tijd*, 12 December 2007; Bat Ye'or, *Eurabia. The Euro–Arab Axis*, New York: Fairleigh Dickinson University Press, 2005; *Islam and Dhimmitude: Where Civilizations Collide*, New York: Fairleigh Dickinson University Press, 2001.
17 H. Jansen, *Islam voor varkens, apen, ezels en andere beesten*, Amsterdam: Van Praag, 2008.
18 M. Carr, 'You Are Now Entering Eurabia', *Race & Class* 48 (2006) 1–22; H.G. Betz, 'Against the Green Totalitarianism. Anti-Islamic Nativism in Contemporary Radical Right-Wing Populism in Western Europe', in *Europe for the Europeans. The Foreign and Security Policy of the Populist Radical Right*, Chr. Schori Liang, ed., Aldershot; Burlington: Ashgate Publishing House, 2007; S. Bangstad, *Anders Breivik and the Rise of Islamophobia*, London: Zed Books, 2014; J.P. Zúquete, 'The European Extreme-Right and Islam. New Directions', *Journal of Political Ideologies* 10 (2008): 321–344.
19 H. Jansen and B. Snel, eds, *Eindstrijd. De finale clash tussen het liberale Westen en een traditionele islam*, Amsterdam: Van Praag, 2009.
20 Quote, Bawer on www.militantislammonitor.org/article/id/1675
21 B. Bawer, *While Europe Slept. How Radical Islam is Destroying the West From Within*, Amsterdam: Meulenhoff, 2006; C. Caldwell, *Reflections on the Revolution in Europe. Immigration, Islam and the West*, New York: Knopf Double Day, 2009; E. Al Maqdisi and S. Solomon, *Modern Day Trojan Horse: Al Hijra, the Islamic Doctrine of Migration* [n.p.] 2009; M. Steyn, *America Alone. The End of the World as We Know It*, Washington, DC: Regnery Publishing, 2006.
22 G. Komrij, *Morgen heten we allemaal Ali*, Amsterdam: De Bezige Bij, 2010.
23 C. Mudde, 'The Populist Zeitgeist', *Government and Opposition* 39 (4) 2004: 542–563; B. Stanley, 'The Thin Ideology of Populism', *Journal of Political Ideologies* 13 (1) (2008): 95–110; D. Albertazzi and D. McDonnell, *Twenty-First Century Populism. The Spectre of Western European Democracy*, New York: Palgrave Macmillan, 2008; P. Taggart, *Populism*, Buckingham: Open University Press, 2000.
24 E. Laclau, *On Populist Reason*, 69–83, 103–107, New York: Verso, 2005.
25 Bosma, *De Schijnélite*, 71, 319.
26 Wilders, *Marked for Death*, 180.
27 Bosma, *De Schijnélite*, 325.
28 *De Agenda van Hoop en Optimisme. Een tijd om te kiezen. PVV 2010–2015*.
29 M. Beyen and H. te Velde. 'Passion and Reason. Modern Parliaments in the Low Countries', in *Parliament and Parliamentarism. A Comparative History of a European Concept*, P. Ihalainen, C. Ilie, and K. Palonen, eds, 81–96, New York: Berghahn Books, 2016; H. te Velde, *Van regentenmentaliteit tot populisme. Politieke tradities in Nederland*, 75–96, Amsterdam: Bert Bakker, 2010.
30 E. Gellner, *Nationalism*, London: Weidenfeld & Nicolson, 1997; P. Alter, *Nationalism*, London: Edward Arnold, 1994.

60 The four pillars of PVV ideology

31 Wilders, *Marked for Death*, 215.
32 *De Volkskrant*, 15 February 2005.
33 *Hún Brussel, óns Nederland. Verkiezingsprogramma, 2012.*
34 *Hún Brussel, óns Nederland. Verkiezingsprogramma*, 2012; *De Agenda van Hoop en Optimisme. Een tijd om te kiezen. PVV 2010–2015.*
35 Speech, Geert Wilders, Ahoy Rotterdam, 24 August 2012. Available on www.pvv.nl.
36 Speech, Bosma in House of Representatives, 9 April 2009.
37 M. Bosma, *Minderheid in eigen land. Hoe progressieve strijd ontaardt in genocide en ANC-apartheid*, Amsterdam: Uitgeverij Van Praag, 2015.
38 Interview, Jhim van Bemmel.
39 G. Wilders and M. Bosma, 'Nederland en Vlaanderen horen bij elkaar', *NRC Handelsblad*, 31 July 2008.
40 P. Blaas, 'Gerretson en Geyl: de doolhof der Grootnederlandse gedachte', *Tijdschrift voor geschiedenis* (1984).
41 Speech, Geert Wilders, House of Representatives, 26 March 2009.
42 Speech, Geert Wilders, House of Representatives, 19 June 2007 and 18 February 2009; The PVV also launched a website 'What Does Mass Immigration Cost Us'; www.watkostdemassaimmigratie.nl/ and 'An Immigration Plan: Eighteen Measures to Really End Mass Immigration', 26 October, 2007.
43 Interview with PVV candidate, Sheren Cheng on www.Geledraak.nl, 31 October, 2006.
44 Betz, 'Against the Green Totalitarianism'; C. Mudde, *Populist Radical-Right Parties in Europe*, 18–21, Cambridge: Cambridge University Press, 2007.
45 *De Standaard*, 20 November 2004.
46 *De Agenda van Hoop en Optimisme. Een tijd om te kiezen. PVV 2010–2015.*
47 Wilders, *Kies voor vrijheid*, 107.
48 J. Kuitenbrouwer, *De woorden van Wilders & hoe ze werken*, Amsterdam: De Bezige Bij, 2010; H. de Bruijn, *Geert Wilders Speaks Out. The Rhetorical Frames of a European Populist*, The Hague, 2011.
49 Speech, Fleur Agema, *House of Representatives*, 12 December 2007.
50 *Justitie en Politie met Ambitie. Plan PVV voor een effectieve aanpak van de criminaliteit.*
51 On Joe Arpaio, J. Hagan, 'The Long, Lawless Ride of Sheriff Joe Arpaio', *Rolling Stone*, 2 August 2012.
52 Speech, Four Seasons, New York, 23 February 2009.
53 Interview, Johan Driessen.
54 *NRC Handelsblad*, 4 November 2009.
55 On this discussion; R. te Slaa, *Is Wilders een fascist?*, Amsterdam: Boom, 2012.
56 R. Stolk, 'New Words for an Old Fear? Opposition to Catholicism and Islam'. Master's thesis, Leiden University, 2010. Available via www.openacces.leidenuniv.nl.
57 Interview, Joram van Klaveren.
58 M. Davidovic, J. van Donselaar, P.R. Rodrigues and W. Wagenaar, 'Het extreemrechtse en discriminatoire gehalte van de PVV', *Monitor Racisme Anne Frank-Stichting* (2008); G. Wilders and M. Bosma, 'WC-eend adviseert Ter Horst', *De Volkskrant*, 30 January 2010.
59 Lucardie and Voerman, 'Rootless Populists?'; Vossen, 'Classifying Wilders'.
60 Mudde, *Populist Radical-Right Parties in Europe*; Albertazzi and McDonnell, *Twenty-First Century Populism*; Y. Mény, and Y. Surel, eds, *Democracies and the Populist Challenge*, New York: Palgrave, 2002; A. Zaslove, *The Re-Invention of the European Radical Right. Populism, Regionalism and the Italian Lega Nord*, Montreal; Ithaca, NY: McGill-Queen's University Press, 2011; T. Pauwels, *Populism in Western Europe. Comparing Belgium, Germany and the Netherlands*, London: Routledge, 2014. Extremism and Democracy series.

61 W. van der Brug, M. Fennema and J. Tillie, 'Anti-Immigrant Parties in Europe: Ideological or Protest Vote?' *European Journal of Political Research* 37 (2000): 77–102.
62 The motion was submitted by Hero Brinkman on 15 January 2009 and was eventually accepted.
63 In an interview with Israeli newspaper *Haaretz*, Wilders said on Lieberman: 'Our parties may not be identical, but there are certainly more similarities than dissimilarities, and I am proud of that', *Haaretz*, 18 June 2009.
64 Geert Mak, *Gedoemd tot kwetsbaarheid*, Amsterdam: Atlas, 2005.
65 P. Jansen, 'Geert Wilders: Mijn focus is altijd op Islam gericht', *De Telegraaf*, 28 February 2015.
66 *Psychosociale gevolgen van dreiging en beveiliging*. Rapport Nationale Coördinator Terrorismebestrijding, Maart 2008 (Psychosocial consequences of threats and security; Report National Coordinator for Counterterrorism, March 2008).

3 The PVV in action
National and international activities

Politics is not just about propounding ideas, but also about achieving concrete results. Not all parties are after the same kind of result, however. For example, political scientists Kaare Strøm and Wolfgang C. Müller distinguish between parties who prioritise votes (vote-seeking), those more focused on influencing policy (policy-seeking) and those that put positions of power first (office-seeking).[1] These three positions are, of course, model types: in practice, every party moves between these three extremes. Where should we place the PVV? What result do they aim for and to what extent are they successful? In order to answer this we can look at the party's practical political activities. As we will see, the most significant of these play out at the Binnenhof in The Hague. There the party has fiercely opposed the government since 2006, with the exception of a short period between October 2010 and April 2012 in which the party supported a minority government. The PVV's extra-parliamentary activities in the Netherlands have been limited to a few small demonstrations or support to citizens' initiatives against the construction of windmills or mosques. Beyond the Dutch borders, however, Wilders has been particularly active as a speaker at a number of conferences and party events, as well as acting as an architect of a collaboration of several national populist parties.

Representatives of the people: the PVV in the House of Representatives

If there is a single constant in Wilders' political career, it is his enormous passion for parliamentary politics. 'I love being able to walk around here every day; I enjoy signing the attendance list and heckling during debates. It is a privilege to be able to give your opinion here as a representative of the people', the daily newspaper *Trouw* quoted him in 1999. Five years on, that enthusiasm had only increased, as Wilders is documented in the same paper as saying, 'I hear the rush of adrenalin in my ears. Do you have any idea how proud I am to be able to do my work? I wish I could raise a question in the House of Representatives every day.'[2] Although he has been highly critical of the political elite since 2004, he continues to consider the role of people's representative to be a 'fantastic job' and an 'immense privilege', as he emphasises time and time again. According to various sources the temporary loss of his seat in parliament in May 2002 was a traumatic experience. Characteristic also of his devotion to the House of Representatives is his membership of the Presidium – the organisation responsible for the daily running of the House of Representatives – from 2006 to 2010, where he even acted as a remarkably neutral chairman on several occasions.

This passion for parliamentary politics tends to be forgotten when Wilders is mentioned, probably because such parliamentarianism does not sit well with his usual populist image.[3] After all, the archetypal populist politician, as portrayed in the literature on populism, is the opposite of an enthusiastic parliamentarian. In order to underline their disgust at politics, populists usually present themselves as untainted outsiders who apply themselves with undisguised distaste to the parliamentary work they consider so pointless. 'In Parliament, but not *of* Parliament', was the motto of the national populist Flemish Bloc MPs. Extra-parliamentary campaigns and direct communication with the voter were considered more important than the tedious and frustrating toil in parliament, where they ran the risk of becoming 'hedged in and stupefied by the Belgian political establishment'.[4]

When Wilders established the PVV at the start of 2006, by contrast, he had already been active in the House of Representatives for almost half his life. At the age of 26, when he started out as a VVD employee, the House of Representatives still met in the Old Chamber, Ruud Lubbers was prime minister and the CDA and PvdA were calling the shots with 54 and 49 seats respectively. After his disappointing office job for the Health Care Insurance Board, Wilders found his destiny at the Binnenhof and immersed himself in the parliamentary politics of The Hague. From the outset he studied the other MPs carefully, as he mentioned in an interview: 'That way you get to see what makes a good or a not so good MP.'[5] He learnt which parliamentary instruments could be used and what effect they could have, got to know the complicated procedures and mores of parliament, built up a large network of journalists, lobbyists, politicians and party specialists and grew to be a top-notch political professional.

The PVV's character and success has been largely fuelled by its leader's passion for parliamentary politics. This makes the PVV a parliamentary party first and foremost. In the manifesto it calls itself a party of 'ordinary citizens who come to The Hague to reclaim the square kilometre that is the Binnenhof as part of the Netherlands'. In reality, however, the PVV came into being in parliament and has its headquarters in the building of the House of Representatives, where, on the heavily guarded third floor of a side wing, the campaigns are organised, candidates selected and trained, and decisions made. There is no separate party office. Only since 2009 has the PVV had a representation in forums other than the House of Representatives, but these offices in Brussels (European Parliament), The Hague and Almere (municipal councils) and provincial capitals (the States Provincial) are connected only through the Binnenhof. This choice in favour of parliamentary politics is partly necessitated by security risks. Wilders can move in relative safety at the Binnenhof, although he is constantly accompanied by bodyguards there too. That does not change the fact that the PVV's strong focus on the House of Representatives coincides with Wilders' fixations and predilections dating back to before 2004.

Second, Wilders' extensive knowledge and love of parliamentary work has enabled the PVV to build a reputation as an anti-establishment party. Paradoxical as it may sound, anyone wanting to give the impression that they wish to distance themselves from the game must have a good understanding of its rules and customs to do so effectively, just as a striker in a football team knows precisely when he is offside. Voters who have cast a protest vote want to be represented by skilled, capable people who are not always at loggerheads with one another. With all his political knowledge Wilders did succeed in forming a reasonably solid, professional-looking party for the House of Representatives, which stood out favourably among many other newcomers. Along with Bosma he personally selected the MPs in 2006 and trained them in a whole series of classes he chaired himself. That must have been a time-consuming task, but the nine candidates who sat for the PVV in the House of Representatives from 2006 to 2010 surprised friend and foe with their thorough knowledge of the procedures and mores, active participation in debates and extensive use of the various parliamentary tools.[6]

The PVV was also fortunate that interest in the House of Representatives in the Netherlands has increased substantially in recent years. For years a large part of the political battle had proceeded outside parliament, in the large party organisations, trade unions, social campaigns such as the women's movement, or environmental movement. Although a great deal of power currently resides in Brussels, the House of Representatives is again the centre of politics and social debate in the Netherlands, where the political heavyweights of each party are to be found, ready to be questioned by ever more journalists from serious current affairs programmes as well as, increasingly, more light-hearted features. Election campaigns for municipal councils, the States Provincial or the European Parliament are dominated by national politics, and the results gain significance largely by their effects within the House of Representatives. Ever fewer Dutch citizens show an interest in political life outside parliament: memberships of political parties and social organisations have dropped significantly and the willingness to engage in political activism has declined.[7] To put it another way, a party like the PVV, focused purely on the Binnenhof, without departments, member participation or conferences, would have been inconceivable 20 years ago. If, as some political scientists claim, Dutch democracy has really become an 'audience democracy', then the House of Representatives is the stage those spectators are watching, and it is on that stage that Wilders has excelled.[8]

On this national platform at the end of 2006, seven new PVV members made their entry into the House of Representatives in the wake of their guru Wilders and his assistant Martin Bosma. 'We are a nine-headed phalanx, a vigilante group in Parliament', Martin Bosma stated.[9] The first group of PVV MPs certainly stood out for their fanaticism, work ethic and strict, almost military discipline. No one defied the whip, nothing was known of possible internal conflicts and in the media the various MPs told the same story of 'Islamisation', 'mass immigration', the 'dreadful left-wing elite' and the 'European superstate' in almost exactly the same words. Like a greedy child in a sweet shop the party also made enthusiastic use of the various powers of the House of Representatives, such as the right to put verbal and written questions to cabinet members. The annual reports of the House of Representatives show that between 2007 and 2010 the PVV, with its nine seats, put as many as 1313 questions to parliament, or 15.2% of the total of 8702 questions in writing.

Fleur Agema, the only female PVV MP, stood out as a particularly active questioner. This art school graduate and architect became vice party chair and Chief Whip. As spokesperson for care she raised a number of questions regarding abuses in the sector and in care homes, where 'our parents' are the victims of government failure and mismanagement. Many of these questions had an anti-Islamic alarmist edge to them, as witnessed by many questions on subsidies for Islamic homecare, halal food in hospitals and muggings of the elderly by Moroccan 'street terrorists'.

In general the PVV was not quick to run out of questions when it came to Islam, according to data from the House of Representatives Central Information Point. The PVV raised questions on segregated swimming lessons for Muslim women, the removal of a Christmas tree under suspected pressure from Muslims and even what they viewed as overly positive attention for Islam in children's television programmes. Overly lenient judges, weak police officers and soft treatment of criminals in prison also emerged as almost inexhaustible sources of questions in parliament. The populist pillar is ultimately also recognisable in questions on the squandering of tax funds by the elite through favourable redundancy schemes for civil servants, subsidised 'jollies', expensive receptions and extravagant prestige projects.

By raising questions verbally during Question Time on Tuesday afternoons, requesting emergency debates and interpellations, the PVV made its voice heard quite extensively. In the parliamentary year 2008–2009, the media monitoring organisation Nieuwsmonitor counted 68 emergency debates, of which slightly more than a third were requested by PVV MPs. Between 2007 and 2010, the PVV submitted 939 motions, 13.2% of the total; only the SP submitted more.[10] No other party submitted so many votes of no confidence, however. The PVV made use of this serious measure, which entails calling on a particular cabinet member or the entire government to step down, as many as ten times: three times against the entire cabinet and seven on individual cabinet members and secretaries of state. Since no other party was willing to support these motions in most cases, none of them achieved a majority. The same goes for almost all the motions the PVV has submitted: not a single party in the House of Representatives saw as many motions rejected as the PVV between 2006 and 2010.[11]

In fact, many of those motions were not intended to achieve a majority, but to provoke debate both inside and outside the House of Representatives, often demanding impossible measures and worded in such a way as to force a prompt reaction. For example, immediately after Balkenende's cabinet was formed in February 2007, the PVV submitted a vote of no confidence against Secretaries of

State Nebahat Albayrak and Ahmet Aboutaleb, because they had dual nationality (Dutch combined with Turkish and Moroccan respectively), which the PVV claimed might lead to a conflict of interest. More than half a year later Geert Wilders submitted a motion to ban the Koran, calling it the Islamic *Mein Kampf*. Two months later his fellow party member, Hero Brinkman, submitted a motion in which he proposed to break all political ties with the Netherlands Antilles, calling this Caribbean part of the Kingdom a 'largely corrupt den of thieves'. In April 2008, Wilders submitted a vote of no confidence against the entire cabinet after a fierce debate on his film, *Fitna*. In the subsequent debate he accused the minister of justice of lying and deception because he had read out a written declaration claiming that Wilders had stated his intention of tearing up and burning the Koran in the film. Finally, in September 2009, Wilders submitted a motion to tax people for wearing headscarves, which he insultingly dubbed *kopvoddentaks* (tax on head rags) to the disgust of many MPs.

But the PVV succeeded in getting a rise out of large swathes of the House of Representatives in other ways too. For example, at the end of March 2009 the entire PVV parliamentary group walked out on a debate on the new package of government crisis measures because the opposition parties were given too little opportunity to exert an influence. The choice of words and tone of PVV MPs also strike many as offensive. It was hardly customary in the generally genteel Binnenhof for a minister to be called 'barking mad', or the overseas territories to be portrayed as corrupt dens of thieves, nor was it usual to use words such as 'bastard' or 'arsehole', to accuse another party of 'not giving a damn' or suggest, as Dion Graus did, that a fellow MP was 'beginning to suffer from Alzheimer's. Expressions used by the PVV such as 'go to hell' and 'talking out of your arse', and labelling politicians as 'cowards' or 'liars' were similarly seen as less than model parliamentary behaviour. Social media, YouTube and popular websites, such as the Dutch blog *GeenStijl*, rapidly brought many such incidents to a large audience. Wilders' speeches in particular, due to their biting satire, neologisms and coarse comparisons, were soon watched and discussed by many.

Besides leading to hilarity, the PVV's behaviour was also a source of serious concern. Many politicians and opinion-formers felt that its members were violating a certain Dutch standard of behaviour in their language use and style of discussion. Politicians should not behave or express themselves in that way; it was bad for the image of politics, and various commentators and politicians felt that the PVV was increasingly distracting attention from the content of the debate. A specially set up parliamentary steering committee, in which the PVV did not wish to participate, set to work on the behaviour of the PVV parliamentary group and operations of the House of Representatives. According to the Christian Democrat chair of this steering committee, Jan Schinkelshoek, the PVV seemed to see the parliament as 'a political café, a platform for mobilising dissatisfaction among voters', while the other parties were used to seeing the Binnenhof as 'a market where you negotiate, where you have to make decisions'.[12] In response, PVV MP Hero Brinkman stated that it is 'precisely our job in parliament to give voice to what you pick up in cafés, on the shop floor, in the street. Citizens make politics, we carry it out.' His party, with its 'plain, clear use of language' reduced the gap between citizens and politicians, 'thereby elevating the image of parliament which Schinkelshoek is so worried about', said Brinkman. His fellow member, Martin Bosma saw Schinkelhoek's mission as a veiled attempt by the centre parties to block the path of the new opposition parties. 'They yearn for the time when MPs called one another "old boy" and could set the world to rights over a cigar and a gin', Bosma said. 'We're spoiling it for them, like a group of disciplined fighters, we don't go brawling in the streets.'[13]

This parliamentary self-reflection illustrates the extent of the uncertainty among MPs as to how to deal with the PVV. Should they revert to the strategy used against the Centre Party and Centre Democrats in the 80s and 90s? These national populist parties led by Hans Janmaat were completely ignored and excluded in the House of Representatives and the media. No one was willing to work with, listen to or even be seen with Janmaat, but the result was not particularly satisfactory – had it not led to excessive neglect of the problems of immigration and integration raised by Janmaat? Was it not this which enabled Fortuyn to set himself up as an outsider who dared to break 'the Left Church's taboos'? Fortuyn's subsequent murder by an extreme-left animal rights activist also lent the debate over the desirability of certain taboos a whole new dimension. Was Fortuyn's murder not a consequence of 'demonisation' by the left-wing parties ('the bullet came from the left')? The murder of Theo van Gogh, the critic of Islam, increased the rage and confirmed the analysis of those who saw freedom of expression as coming under threat from the Left Church and Islam.

After Fortuyn and Van Gogh, the Netherlands suddenly adopted the rule that ignoring certain opinions was no longer an option. At the same time, opposing them too fiercely was not without risk. Many MPs were certainly reticent about criticising Wilders too strongly in the initial years. Besides fear of the possible consequences, the fact that Wilders, unlike Janmaat or the LPF after him, was not an outsider but a political animal, well-integrated into the Binnenhof, undoubtedly played a role. Many MPs, journalists and House of Representatives employees had known him for years and felt some admiration or sympathy for him over the heavy security measures he was subject to. That is not to say that the PVV was popular, but, unlike previous anti-establishment parties such as the Centre Democrats or the Farmers' Party, it was an inextricable part of political and social life at the Binnenhof. There were PVV members on all parliamentary committees, some even acting as chair. The PVV regularly put questions on Israel or Christian minorities in the Middle East to the smaller orthodox Protestant parties, submitted some motions on crime and immigration to the VVD, while sometimes receiving support from the Party for the Animals (PvdD) for issues regarding animal welfare. The party, however, tended to remain somewhat aloof from social activities. The PVV members did not show their faces at what Wilders termed the 'dreadful journalist haunt' of Bar Nieuwspoort (next door to parliament), and the party consistently refused to take part in surveys, conferences and journalists' background reports.

How successful has the PVV's strategy of head-on opposition been? Of course that depends on how success is defined. If we join Schinkelshoek in seeing the parliament as a kind of market where business is done, the party initially appears extremely unsuccessful. The PVV has barely made use of the legislative powers of the House of Representatives, only submitting two private member's bills in three and a half years, which is far fewer than the other parties, and making relatively little use of the right of amendment. Of the 1500 amendments submitted between 2007 and 2010, only 39 (2.5%) came from the PVV, with only five adopted, making the PVV the lowest-scoring party. Likewise, of all the motions submitted by the PVV only a couple have been accepted, generally those which they submitted in conjunction with another party. Whether the government actually adopted the accepted motions remains unclear. Bearing in mind that the PVV often voted alone (or with other opposition parties), it seems reasonable to pronounce the PVV fairly ineffectual in parliament, at least if we view the parliament as a marketplace.

If we see the parliament more as 'a political café, a platform for mobilising dissatisfaction', as Schinkelshoek put it, then of course the criteria for success are completely different. An important criterion in that case is, for example, the extent to which a party succeeds in cranking up a debate on particular topics in parliament. It is difficult to pass precise judgements on this, but a number of examples of PVV motions and actions which have led to the desired effect are discussed below. We do not need a calculator to tell us that topics such as Islam, immigration and integration have risen on the agenda due to the PVV, which is not to suggest that the approach to 'Islamisation' and 'mass integration' introduced by the PVV has been adopted, but that other parties have been forced to react in some way or other. They had a choice between refuting the PVV's account, combating it, presenting a more nuanced view or ignoring it, but even this last option required effort and explanation.

Another criterion for success is the extent to which the PVV has succeeded in generating media attention. How would citizens have heard that the PVV is trying (in Brinkman's words) 'to give voice to what you pick up in cafés, on the shop floor, in the street'? Of course they have been able to control their own publicity to some extent on their own website, slots in the Airtime for Political Parties and increasingly also through social media (Twitter, Facebook), but for the most part the party has remained dependent on less controllable newspaper, television and radio journalists. Media attention has in fact been a little more important to the PVV than to most other parties because they had no departments across the country, with no local or provincial representatives until 2010, and because they never took part in initiatives outside parliament. As we will see, unlike other political parties, the PVV has no classic party organisation. In short, there has really been no way of learning about the party other than through the media.

If we take media attention as our criterion for parliamentary success, the PVV is clearly a decisive success story, as we can show with a simple search of the newspaper database LexisNexis. Although the PVV was not yet active on municipal and provincial councils at the time, in 2007, 2008 and 2009 it was already mentioned far more often in the newspapers than parties such as D66, the

Christian Union and GreenLeft (although significantly less often than the three main parties). Between 2007 and 2010, Geert Wilders saw his name in Dutch newspapers more often than any other Dutch politician with the exception of Prime Minister Jan Peter Balkenende. Of the prominent foreign politicians, only American President Barack Obama was ahead of him: German Chancellor Angela Merkel, former French President Nicolas Sarkozy, Russian President Vladimir Putin and former President George W. Bush were all mentioned less often in the Dutch papers in these years than Wilders, who at the time was still only the party chair of the fifth largest party in the country.[14] Other MPs such as Fleur Agema, Hero Brinkman and Dion Graus became Dutch celebrities in these years too. A study in the catalogue of the Netherlands Institute for Sound and Vision offers a similar picture from the public television and radio broadcasters. Since September 2006, Wilders has featured more than many other Dutch politicians as a topic on radio and television, although unlike other politicians he is generally the subject of conversation, appearing as an interviewed speaker far less often than his peers. In other words, people talk about Wilders far more than they talk with him. This is in part a consequence of Wilders' own media policy: for years he has refused to appear in most talk shows and current affairs programmes, which he views as left wing. The fact that there is so much talk of Wilders in the media should also be taken in conjunction with all his spectacular, mediagenic acts and shocking statements between 2007 and 2010. Whether people wanted it or not, Wilders has produced a continual supply of topics for the various Dutch talk shows and current affairs programmes.[15]

Although the PVV had little to show in the way of concrete results at the time, the 'PVV brand' enjoyed overwhelming market success. That success was almost entirely down to free newspaper and television publicity, as the party even lacked the financial means and organisation for an advertising campaign; in fact, generating publicity for the party and its programme was one of the main aims of these years. The PVV achieved this in part by organising its own media events (particularly *Fitna*), and in part by perfecting a parliamentary strategy previously introduced by the SP. This strategy rested on making maximum use of the checking powers of the House of Representatives, such as putting questions to the House verbally and in writing, applying for emergency debates or interpellation and submitting motions. In terms of direct results this activity was rather limited in its effects, but it did ensure a continuous stream of publicity which, above all, created the impression of strong commitment and activism. Of course most of the questions and motions received no attention from the national press, but sometimes they were picked up by organisations and communities which identified with these issues. These groups felt strengthened in the knowledge that there was a party in the House of Representatives sharing their wishes and fears.

Like the SP, the PVV also introduced its own recognisable idiom. Whichever MP was speaking, they all used a fixed repertoire of terms and expressions. At all levels of the party, PVV members consistently spoke of 'Islamisation', 'mass immigration', 'dhimmis', 'street terrorists', 'left-wing hobbies', 'hate imams', 'climate madness' and 'Henk and Ingrid'. This communicative discipline not only created the impression of great homogeneity, but also ensured the continual repetition of the core message, even outside the campaign period. By the time the 2010 election campaign for the House of Representatives began, the PVV message had reached the most remote geographical and social corners of the country.

At the centre of power

In 2009 and 2010, the PVV reaped what it had sowed. The 2009 European elections won the party 17% of the vote, making it the second party in a single stroke. In March 2010, the PVV also took part in local council elections in two cities, The Hague and Almere. These specific cities were selected on the one hand because they were known as PVV strongholds, and on the other because, unlike in many other cities, there were enough good candidates available there. 'Wilders refused to run the risk of just any old idiot speaking for the party. He wanted to maintain control', says Johan Driessen.[16] In The Hague, with 19.9% of the vote, the PVV just missed becoming the largest party, a position which it achieved in Almere with 27.4%. Because of the PVV's demand for a ban on headscarves in public buildings, it was not admitted to the local authorities in either city. As opposition parties, the PVV members in The Hague and Almere would follow the example of their group in the House of Representatives in subsequent years: lots of questions and motions, coarse language and mediagenic action.

The important elections, of course, were those for the House of Representatives held in June 2010. Although the campaign focused firmly on the economy, not integration and immigration, 1.5 million of the electorate voted for the PVV, or 15.5% of the total votes. With 24 seats the PVV had now become the third party in the country. The party celebrated all night long in a beach café in Scheveningen. 'That was a magnificent moment. Now we could really change things, we all thought', one dissident reminisces.[17]

In order for that to happen, however, the party needed to enter a government coalition, which demands considerable patience and ideological flexibility: House of Representatives elections in the Netherlands are often the beginning of a complicated, nebulous process of government formation. The fragmented party landscape makes finding majorities an increasingly complex puzzle – besides a majority of seats in the House of Representatives (at least 76), a majority in the Senate must also be taken into consideration. It is also an unwritten rule that the largest party should take the initiative in forming the coalition and that at least one big winner should be included in the new coalition. Along with the VVD, the PVV came through as the biggest winner, so it was obvious that both parties would participate. Various parties such as the PvdA and D66, however, had already indicated before the elections that they would not work with the PVV under any circumstances. Taking the initiative as the largest party, the VVD therefore started by exploring other options, but those turned out to be unattainable – having excluded the PVV, the liberals now depended on collaboration with left-wing parties, which proved unpalatable to many of their voters. The VVD party office received countless angry emails and phone calls after cautiously probing this option. The problem was that a centre-right coalition with the CDA did not have a majority, given that the CDA had been almost halved in these elections. With the PVV there would be a majority, albeit a very small one (76 of 150 seats).

Within the VVD many people were prepared to consider cooperating with Wilders. After all, he was in some ways a lost son with a long history within the party, and many of its other members still regretted the loss of this talented young liberal. VVD leader Mark Rutte, too, was on good terms with Wilders, having shown him the ropes in 2002 when he entered the House of Representatives.

For the CDA, however, cooperation with the PVV was a rather more sensitive matter. The Christian Democrats were recovering from an enormous election defeat (in which they had lost almost half their seats) and the subsequent departure of Jan Peter Balkenende as party leader. Maxime Verhagen, negotiating for the CDA as interim leader, ultimately decided to endorse cooperation with the PVV, probably in the hope that giving the party responsibility would lead to its elimination – a strategy that had, after all, worked in the case of the LPF. Within the CDA, however, many members fiercely resisted a possible collaboration with the PVV, including two former prime ministers in the party, Dries van Agt and Piet de Jong. Christian Democrats abroad, including Angela Merkel, also stated publicly that they were following the developments in the Netherlands with serious concern.[18]

Wilders, by contrast, had already stated several times before the election that he was ready for government. In the months leading up to the elections he had often shown his most reasonable side. In order to emphasise his readiness, the day after the elections, he conceded an important sticking point, namely raising pension age. But Wilders was also dealing with serious internal party doubts over participation in government, as various sources reveal. 'He had no idea who might become a minister for the PVV if it came to it: there weren't that many good people and Wilders is scared to death of people he can't control', Louis Bontes, who was on the party board, explains.[19]

Nevertheless, after a summer of laborious negotiations, the VVD, CDA and PVV finally came up with a structure acceptable to all parties. Denmark served as an example for the model: liberals and conservatives there had formed a minority cabinet supported in parliament by Pia Kjærsgaard's Danish People's Party in exchange for commitments in a number of areas important to the party, such as immigration and integration. From as early as the summer of 2008, the PVV had enjoyed friendly relations with the Danish People's Party, and Danish MEP, Morten Messerschmidt gave Wilders and his co-negotiator, Barry Madlener negotiating advice over the phone.[20] Following the Danish example, the parties came to a parliamentary agreement including clear commitments by the PVV to support the cabinet in exchange for influence in various policy areas. The Danish structure appeared to offer advantages to all parties. The CDA and

VVD could maintain before critics within and outside their parties that they were only 'indirectly' working with the PVV, while Wilders, on the other hand, was not completely bound to the coalition agreement and could allow his own voice to be heard in certain areas, such as the European Union and foreign politics. An additional advantage was the fact that Wilders was relieved of the task of finding competent cabinet members.

On 14 October 2010, Rutte's cabinet was officially sworn in, making Mark Rutte the first liberal prime minister in the Netherlands since 1918. Although the CDA was significantly smaller, both parties supplied the same number of ministers, a clear concession to the CDA. Many of the ministers were rather older gentlemen, which was seen by some commentators as an indication that both the CDA and the VVD themselves were unsure of a good outcome and wanted to avoid risking promising careers. In contrast with Spain and the Scandinavian countries, for example, the Netherlands had little experience with minority governments.

Both Prime Minister Mark Rutte and Geert Wilders spoke triumphantly at the first press conference of a clear victory for right-wing politics in the Netherlands. The left-wing parties 'are playing cry-baby in the corridor. Look at them whining', Wilders remarked scornfully in the House of Representatives.[21] Indeed it was without a doubt the most right-wing coalition agreement the Netherlands had seen in recent decades. The emphasis was firmly on 'restoring state finances to health' by means of cuts as high as 18 billion euros in areas such as development aid, social security, climate policy and art and culture. The government intended to make the Netherlands 'safer' by means of stricter punishment of criminals and appointment of more police officers. The cabinet also set the goal of substantially reducing immigration through stricter regulations for family immigration and citizenship, and wanted to be able to deport illegal immigrants faster. Only the most extreme suggestions by the PVV – halting immigration from Islamic countries, closing the borders to Bulgarians and Romanians, a tax on headscarves – were not included in the agreement. Wilders enthusiastically predicted a halving of the number of non-Western immigrants, and with it a considerable reduction in Islam in the Netherlands. A striking feature with respect to the nature of Islam, with the CDA and VVD on one side and the PVV on the other, was a separate paragraph stating an agreement to disagree: the CDA and VVD considered Islam a religion, whereas to the PVV it was an ideology. The precise impact of this paragraph remained unclear, but it did show how much significance the PVV attached to this doctrine. No compromise was possible on this subject.[22]

The PVV-supported cabinet would ultimately govern for 18 months: on 23 April 2012, the PVV decided to withdraw its support. That might seem a short time, but given the shaky basis for this coalition and the many incidents which arose, it is almost a miracle that it survived so long. As stated, the coalition only had a narrow majority in the House of Representatives, and the PVV maintained its traditional opposition in certain areas, such as foreign policy. Rutte therefore had to seek backing from other parties for the necessary financial support of

Greece due to the euro crisis and the extension of the military mission in Afghanistan. In the Senate, the coalition did not even have a majority, because the PVV was not represented there. The Senate is indirectly selected by the States Provincial, so Wilders was compelled to participate in elections for the States Provincial in 2011 against his will. In these provincial elections the PVV received 12.4% of the vote, which turned out to be too little to give the coalition a majority in the Senate. The PVV did succeed in entering provincial government in Limburg, where the party formed a coalition with the VVD and CDA, supplying two of the six delegates. This was the PVV's first real taste of government responsibility, albeit at the provincial level. In the Senate, however, Prime Minister Rutte again had to negotiate with other parties to attain majorities. The socially skilled and apparently always optimistic Rutte succeeded astonishingly well at this, albeit by continually making concessions.

However, the primary threat to the stability of the coalition was the behaviour of the PVV. In these years the PVV confirmed the position of Austrian political scientist Reinhard Heinisch that right-wing populist parties by nature have little success as partners in government. 'Their nature as relatively de-institutionalised parties oriented towards charismatic personalities and as organisations seeking to maintain "movement-character" while engaging in spectacular acts of self-presentation is a poor match for specific constraints of public office', according to Heinisch.[23] Although the PVV was not a partner in government but a parliamentary supporter, this observation also turned out to apply to Wilders and co.

First of all, a number of new PVV MPs were discredited. Due to its weak organisational structure and lack of finances, the party was not capable of conducting proper candidate screening. Journalists did a better job of mapping out the backgrounds of the new PVV MPs, bringing all kinds of less wholesome facts to light. One MP had been convicted of forgery in the past, another was imprisoned for a bar brawl shortly after being sworn in, and another newcomer turned out to earn his living with shady dealings in the sex industry. One became known nationally as 'the letter box pisser' when former neighbours claimed that the PVV MP had threatened to urinate into their letter box after repeated disputes. As Wilders was forced to admit publicly, the screening had not been up to scratch. Dutch electoral law, however, did not allow him to fire these MPs and replace them. Wilders also had his hands full with former MP Hero Brinkman, who, since entering the House of Representatives, had increasingly emerged as the most mediagenic but also the most self-willed PVV member. In protest against the lack of democracy within the PVV, he had started a campaign on the eve of the elections for the House of Representatives to force Wilders to open the party up to take on members in an official sense. Brinkman was not particularly successful, and at the end of March 2012, he decided to leave the PVV and proceed independently. Although Brinkman announced that he would continue to support the cabinet, it was now more difficult to find majorities.

Furthermore, the PVV itself caused a great deal of fuss by launching in December 2011 an online registration centre for problems with employees from central and eastern European countries. On this website, which soon became publicly known as the *Polenmeldpunt* or 'Poles complaints centre', Dutch citizens could submit complaints about objectionable behaviour or competition for jobs from Polish, Czech, Bulgarian and Romanian citizens who had come to the Netherlands. The Dutch diplomatic services worked overtime convincing their enraged eastern European colleagues that this was not cabinet policy. It was also difficult for Wilders to exchange his role as opposition leader for that of parliamentary supporter. In the House of Representatives, Wilders went to work in traditional fashion opposing government proposals which fell outside the agreement, such as the billions of euros of support to the 'crazy Greeks'. He was also increasingly dissatisfied with the agreements he had made. 'In retrospect Geert felt that he had received too little in the negotiations. There was also less and less left of it as new concessions to other parties kept becoming necessary, especially with the European Union', according to then PVV MP Louis Bontes.[24] In the House of Representatives and in messages on Twitter, Wilders often made his dissatisfaction publicly known in less than diplomatic terms. In particular the Christian Democratic minister for immigration, Gerd Leers, came under fire. Leers had been told repeatedly in Brussels that the Netherlands was bound by European agreements with respect to immigration and asylum. Wilders, however, accused Leers of poor negotiating skills and blamed him for the fact that the number of immigrants had not significantly dropped. Wilders also embarrassed the government with certain tweets. He denounced Queen Beatrix for visiting a mosque in Oman wearing a headscarf and offended Turkish President Abdullah Gül when he visited the Netherlands, calling the friendly allied head of state a 'Christian-bully, Kurd-basher and friend of Hamas' on Twitter. Wilders told the two PVV representatives in Limburg's provincial government that it was best for them not to attend a banquet organised by the queen to honour the visit of the Turkish president to the province. For the Christian Democrats in Limburg this was reason enough to revoke their confidence in cooperation with the PVV.

In short, Wilders' behaviour and that of the PVV was a constant source of disquiet. An exhaustive reconstruction in the national newspaper *De Volkskrant*, based on interviews with various ministers and journal notes by Gerd Leers, reveals that the coalition was treading on eggshells for 18 months due to Wilders' unpredictable reactions. Rutte maintained to his fellow ministers, parliament and the media that they should not respond to 'every piece of red meat the PVV throw into the arena'. At the same time the pragmatic prime minister continued to emphasise internally that Wilders was a trustworthy partner as long as 'we keep him happy', taking his wishes into account.[25]

That turned out to be a miscalculation on the prime minister's part. On 23 April 2012, Wilders suddenly and completely unexpectedly decided to withdraw his support, a decision which took even most of his fellow party members by surprise. In the previous weeks new negotiations had been conducted between the VVD, CDA and PVV on the 2013 budget. New cuts were needed to fulfil the demand of the European Union that the budget deficit should not rise above 3%. Figures from the CPB Netherlands Bureau for Economic Policy Analysis had pointed out that the government was heading for a budget deficit of 4.5% in 2013. Wilders, however, refused to put his name to the required cuts. In front of the TV cameras he declared that hard-working Dutch citizens and elderly people could not be expected to play along with 'the ridiculous demands from Brussels'. Wilders believed the Netherlands would be better off leaving the European Union and dropping the euro; in his view, maintaining national sovereignty and leaving the EU were now required as the central themes of the new elections.

Since then, there has been much speculation in the Dutch media as to the deeper reasons for the fall of the cabinet. The fact is that the balance of the cabinet was always very delicate, in spite of the appearance Rutte managed to create to the contrary. After Brinkman's departure he did not even have a formal majority in the House of Representatives. Various dissidents claimed that Wilders was also very worried that more PVV members would split from the party. 'New elections allowed him to draw up a new list of candidates and also to restore his power internally. From that moment on, everyone kept their heads down out of fear for their own political careers', one of them said.[26] Wilders was also absolutely livid about the CDA in Limburg deciding to end the provincial cooperation with the PVV. The PVV's Limburg branch had been severely watered down and had supplied two moderate delegates, but the Limburg Christian Democrats nevertheless decided to drop the coalition over a relatively minor incident. According to Louis Bontes, the fall of the coalition eventually became inevitable because Wilders is not suited by character to govern in a coalition country such as the Netherlands. He went on,

> Above all Wilders wants a platform to disseminate his message. All that negotiating and the agreements that have to be made just aren't his thing. It just wasn't in his nature. One day he couldn't stand it anymore and pulled the plug.[27]

The decision to drop the coalition can be viewed as an important hiatus in the history of the PVV. In the September 2012 elections for the House of Representatives the PVV suffered a sensitive loss for the first time. The party lost a third of its voters, dropping back to 10% of the vote, or 15 seats. Wilders had not succeeded in making the EU the central theme of the elections. In August and September 2012, the election campaign quickly came down to a neck-and-neck race between Rutte's VVD and the PvdA. In this kind of situation many voters are swayed by strategic considerations towards one of the two parties out of fear that the other will become the largest. Analyses showed that many potential PVV voters chose Rutte at the last minute because of this.

Wilders, however, lost something even more important in 2012. After suddenly abandoning negotiations he was no longer seen as a trustworthy partner who stuck to agreements and behaved sensibly. In a coalition country such as the Netherlands that is fatal. Not a single party, not even the VVD, was keen to work with Wilders. Since 2012, responsibility for government or even a role as parliamentary supporter has therefore been less likely than ever.

The fall of the first Rutte cabinet also abruptly ended a process of the PVV settling down and taking roots in the system. As parliamentary supporter between 2010 and 2012, despite the incidents, the PVV party had become a relatively ordinary party which no longer only focused its energy on head-on opposition but also played a part in legislation by submitting amendments and private members' bills. In 2011, the PVV submitted twice as many amendments as in previous years. Moreover, half of these were accepted, something which only happened for 10% of cases before 2011. In 2011, the PVV submitted six private members' bills, twice as many as in the previous four years. Despite the substantial increase in number of MPs, the number of motions and questions submitted barely rose in relative terms (11% and 15.6% of the total respectively, in 2011).[28]

After the fall of the cabinet, the PVV returned to its previous mode of opposition. True to tradition, Wilders sought the boundaries of parliamentary mores, for instance by threatening to sue the government and by filibustering. The number of motions and questions in parliament again increased significantly at the expense of more labour-intensive legislation. Thus after 2012, the PVV seemed in many respects to be back to square one. The big difference, however, was a change in perspective. Before 2010, Wilders could still work towards the moment when he was admitted to the centre of power, but after 2012 that perspective seemed to have vanished completely. The PVV's isolation was greater than ever after his call for 'fewer Moroccans' in a speech in March 2014. A storm of indignation flared up in the Netherlands with more than 5000 people reporting Wilders for discrimination. Most parties announced that they would avoid any form of cooperation with the PVV from then on. A cordon sanitaire was placed around Wilders and his party. Various PVV members, including two MPs and two MEPs, left the party. The PVV compensated for its domestic isolation by expanding its international network. After the failed venture with the VVD and CDA, Wilders stepped up his search for support from abroad. In April 2013, he paid his first visit to Marine Le Pen of the Front National, followed by visits to the Austrian FPÖ, Flemish party Flemish Interest, Italian Lega Nord and Swedish Democrats. His new goal was the European elections of May 2014. 'If we gather our strength, we can achieve an enormous amount. We have the momentum', he announced. In response to questions from journalists as to whether he knew which parties he would work with he replied briefly, 'I have more in common with these parties abroad than with the entire House of Representatives.'[29]

In search of allies in Europe

Wilders' decision to look beyond the borders was not simply a consequence of increasing isolation at home. From the start of his political career he was very much involved in international as well as national politics, as we have already seen. With his anti-Islamic alarmism he was clinging to an ideology that was eminently international, as he himself acknowledged in *Marked for Death*:

'Since Islam has global ambitions, we are all in danger and we should stand with every nation and every people that is threatened by jihad', he stated.[30] From as early as 2005, he was involved in all kinds of anti-Islamic alarmist organisations abroad and travelled the whole world. It nevertheless came as a surprise to many, even within his own party, when he sought contact with the Front National and Flemish Interest. In the past he had always clearly distanced himself from Jean-Marie Le Pen, Jörg Haider and Filip Dewinter. When the PVV decided to take part in the European elections in 2009, Wilders immediately announced that his party would not seek cooperation with the newly formed parliamentary group, Identity, Sovereignty and Transparency (IST), which had populist nationalist parties such as Flemish Interest, the Front National and the Bulgarian Ataka as members. 'A "no" with an exclamation mark', Wilders stated firmly. 'I never had anything to do with Le Pen. When you read the programmes of those Eastern European parties, they send shivers down your spine.'[31] Once elected, Wilders gave the PVV delegation in the European Parliament clear instructions not to appear in the vicinity of Le Pen or members of Flemish Interest. 'We even had to change seats in parliament because old Le Pen sat a couple of seats behind us and we could easily have ended up in a photo together that way. Geert wouldn't allow that under any circumstances', says Louis Bontes, who represented the party in the European Parliament between 2009 and 2010.[32]

Because the PVV delegation did not enter any of the other parties, they sat as a four-man independent party in the immense European Parliament, completely sidelined. Now and again the delegation would submit an amendment, generally with no prospect of success, and twice they tried in vain to get a resolution on the plenary agenda. Following the example of the PVV in The Hague, the delegation did submit many critical questions regarding unnecessary spending, while also hoping to attract attention through unparliamentary behaviour and robust use of language. For instance, the PVV delegation demonstratively remained seated during applause after a speech by Václav Havel (who they considered too pro-European) and refused to participate in the commemoration of the dead in the Arab Spring.[33] But where the party in the House of Representatives regularly made the front page with such actions, the capers of the PVV MEPs were never picked up by the Dutch media, which had little overall interest in the European Parliament. The delegation's behaviour in Brussels thus mainly illustrated how dependent the PVV is on the media. Just as a candle without oxygen is slowly extinguished, so the PVV delegation was slowly extinguished without media attention.

Where they did collaborate, it was often with the United Kingdom Independence Party (UKIP), the Finns Party and the Danish People's Party (DFP), which had joined forces. Like the PVV, these parties consciously distanced themselves from extreme right circles, and would not be caught making anti-Semitic remarks. They also enjoyed a certain level of respectability in comparison with the Front National and Flemish Interest. Many former Conservative politicians were active in UKIP, while the DFP was parliamentary supporter to the Danish government. In addition to their aversion to the EU, these parties shared a fear of immigration and of Islam. The DFP had a strong anti-Islamic–alarmist contingent and, under the leadership of Malcolm Pearson, UKIP also appeared more interested in the danger of Islam. It seemed only to be a matter of time before the PVV would join the party with UKIP and the DFP.

In summer 2011, however, Wilders decided quite unexpectedly to end talks with UKIP and the Danish People's Party. Opinions differ somewhat as to the precise reason for the sudden break.[34] One reason often suggested by insiders is bad relations between Wilders and Nigel Farage, Pearson's successor as UKIP leader. Farage was critical of what he saw as Wilders' exaggerated views on Islam and especially his proposal to ban the Koran. Wilders in turn feared that the popular and well-spoken Farage would exert too much influence in the new party, silencing the PVV. He opted for a strategy that had proven useful before (and has since): retreating in the hope that in time the other party would come after him, but on his own terms. 'Geert never wanted to definitively break with UKIP', one insider tells us. 'He probably still hopes they'll come after us later.'[35]

A new, attractive candidate had also emerged in the form of Marine Le Pen. When she was selected as successor to her father, she embarked on a process of ideological moderation and cleansing of overly radical elements. This process of 'dédiabolisation' was supposed to make the Front National a catch-all party, attractive to all nationalistically minded French citizens. Like Wilders, Marine Le Pen accused the elite of throwing away the liberal values and achievements of the republic in the name of multiculturalism.[36] She also stood for the same brand of welfare chauvinism as Wilders and distanced herself from the anti-Semitism and racism of her father, who was eventually expelled from the party. Marine Le Pen's new course was not without success: by 2013 the Front National had been the highest polling party in France for some time.

On 13 November 2013, Wilders and Marine Le Pen announced at a press conference in The Hague that their parties would cooperate after the 2014 European elections. Wilders, who also announced Marine Le Pen as 'the next president of France', said,

> Today is the beginning of the liberation from the European elite, liberation from the monster of Brussels. We will embark on collaboration to restore the nation state. We want to return sovereignty from Brussels and become our own boss again. We want to combat mass immigration and regain control of our own money and legislation.[37]

The two had first met in Paris precisely half a year previously, on Wilders' initiative. Wilders had trawled half of Europe in spring and summer 2013 in search of allies. In Prague he met former Czech President Václav Klaus, in Vienna, Heinz Christian Strache of the FPÖ, in Milan he spoke with Robert Maroni of Lega Nord, and in Malmö with Jimmie Åkesson of the Swedish Democrats. He also travelled back and forth to Antwerp for a 'fantastic meeting' with Filip Dewinter and Gerolf Annemans of Flemish Interest. With the exception of Klaus, all were enthusiastic about the cooperation Wilders proposed. They all also welcomed Wilders as though he were a long-lost son.

This made the results of the European elections in May 2014 all the more disappointing for Wilders. With 13.3% of the vote the PVV might have done better than in the 2012 elections for the House of Representatives, but the polls had predicted a much better result. In comparison with the 2009 European elections, the PVV had lost almost a quarter of its voters. To make matters even worse, UKIP and the Danish People's Party, having been dumped, had scored spectacularly: the two parties achieved 26.6% of the vote, precisely double the PVV's score. Among Wilders' new friends, Marine Le Pen had also achieved an excellent score with 25%, but she was the only one. The remaining allies all achieved disappointing results. After the elections, Wilders and Le Pen initially failed to gain the necessary number of seats and supporters behind them to form a parliamentary party. In June 2015, they managed this with the help of Janice Atkinson, who had been expelled from UKIP, two dissidents from a Polish Eurosceptic party and a Romanian dissident. The party was named Europe of Nations and Freedom and had 37 members. This made it the smallest party in the European Parliament, but it was able to claim more speaking time and higher subsidies from then on. The refugee crisis in the summer of 2015 also threw a favourite theme into the lap of the new party. How much they manage to profit from it remains to be seen.

Nevertheless, the overriding impression was that the entire European venture had failed to live up to Wilders' predictions. He had hoped to attain a pivotal position within a large Eurosceptic party, to be joined by the Front National, UKIP and perhaps even Alternative für Deutschland. The disappointing results in the European Parliamentary elections and subsequent difficulties forming a party prevented this scenario from working out. To Wilders, the failed 2014 European campaign was a reason to focus even more than previously on his other big international pursuit, warning the entire world of the dangers of Islam by holding lectures, showing his documentary, *Fitna*, and publishing articles and a book in English. The Netherlands and even Europe seem too small for Geert Wilders' ambitions.

The flying Dutchman

One would be hard pressed to find another politician still in office who has given lectures in as many different countries in the last ten years as Geert Wilders. Since 2007, the PVV politician has literally travelled around the world with his lectures on the malicious and dangerous nature of Islam. His international tour has taken him to Belgium, Germany, Switzerland, Austria, the Scandinavian countries, the United Kingdom, France, Italy, the United States, Canada, Israel and even Australia. He would like to add countries such as India and Nigeria to the list, a former co-worker claims, but for the moment he considers that 'too risky'. Where does Wilders' international status come from? And why does he put so much energy into his international career?

To begin with the second question, Wilders has always emphasised that Islam represents a threat to the entire world, not just the Netherlands. The entire world is the stage for the clash between Islam and Western, Judeo-Christian civilisation, so the battle against Islam is inevitably an international battle. The primary dilemma is that such a worldwide battle demands that of which Wilders is so wary, namely far-reaching international cooperation or in any case an international organisation with extensive authority. A second problem is that the danger observed by Wilders is not recognised by many people. In his view the cosmopolitan elite in particular, thanks to their belief in multiculturalism, will not listen to reason, but Wilders also feels there is a great deal of ignorance among ordinary Westerners: there may be a widespread sense of unease in Europe, but few realise that Islam really plans to subdue the West. Before the step towards an international coalition against Islam can be made, there is a great deal of missionary work to be done. Wilders sees himself as the whistle-blower needed to warn the often ignorant and naïve Westerners of the new threat. 'Wilders really wants to become a historic figure, someone who saw impending danger in good time, a bit like Churchill, his great model', a former colleague states. In his published memoir, former PVV MP Marcial Hernandez also expresses his suspicion that Wilders sees his parliamentary membership first and foremost as a platform necessary for 'promoting his anti-Islamic agenda worldwide' in order subsequently 'to go down in history as a great seer'.[38]

It remains to be seen whether Wilders will indeed go down in history. In any case we do know that he has grown in the last ten years into the most famous and influential anti-Islamic alarmist. This fame is down to a combination of factors. As a member of parliament under constant protection and coming from a once so tolerant country which has recently seen two political murders, he offers the international media an attractive storyline. Wilders effectively embodies both dramatic change in the little, innocent Netherlands and the clash between the West and Islam. His remarkable appearance no doubt adds to his newsworthiness. Wilders is of course also very adept in playing the media, both nationally and internationally. He fully exploits his status as a politician under constant protection and it gives him a certain credibility. The full title of his autobiography, written in English, tellingly reads *Marked for Death. Islam's War against the West and Me*. His remarkable talent for attracting attention was also demonstrated at the online launch of his documentary film, *Fitna*, on 27 March 2008. As a film, *Fitna* was little more than a slapdash collage of images intended to reveal the wickedness of Islam, but from a publicity perspective it was successful. In the months before the showing of the film, Wilders had hinted that he would burn or tear up a Koran. The Danish cartoon crisis in the winter of 2005 had shown the possible consequences of such insults. The Dutch government and European Union, as well as a number of international organisations, publicly distanced themselves from the documentary, even before it had been properly launched. UN Secretary General Ban Ki-moon called the film 'offensively anti-Islamic' and 'appealed for calm to those understandably offended by it'. In part due to all the reactions before the documentary appeared, Wilders suddenly became one of the most prominent anti-Islamic alarmists worldwide. Journalists from a number of countries flocked to the Netherlands for an interview, and Wilders received many invitations to speak at international conferences and meetings.

Finally, Wilders also clearly met an existing need in both Europe and the United States for an anti-Islamic alarmist figurehead, untainted by a background in radical right-wing circles. From as early as 2001, there existed a small international network of people and organisations who shared Wilders' essentialist vision of Islam. Due to the continual advance of the Internet worldwide, this international network, sometimes also known as the Counter-Jihad Movement, found a virtual platform and meeting place where the anonymity of both authors and readers was guaranteed. Particularly after the attacks of 11 September 2001, many anti-Islamic alarmist websites were launched, each one more serious and professional than the last. Well known, heavily trafficked sites include Stefan Herre's German pi-news.net, Paul Beliën's Brussels Journal (which has served Wilders since 2010), American Pamela Geller's Atlas Shrugs, Robert Spencer's Jihad Watch, TheReligionofPeace.com and Edward S. May's Gates of Vienna.[39] The latter website in particular, whose name refers to the Ottoman invasion repelled at Vienna in 1683, has become a meeting place for anti-Islamic alarmists from all over the world. Some meet at international conferences organised by small think tanks and institutes such as the American Gatestone Institute, Israeli Ariel Center for Policy Research and Lars Hedegaard's Scandinavian Free Press Society. In 2006, as we saw, the scientific institute of the LPF, together with Hans Jansen, also held a conference in The Hague, attended by Wilders.

In the United States in particular, anti-Islamic alarmism corresponded strongly with fear for the future of the state of Israel.[40] Many 'friends of Israel' looked on in sorrow as support for the country in the United States and especially in Europe seemed to crumble, and understanding for the Palestinian demands increased. Anti-Islamic alarmism was attractive to some of them because it gave the conflict a completely new significance, making support for Israel seem more urgent. According to anti-Islamic alarmism, after all, this was not a battle between Israel and the Palestinians striving for their own state, but a clash between Western Judeo-Christian civilisation and Islam. This gave Israel the status of West Berlin during the Cold War, a kind of remote outpost of civilisation to be protected at all times. This was also the analysis of Wilders, who had given Israel the title 'first line of defence of the West' and 'Jihad buffer'.[41] As mentioned above, Wilders had often visited Israel, had an extensive network there and was familiar with Israeli politics. He had, however, ended up in ever more radical circles, maintaining good contacts with the ultranationalist Aryeh Eldad's Hatikva party and the Ariel Center for Policy Research, a study centre set up by colonists on the West Bank. In Europe, however, Wilders initially distanced himself from politicians such as Jean-Marie Le Pen, Jörg Haider and other politicians and parties accused of anti-Semitism and Holocaust denial.

Because of his anti-Islamic alarmist and pro-Israeli views, Wilders was invited by alarmists in the United States, Canada, Israel and even Australia to hold public lectures on the current situation in Europe. Between 2008 and 2015, Wilders travelled to the United States at least nine times to speak in North American cities such as New York, Los Angeles, Philadelphia, Washington DC,

Boston and Toronto, as well as smaller places such as Orange County (California), Garland (Texas), Nashville (Tennessee), Boca Raton (Florida) and the Canadian city of London (Ontario). On 11 September 2010, Wilders acted as a keynote speaker at the 'No Mosque on Ground Zero' demonstration in New York, organised by Pamela Geller and Robert Spencer. On other occasions he was invited by Christian Republican members of congress such as Michelle Bachman, Louis Gohmert and Jon Kyle. Early in 2014, Wilders also went to Australia at the invitation of a small organisation called the Q Society, and set off for Australia for a second time in autumn 2015 to attend the foundation of the anti-Islamic alarmist Australia Liberty Alliance.

After 2013, he also became a popular speaker at meetings of allied parties such as Lega Nord, Flemish Interest, the FPÖ, the Swedish Democrats and the Front National. UKIP leader Malcolm Pearson invited Wilders to show *Fitna* in the House of Lords. In Germany he attended the founding congress of former CDU member René Stadtkewitz's strongly PVV-oriented party, Die Freiheit. This party, however, failed to effect the hoped-for breakthrough and became radicalised. The German grassroots movement Pegida (Patriotic Europeans Against the Islamisation of the Occident) enjoyed greater success, at least initially, mobilising tens of thousands of people for demonstrations. At one of these demonstrations, on 13 April 2015 in Dresden, Wilders was guest of honour and gave a speech in German.

What did all these lectures achieve for Wilders? They probably provided some funds for his party and financed his lawyers, though as we will see in a later chapter it is difficult to estimate the amounts involved. In any case, all these invitations enabled him to disseminate his message abroad as well. Armed with a whole series of worrying facts, figures and authoritative quotes, he warned his audiences of the dangers of Islam. In Australia and North America he gave the impression that Europe was on the point of surrender and that entire neighbourhoods of many European cities had been taken over by Muslims, giving rise to parallel communities where Sharia law applied and polygamy, female genital mutilation and honour killings were the order of the day. Blinded by cultural relativism, progressive politicians would not put any obstacle in the way of Islam. 'Learn from the European lesson', Wilders warned his Australian and American audiences. 'The more Islam you get into your society, the less civilized it becomes and the less free.'[42]

These visits also gained Wilders the publicity he needed, both in the Netherlands and in the countries he visited. In fact, Wilders had his opponents to thank for much of the publicity: almost everywhere he went there were demonstrations against him and his ideas. Sometimes appearances were cancelled for safety considerations or because a venue owner feared negative publicity. In 2009, Wilders received free publicity from the British government when the UK Home Secretary, fearing possible unrest, decided to deny Wilders entry to the United Kingdom. Cunning Wilders did not pass up this opportunity, flying to Heathrow all the same to be sent back under the watchful eye of a host of media organisations. On 2 May 2015, Wilders again reached the world press after two Islamic fundamentalists were shot down just before an intended attack at a meeting in Garland, Texas, where he was the keynote speaker.

As a figurehead of anti-Islamic alarmism in the last ten years, Wilders has become the most famous Dutch politician by a long way. A simple search of the online archives of foreign newspapers such as the *Frankfurter Allgemeine Zeitung*, *The Times*, *Le Monde*, *El Pais* and the *Wall Street Journal* shows that Wilders is the most frequently mentioned Dutch politician of the past decade. He has acquired admirers in a wide range of circles, from the German Pegida movement to the English Defence League, and from the Israeli settlement movement to the French Front National. Certainly for a politician from a small country like the Netherlands that is a remarkable achievement.

By far his most notorious admirer, however, was a Norwegian named Anders Behring Breivik. On 22 July 2011, Breivik launched a double attack in which a total of 77 people lost their lives. In a manifesto posted on the Internet, Breivik appeared to have been strongly inspired by the anti-Islamic alarmism of Geert Wilders and others, mentioning the politician's name with approval more than 30 times.[43] 'A slap in the face for the anti-Islam movement worldwide', Wilders was forced to acknowledge as he did his best to deny any connection with this disturbed madman.[44] It took a while for the 'anti-Islam movement worldwide' to recover from this blow. Only with the rise of the Islamic State in the summer of 2014 and the attacks in Paris and Copenhagen in 2015 did anti-Islamic alarmism get the wind in its sails again. How long it will last this time remains unpredictable. It certainly appears that in the coming years, Geert Wilders will remain one of the most important figureheads for anti-Islamic alarmism.

Parliamentarian, whistle-blower and media strategist

What exactly is Wilders trying to do? What does he seek to achieve with the PVV? This is the question asked by the many 'Wilders watchers' since the fall of the coalition he supported. The PVV is not likely to regain direct political influence in the Netherlands as both VVD and CDA have excluded Wilders from future coalitions. After his decision to withdraw his support for the first Rutte coalition the PVV leader is no longer seen as a trustworthy partner. Where a party such as the Front National in France is trying to free itself from isolation, in the Netherlands Wilders appears to have chosen isolation as the best place for his party. At the same time his star continues to rise abroad and he receives invitations from all over the globe to proclaim his anti-Islamic alarmist message. Moreover, the polls in 2015 and early 2016 show a steady rise in support for the PVV, reaching more than 25% for the first time in December 2015, such that the PVV has become by far the largest party, even larger than the coalition parties VVD and PvdA combined. Among his former colleagues, too, there is little agreement as to what Wilders is up to. 'Wilders is really more of a media strategist than a politician. He is always coming up with plans to get the media to do his dirty work for him', says Louis Bontes, for example.[45] If one thing is clear from the previous chapter, it is Wilders' talent for attracting media attention, but what is it all for in the end? Some dissidents believe Wilders wants to go down in history as a new Churchill, as a severely tested self-made man grown into an international statesman. Others are more sceptical. 'Ultimately, Wilders wants one thing above all: to keep his seat in the House of Representatives', says Johan Driessen. 'He's addicted to the political game: the parliamentary debates, the media attention, coming up with one-liners. He never wants to do anything else, even if he has to sit there on his own. What alternative does he have anyway?'[46]

It is true that Wilders has few alternatives. He is not cut out for high office outside politics and has made too many enemies for a coalition country such as the Netherlands. Nor is living a quiet life of anonymity likely to be an option, since he will remain a target for Islamic fundamentalist terrorists for the foreseeable future. For that reason he will need security for some time to come. As long as he sits in the Dutch parliament, the Dutch state provides security, but as a private citizen he may well eventually have to cover it himself.

At the same time, his passion for parliament seems to have been diminished somewhat as a result of the enduring isolation. At least, Wilders has begun to question the legitimacy and representativeness of the Dutch parliament. In the wake of the refugee crisis in September 2015 he called the House of Representatives a 'fake parliament' after appealing for the borders to be closed, a wish he claimed the PVV, as the only parliamentary party, shared with millions of Dutch people. In his opinion the stream of refugees was in fact an Islamic invasion and the many young male Muslims were 'testosterone bombs' who put the lives of Dutch wives and daughters in danger. He appealed to the citizens of the Netherlands to actively resist the arrival of asylum seeker centres in their communities. In autumn 2015 and winter 2016 many public village and neighborhood information meetings about the housing of asylum seekers ended in turmoil. These sometimes fierce protests were not, however, organised by the PVV which, as we will see in the next chapter, lacks the organisation and manpower for extra-parliamentary activities.

Notes

1 W.C. Müller and K. Strøm, *Policy, Office or Votes. How Political Parties in Western Europe Make Hard Choices*, Cambridge: Cambridge University Press, 1999.
2 *Trouw*, 17 December 1999; *Trouw*, 16 October, 2004.
3 F.i. Paul Taggart's statement: 'Populism is Reluctantly Political'. Taggart, *Populism*, 3.
4 M. Spruyt, *Wat het Vlaams Blok verzwijgt*, 53–54, Leuven: Van Halewyck, 2000.
5 *Trouw*, 17 December 1999.
6 D. Art and S.L. de Lange, 'Fortuyn versus Wilders. An Agency-Based Approach to Radical Right Party Building', *West European Politics* 34 (6) (2011): 1229–1249.
7 H. te Velde, *Van regentenmentaliteit tot populisme*, 120.
8 J. de Beus, 'Audience Democracy. An Emerging Pattern in Postmodern Political Communication', in *Political Communication in Postmodern Democracy*, K. Brants and K. Volmer, eds, 19–36, New York: Palgrave Macmillan, 2011; B. Manin, *The Principles of Representative Government*, Cambridge: Cambridge University Press, 1997.
9 *Vrij Nederland*, 27 June 2009.
10 O. Scholten, N. Ruigrok et al., eds, *Stemmen krijgen of stemming maken?* Nieuwsmonitor Vrije Universiteit Amsterdam, September 2009.

11 T. Louwerse and S. Otjes, *Kiezen voor confrontatie. Hoe stelt de PVV zich op in de Tweede Kamer* (Leiden, 2010); T. Louwerse and S. Otjes, *Loyaal met een scherpe rand. Stemgedrag PVV 2010–2011 in kaart gebracht* (Leiden, 2011); Also S. Otjes and T. Louwerse, 'Populists in Parliament: Comparing Left-Wing and Right-Wing Populism in the Netherlands', *Political Studies* 63 (1) 2015: 60–79.
12 *De Volkskrant*, 23 March 2009.
13 *NRC Handelsblad*, 10 January 2009.
14 Research in LexisNexis in following newspapers *NRC Handelsblad, Trouw, De Volkskrant, Telegraaf, AD, Spits, Metro, Dag.*

Table 3.1 LexisNexis newspaper research results, 1 January 2007–31 December 2009

	2007	2008	2009
Geert Wilders	1799	2509	2362
Rita Verdonk	1152	1419	549
Wouter Bos	1754	2013	1942
Mark Rutte	845	526	584
Jan Peter Balkenende	4091	4138	4474
Nicolas Sarkozy	1701	2118	1419
Barack Obama	4500	5711	6701

15 Research in catalogue Institute for Vision and Sound:

Table 3.2 Institute for Vision and Sound research results, 1 September 2006–1 March 2012

	Total	Interview	Subject
Geert Wilders (PVV)	2756	933	1823
Mark Rutte (VVD)	2420	1627	793
Wouter Bos (PvdA)	1752	1115	637
J.P. Balkenende (CDA)	2330	1404	926
Femke Halsema (GL)	832	717	115
Alexander Pechtold (D66)	1380	1214	166

16 Interview, Johan Driessen.
17 Interview, Marcial Hernandez in the documentary *Wilders' Wereld*. NPO, 5 July 2014.
18 On the formation: J. Heymans, *Over Rechts. De formative* (Amsterdam, 2010); B. Bukman, *Het slagveld. De lange weg naar het kabinet Rutte*, Amsterdam: Meulenhoff, 2011.
19 Interview, Louis Bontes.
20 J. Albers, 'Hoe Wilders over zijn eigen grens ging', *Vrij Nederland*, 21 May 2014.
21 Speech, Geert Wilders, House of Representatives, 27 October, 2010.
22 'Concept-Gedoogakkoord', VVD-PVV-CDA, 30 September 2010. www.kabinetsformatie2010.nl. Accessed 12 September 2012.
23 R. Heinisch, 'Success in Opposition – Failure in Government: Explaining the Performance of Rightwing Populist Parties in Public Office', *West European Politics* 26 (3) (2003): 91–130.
24 Interview, Louis Bontes.
25 J. Hoedeman and R. Meijer, 'Alles voor Geerts gerief', *De Volkskrant*, 22 February 2014.

26 Interview, anonymous IV; confirmed by Bontes and Van Bemmel.
27 Interview, Louis Bontes.
28 Louwerse and Otjes, *Loyaal met een scherpe rand.*
29 *Algemeen Dagblad*, 27 April 2013.
30 Wilders, *Marked for Death*, 215.
31 *NRC Handelsblad*, 10 January 2007.
32 Interview, Louis Bontes.
33 Tj. Bosma, '*Het parlement van binnenuit onderuit halen. Een onderzoek naar het gedrag van de Partij voor de Vrijheid in het Europees Parlement*'. Masters thesis, Leiden University, June 2012, via openacces.leidenuniv.nl.
34 Albers, 'Hoe Wilders over zijn eigen grens ging'.
35 Anonymous, Interview III.
36 N. Genga, 'The Front National and the National-Populist Right in France', in *The Changing Faces of Populism. Systemic Challengers in Europe and the US*, H. Giusto, D. Kitching, S. Rizzo, eds, 69–86, Brussels; Rome: Foundation for European Progressive Studies, 2014.
37 *NRC Handelsblad*, 13 November 2013.
38 Interview, anonymous III; M. Hernandez, *Geert Wilders ontmaskerd. Van messias tot politieke klaploper* (Soesterberg, 2012) 95–97.
39 M. Ekman, 'Online Islamophobia and the Politics of Fear: Manufacturing the Green Scare', *Ethnic and Racial Studies*, 38 (11) (2015): 1986–2002; Bangstad, *Anders Breivik*.
40 W. Ali and E. Clifton, eds, *Fear, Inc. The Roots of the Islamophobia Network in America* [n.p.] 2011; J. Heilbrunn, *They Knew They Were Right. The Rise of the Neocons*, New York: Doubleday, 2009; J.J. Mearsheimer and S. Walt, *The Israel Lobby and US Foreign Policy*, Chicago: Farrar, Straud and Giroux, 2008.
41 Dutch anti-Islam MP: 'Israel Is West's First Line of Defence', *Haaretz*, 18 June 2009.
42 Speech, Wilders, Melbourne, 19 February 2013; Los Angeles, 9 June 2013. English speeches can be found on www.geertwilders.nl.
43 Anders Behring Breivik/aka Andrew Berwick, '*2083 – A European Declaration of Independence*'. Bangstad, *Anders Breivik*.
44 *De Volkskrant*, 27 February 2011.
45 Interview, Louis Bontes.
46 Interview, Johan Driessen.

4 A unique party
The PVV as a party organisation

The PVV's ideology and behaviour in parliament caused a considerable stir. Nevertheless, political scientists and parliamentary historians will note that the party is not entirely unique in this respect. The combination of anti-Islamic alarmism, nationalism, populism and a focus on law and order are features we also find to a greater or lesser extent in the programmes of parties such as the DFP, the FPÖ, the Front National and also in other Dutch parties such as the LPF. Neither is provocative parliamentary behaviour, colourful language or intensive use of parliamentary powers exceptional. The PVV copied the socialist-populist SP to a large extent, while in the more distant past communists, anarchists and fascists often succeeded in causing uproar. In one area, however, the PVV is unique, namely, in its organisation. As far as I am aware, the PVV is the only party in the world formally based on a single-member organisation. Strictly speaking, none of the members of the Senate and House of Representatives, delegates, MEPs or members of municipal councils who have represented the PVV are members of the party. That privilege is reserved for just one person, Geert Wilders.

Anyone wanting to study the PVV party structure therefore has an easy job. In formal organisational terms, the PVV is nothing more than the Wilders Group Association, founded on 30 March 2005 by Geert Wilders and the Wilders Group Foundation, which was established on 20 November 2004 to acquire funds, again with Wilders as its sole member. The two official founders of the association, Geert Wilders and the Wilders Group Foundation, immediately decided to halt recruitment of new members, leaving the PVV with just one member, legally speaking.

Of course that is not particularly satisfactory. In organisational terms, the PVV is more than just a legal casing for 'Mr G. Wilders' views on politics and society'. The party has 17 different parliamentary groups, each with its own internal organisation, and has participated in nine election campaigns. Candidates have been selected and trained for this purpose, funds acquired, advertisements placed on the radio and television, posters put up, flyers distributed, meetings convened; all activities requiring organisation and staff. In other words, a great many people have contributed their efforts to the party, from poster distributors to MPs and from press officer to number 20 on a provincial candidate list. How many people are there and how are they organised? What does the internal hierarchy look like and what are the channels of internal communication? How are all the activities paid for?

It is as difficult to obtain an answer to these questions as it was easy to gain an overview of the formal structure of the PVV. Unlike most parties, after all, the PVV has no public party conferences, no departments organising meetings, no party newspaper with information on the organisation, no think tank publishing working papers, and no youth organisation supplying fresh blood. The party also systematically refuses to assist with investigations or interviews into its internal operations. Emails from journalists, students and scientists wanting to study the party almost always remain unanswered; the party rarely takes part in surveys or political conferences. The extremely closed character of the PVV means that speculation as to the internal balance of power resembles the work of Kremlin watchers during the Cold War. Outsiders attempt to form a picture of what goes on in this secretive stronghold based on a few snippets of information, often supplied by dissidents, and a great deal of circumstantial evidence.

This chapter aims to offer some insight. How does the PVV finance its campaigns? How many people work for the PVV and what are their backgrounds? How are the candidates selected and trained? What is the internal pecking order? The main sources are media statements by various PVV members, interviews with members who have left the party, and journalists' reports. I have also investigated various candidates online using search engines such as Google, Yahoo and LexisNexis to obtain more details on their political and professional backgrounds.

The memberless party: making a virtue of necessity

Why did Wilders choose not to admit members to his party? The most important reason was the fear that his party would become 'a second LPF'. After the loss of its leader, the Pim Fortuyn List split into many factions fighting one another due to lack of organisation. Like many new parties, the LPF turned out to have a magnetic effect on all kinds of political thrill seekers, firebrands and businesspeople with their own agenda. It also attracted individuals from the very narrow and divided circles of the Dutch far right, who hoped to steer the new party in their own direction. All the squabbles and revelations created a near-constant stream of negative publicity, which probably contributed significantly to the rapid electoral demise of the LPF.[1]

The lesson Wilders took from this was that internal disputes must be avoided, and that he must tread carefully with many of those who approached him. The best way to achieve that was to keep the ranks as small and closed as possible. A small organisation also suited a loner like Wilders: in an interview in 2007 he stated that as a VVD member, he had been bothered by the cumbersome party structure with all the powerful party barons and complicated agreements and procedures. 'To stand as a candidate you had to travel all over the country, visit all the chairs of the local branches and tell the biggest idiot he was a genius.'[2]

Wilders also felt that the power of senior party members meant that the wrong candidates were often nominated, as active VVD members were often more progressive than the conservative electorate they hoped to reach. Dutch electoral law allowed Wilders to participate in the elections without a membership structure to his party, although this choice did have substantial financial consequences, since in the Netherlands only parties with a good many members receive a government subsidy.[3]

The choice of this party model seemed to work out nicely at first. In the initial years, the PVV barely had to deal with internal conflicts or revelations regarding dubious volunteers from extreme-right circles. The best method for preventing rumblings in the ranks turned out to be to keep those ranks as small and closed as possible. The lowered security risk in the absence of public meetings was also a consideration, as were the costs saved by not having members, administrative staff, party office premises, newsletters or conferences. Perhaps the most important point, however, was that most voters – at least in the short term – seemed not to care about the PVV's structure. In the polls the PVV continued to score higher until it achieved almost 30 seats in the spring of 2009. Why would the PVV expend finances and energy on something which apparently did not interest most voters? For the time being there were few critical remarks to be heard from within the party either.

That changed in spring 2010, when Hero Brinkman announced that he would work towards opening the party up to members. 'At every party meeting people tell us they want to become members of the PVV. Decent people want to belong to it. The PVV has reached a peak as a political movement, so the moment has come for democratisation', he stated in an interview.[4] In the parliamentary party, however, Brinkman did not find much support, although according to insiders that was mainly because of his personality, which was somewhat controversial within the PVV. 'There were whisperings that Brinkman was primarily dissatisfied with his low position on the candidate list in 2010', says former fellow MP Jhim van Bemmel.[5] Brinkman similarly received little support from the voters, who seemed not to feel much need for a democratic membership structure. He ran his own campaign for the 2010 House of Representatives elections but received a mere 19,000 preference votes, or just over 1% of the PVV vote. Thanks to the PVV's big victory, Brinkman did achieve a seat in the House of Representatives, but his position within the party was severely damaged. As mentioned, his eventual departure from the party on 20 March 2012 was awkward for Wilders because it lost the coalition their majority, but it did not lead to a split in the PVV: only a handful of people followed the former chief of police. Hero Brinkman participated in the 2012 House of Representatives elections with a party of his own, the Democratic Political Turning Point (DPK), but the result – 0.1% of the vote – was thoroughly humiliating, with even a joke party, standing for 'Celebrations every day for everyone', winning more votes.

Another attempt to force Wilders to open the PVV to members also ended in failure. The initiative for this campaign came from two PVV dissidents, Oege Bakker and Geert Tomlow, who were 'inspired by TV images of the protests on

Tahrir Square in Cairo in winter 2011'. 'We called our club's website a "virtual Tahrir Square" on which thousands of PVV voters could have their voices heard', Bakker says.[6] It did not lead to the anticipated onrush of members, though, with fewer than 30 people coming forward in six months. Bakker says only a handful of people turned up to the meetings organised by this Association for the PVV (VvPVV). 'No one wanted to actually do or organise anything. There was no response whatsoever from the PVV itself. We were simply completely ignored. It was a sorry state of affairs.'[7] On 12 December 2011, VvPVV Chairman Bakker sent out a press release stating that the attempt had failed:

> The supporters of the PVV are not interested in a membership association, and they don't feel the need to take part, directly or indirectly, in political discussions within the PVV. I'm sorry to say that Hero Brinkman is probably wrong in his attempts to democratise the PVV and Geert Wilders appears to be right in his decision to manage the PVV as a party with just one member, namely Geert Wilders![8]

Neither voters nor activists felt the need to organise the PVV differently, nor does this seem to have changed. The loss which the PVV suffered in the elections of 2012 and 2014 probably had little to do with the lack of membership structure. The criticism of the party model, however, never completely died down. Dissidents leaving the PVV often justified their decision by pointing to the lack of participation, and the party's amateurism. In 2014, another new movement rose up around a number of former PVV members (called For the Netherlands) who did want to function with a democratic membership structure. In order to better understand this criticism we should first look more closely at the way the PVV operates in practice. Does everyone obsequiously follow Geert Wilders? What is the pecking order? In short, what happens behind the scenes of the PVV?

Behind the scenes

What goes on offstage in the offices of the PVV parliamentary party has been the subject of much speculation, some based on inside information and some not. The PVV itself had effectively asked for this by refusing to provide any information as to its internal organisation and by fobbing off or completely ignoring interested journalists and researchers. They did not wish to be involved with this book either: there was no response to requests for information or interviews. Interviews with PVV dissidents, on the other hand, turned up a wealth of facts and impressions. A few PVV dissidents have also published their experiences in book form or given exhaustive accounts of their experiences in interviews.[9] Of course it should be borne in mind that the testimonies of such dissidents tend to be coloured by a substantial sense of anger towards Wilders and the PVV. With the benefit of hindsight many of them feel short-changed, still have scores to settle and pass severe judgements. More neutral in tone and less spiteful in nature is the book *Undercover bij de PVV. Achter de schermen bij de politieke partij van Geert Wilders* (Undercover in the PVV: Behind the scenes of Geert Wilders' political party), a report in journal form by Karen Geurtsen, a journalist for weekly magazine *HP De Tijd* who worked undercover for a while as an intern for the PVV.[10] Her book offers a number of interesting observations which often agree with dissident testimonies.

The most striking of these observations is the strongly centralised, hierarchical character of the party. When asked by journalists about internal democracy in his party in 2007, Wilders replied in annoyance, 'I'm really not interested in playing Kim Il-sung.'[11] The testimonies of all the PVV dissidents, however, suggest that the organisation of the PVV exhibits many of the traits of an autocracy. In his own party, Wilders acts as if he were some kind of sun god, around whom a small system of planets has formed. These confidants are regularly permitted to enter Wilders' office, hold the main internal positions (such as membership of the parliamentary party board, programme committee or candidate selection) and enjoy special privileges within the party. The composition of this clique varies somewhat; the only constants are Fleur Agema, Martin Bosma and Barry Madlener. According to Louis Bontes, who as treasurer held a place high in the pecking order for a while, Wilders was extremely manipulative:

> Wilders can be very charming. He gives you the feeling that you're one of his confidants, but drops you just as quickly afterwards. Suddenly you're out of favour. That's how he shows that everyone is dependent on him in the end.[12]

Joram van Klaveren, another former confidant, also remembers how a culture of dependence was created. 'At some point during the annual party outing Martin Bosma would always ask us to applaud Wilders, because it was thanks to him we all had decent jobs with good salaries.' All PVV dissidents concur that it was Wilders who personally decided who was placed where on the candidate list. 'Wilders could make or break you. People are constantly afraid of the consequences if they make a mistake. This creates a pervasive culture of fear. It's very unhealthy', says Van Klaveren.[13]

Despite his passion for control, Wilders' style of leadership is very distant. Almost all testimonies show that the PVV leader is not much of a people manager. Outside his little group of confidants he barely speaks with his staff at all. As in his VVD years, Wilders prefers to lock himself up in his office, strewn with files and papers, where he works extremely long days, from half past eight in the morning until at least eleven at night. He demands the same work ethic from his direct employees. 'If he needed you, you had to come right away, even if you were at the cinema on a Saturday evening. All his personal employees suffered burnout sooner or later', a former employee remembers.[14] In return he never showed his face at the coffee machine or lunch table, barely showed an interest in anyone's personal background and avoided socialising as far as possible. In the four months of her internship, Karen Geurtsen only saw him twice in passing and never got to speak to him properly, while another party employee did not meet the PVV leader once in the two years he worked for the party. In his book, Marcial Hernandez states that in two years, Wilders never showed his face on the floor where most of the party was situated.[15] Johan Driessen, who accompanied Wilders for years on trips abroad, does not shrink from describing Wilders as socially maladjusted:

> He can really only talk about politics, as he doesn't have any other interests or hobbies. On Twitter he sometimes pretends to be into football or darts, but it's all for show. As soon as people start talking about something other than politics, he doesn't know what to say anymore. He never felt at ease speaking with ordinary people either.[16]

The PVV leader's somewhat antisocial character makes him as impenetrable to his employees as to outsiders. Whatever is cooked up in Wilders' office remains shrouded in mist to most PVV supporters. At the drop of a hat he will confront fellow party members with sudden changes of course or a fait accompli, as in the case of his proposal for a tax on headscarves, the launch of the 'Poles complaints centre', or critical tweets about the queen. His decision to abandon the first Rutte cabinet in April 2012 was as much of a surprise to the vast majority of the party as it was to Dutch citizens. Most party members heard it from the media.

Various PVV dissidents have expressed a great deal of criticism for Wilders' indecisiveness and lack of resolution. 'Wilders is clearly not a born leader', says Van Bemmel. 'He constantly avoids conflict and often lacks the courage for confrontation. If you were invited to his office, you would often find him at his wits' end.'[17] Other PVV dissidents remember how Wilders sometimes seemed overwhelmed by moments of great indecision and fear of failure. 'He sometimes seemed mentally and physically at the end of his tether. Sometimes he barely ate. Martin Bosma in particular then had to pep him up', Geert Tomlow recounts.[18] Marcial Hernandez describes him in his book as a leader who, when things become stressful, 'changes into a completely uncertain, fearful and neurotic chain-smoker'.[19] According to Johan Driessen, Wilders was always afraid that party members would turn against him. 'As soon as he saw members spending too much time together, he would try to play them off against one another, for instance by putting one and not the other on the list. It really was divide and rule.'[20]

Of course these are dissidents' judgements on Wilders, coloured by hard feelings and disappointment. Neither is Wilders the only political leader to be described by his employees as a socially maladjusted monomaniac who comes across as less decisive and self-assured behind the scenes than in public. Nevertheless, many of the judgements more or less concur with the impressions of his VVD colleagues. The difference is that in his VVD years, he was not yet in a leadership role, with all the burdens that brings. With his loner tendencies, suspicious nature and need for total control, Wilders creates an atmosphere of uncertainty and fear within a party which revolves entirely around him. In the absence of a clear organisation or hierarchy, everyone looks to the great leader to solve all internal problems in person. Mediation by people other than Wilders is only accepted to a limited extent, since they are quickly seen as obstructing the desired direct contact with the leader. In other parties the members are much more attached to the party and its organisation and much less to a party leader, who is generally a transient figure. People are much less likely to expect the leader of the CDA or PvdA to be personally concerned with squabbles in the country or within the party: there are other authorities to take care of that. In this light, the descriptions by dissidents of a distant, indecisive and unpredictable figure tell us not only about Wilders' character and style of leadership, but also about the members' high expectations of a leader with whom they feel they have personally bonded. It appears that many PVV dissidents are mainly disillusioned with Wilders as a person, a former role model who has lost his power of attraction as if by magic, and many now describe him as a narcissistic personality and power-crazed manipulator.

A second observation by Karen Geurtsen which also appears in every testimony is the PVV's emphatic focus on media attention. Media ratings are viewed behind the scenes as the highest good. Geurtsen notes that she received the following fatherly advice from MP Raymond de Roon:

> Don't go too deep into the substance: it's all about the media attention you can earn. Islam is bad, the government is bad, other parties are bad, and the PVV is good of course. That's our point of departure. We might have nuanced discussions of issues internally, but not externally. That would just put everyone to sleep, journalists first of all.[21]

Of course this is an undercover journalist's representation of a conversation, but it corresponds with the statements of almost all dissidents. As a party without departments and without substantial financial means, the PVV is largely dependent on free media publicity. 'Every day we faced the big question of how to get ourselves into the media', Spruyt reminisces about the early days of the PVV.[22] To judge by the other informants, that has never changed. The party is constantly having to come up with something to pique journalists' interest: an unusual proposal, attention-grabbing campaign, sensational statement or remarkable motion. According to a former personal assistant, Wilders also keeps a precise record of where he is mentioned in the media and on websites. Every morning he has a printout delivered of all the newspaper articles in which he has been mentioned. If something has been written about him in South Africa or New Zealand, he reads it. Former MP Louis Bontes says:

> With every step Wilders takes, he considers the media attention. If no media is going to turn up to an event, then he doesn't go either. For instance, once we were going to go to Gouda to show support for people who were being terrorised by Moroccan youths. When it turned out no media would be present, Geert Wilders didn't want to go anymore. He's really not going to go somewhere to meet ten or so people.[24]

In the Netherlands Wilders has gradually developed a clever strategy for getting the television media in particular to do his dirty work. Jhim van Bemmel tells me:

> Wilders deliberately creates scarcity by almost never appearing on a programme. If he then does come, the viewing figures shoot up and journalists daren't ask him critical questions anymore. They're as meek as lambs because they're afraid of antagonising Wilders.[25]

As a result, those who see the rare television interviews with Wilders get the impression that an important statesman is being interviewed.

A third remarkable point in Geurtsen's undercover report is the immense amateurism within the PVV as an organisation. She notes with some surprise that the organisation and application procedures for the 2010 municipal council elections were managed by a 21-year-old intern.[26] The interviews with PVV dissidents also reveal splendid examples of amateurism, ad hoc policy and improvisation. In the broadcasting slot for political parties for the 2012 provincial elections, the party simply displayed the slogan 'Enough is enough' for a full five minutes. 'Some people saw it as a stroke of genius, when actually there was simply no money for a proper broadcast', says Joram van Klaveren.[27] Where many other parties make expensive party political broadcasts for elections, visit lots of cities and organise informal political meetings and youth festivals, the PVV limited itself to the production of clunky, cheap-looking clips, keeping a few websites online and making a few flying visits to cities they think are important. They mainly used the Internet to recruit volunteers for jobs such as putting up posters, but almost no effort was made to maintain contact after the elections. The candidates who were not lucky enough to be elected could also forget any kind of follow-up or interest from the PVV. Geert Tomlow, one of the candidates not elected, noticed to his surprise that volunteers did not even receive a letter of thanks. 'Whether it's ignorance or straightforward rudeness, I don't know, but that's how it always was with the PVV. Personally I didn't hear anything for months after the elections, although I had worked really hard for the campaign.'[28] The provincial parties barely received any practical support or information. 'A couple of posters were sent out and that was it really. You have to do all the rest yourself. You were even expected to pay for part of the campaign yourself', said a former member of the provincial council.[29]

A final recurring theme in Geurtsen's report is the immense secretiveness and strong sense of suspicion within the PVV towards the outside world. 'You can't even tell your colleagues what you're up to', the undercover journalist recounts.[30] Many employees prefer not to say that they work for the PVV, so they only answer the phone with their first name. The mistrust is fed in part by the often hostile or dismissive responses of those around them, but it is also cultivated within the party, as various sources show. Marcial Hernandez, for example, describes how he, along with other newly elected MPs, was subjected to a daily 'intimidation session' by Agema and Bosma after the elections:

Agema painted a picture of an atmosphere in which no one could be trusted. She delivered a tirade about the other political parties and how they smile at you and are nice to you, but as soon as you turn round you can expect a knife in your back. They created an image of a party which had been fighting the outside world, especially the media, from the trenches for the last three years. The media in particular were after our blood; they wanted to break us.[31]

PVV MPs were therefore advised against spending too much time with MPs from other parties, who were only after the demise of the party. The participants in the various classes were constantly reminded to say as little as possible about their experiences. Use of Twitter was sometimes even prohibited. According to Hernandez, employees were even forbidden from speaking with third parties about their poor working conditions, 'on pain of dismissal and a fine of 25,000 euros [sic!] for each violation'.[32] Almost all testimonies also show that leaving the PVV is quite a drastic move: all contacts from that moment are resolutely cut off, personal friendships ended and the departing member is treated as a pariah.

A closed party culture of this kind is by no means unique. Plenty of stories do the rounds about the originally Maoist SP party, telling of rigid discipline and the excommunication of dissidents. On the other hand, this specific party culture in the PVV also follows from the security situation. The constant presence of guards and heavy security measures lend a certain reality to the feeling of being under siege. At a PVV party event members are not welcomed by enthusiastic young members with coffee, tea and balloons, but by strict security officers and detector gates. These unusual circumstances create a different atmosphere from the Dixieland orchestras of political youth events and feed a certain wartime mentality. The same applies to the negative reactions the PVV triggers in the media and society.

Being an activist for the PVV effectively means working for a party which the outside world often labels as fascist or racist and which is seen by many as the enemy. True, besides Wilders not a single PVV member has required constant protection, but various PVV candidates and sympathisers deal with threats, intimidation, vandalism or even physical violence. Joram van Klaveren remembers that they were mainly bothered by extreme-left demonstrators from the Dutch Anti-Fascist Action network and the International Socialists. 'At a meeting in Groningen our bus was besieged. And at election debates people would hiss "fascist" and "racist" at you the whole time. Stickers were placed on candidates' doors. It was extremely threatening.' In Friesland in particular, candidates had to deal with their houses being defaced and noisy demonstrations, probably by Anti-Fascist Action.[33] Various dissidents have also had problems with employers, family or friends due to their sympathy for the PVV.[34] The Complaints Centre for Discrimination also increasingly receives complaints from PVV members who feel 'discriminated against' because of their political views.

In short, it takes some courage to act for the party. What kind of people are prepared to work for the PVV? What do we know about their backgrounds? And how are they selected?

The PVV staff

Finding good staff presents a challenge to any new party. Where capable people give new political parties a wide berth for fear of loss of status, such parties appear to be irresistibly attractive to the type of people one would prefer to avoid: born troublemakers and complainers, people with their own agendas or who are just looking for a job. Of course established parties have to deal with difficult people too, but their age and organisational structure enable them to separate the wheat from the chaff sooner. They have departments, municipal council members, members of the States Provincial and generally also aldermen and delegates all over the country, as well as maintaining political youth organisations, a think tank and a training programme. In short, they have a whole reservoir of aspiring candidates who have already had some opportunity to prove in political practice that they possess the correct skills. The most accident-prone and the biggest troublemakers are filtered out at an early stage.

In its search for good staff, the PVV also encountered an additional obstacle in the form of the leader's awkward security situation. 'If I wanted to talk to a candidate, that had to happen in a secret hotel, on the sixth floor, with agents at the door of my room', Wilders told weekly magazine *HP de Tijd* at the start of 2005.[35] Shortly before that, the NOS Journaal national news programme had announced that the intelligence services considered candidates and employees of the Wilders Group to be at high risk. For example, Bart Jan Spruyt received serious warnings from both the National Coordinator for Security and Counterterrorism and the National Police Services Agency (KLPD) about the consequences of working with Wilders. Many experts predicted that Wilders was on an impossible mission.[36] Who would be prepared to take such risks for a lonely MP?

In the end the mission did not prove impossible, but most dissidents agree that finding sufficient staff has remained a problem. It is difficult to obtain a precise picture because, in the absence of official members, there is no membership administration, nor any information on the number of 'activists'. It is in any case certain that the numbers are quite small. We always come across the same names on the various PVV candidate lists, and many PVV members hold several positions in the party. They combine membership of the States Provincial and House of Representatives or are simultaneously members of municipal councils and policy advisors for the PVV. In some provincial states, PVV supporters have even employed themselves as advisors.

All in all we come to a figure of 368 individual candidates, of whom a good two-thirds have stood as candidates multiple times or been in the paid employment of the PVV. It was more or less expected of party assistants that they would be prepared to have their names placed on a candidate list to pad it out, a former employee remembers. Then of course there are the volunteers doing the many odd jobs in campaign time, such as distributing flyers, putting up posters and collecting the signatures needed for participation in the elections. In 2007, Wilders spoke of 'volunteers, now in their thousands', but the PVV dissidents interviewed offer considerably lower estimations, varying from around 300 to a maximum of 600 volunteers in the entire period between 2004 and 2015.[37] This is closer to estimations by journalists, based on the number of participants at PVV events and campaign activities. Assuming 300–600 more or less active volunteers, 368 individual candidates and perhaps a few dozen more paid employees who have never stood as candidates, we come to the rather generous figure of just over 1000 people who, one way or another, were actively involved in the PVV or the Wilders Group in the period 2004–2012. Of those, fewer than a hundred can be seen as full-time PVV members in the sense that they spend a large portion of their week on work for the party. Besides the members of the House of Representatives and MEPs these are mainly parliamentary party employees and press officers, as well as people who combine membership of various committees.

What kind of candidates were selected? What do we know of their profiles in terms of age, gender, education and political background? One thing we know for certain about all the candidates is their gender. Looking at the ratio of men to women, it seems we are justified in calling the PVV a men's party. Compared with 293 male candidates we see only 75 women, or 20.3% of all candidates – significantly lower than most other Dutch parties, with the exception of the orthodox Protestant SGP, which is still against the right of women to run for office. As far as age is concerned, the PVV has, compared with other parties, many older candidates (over 60) and younger candidates (under 30). So in terms of professional background it follows that the PVV has relatively large proportions of pensioners and students. Of the candidates whose backgrounds we were able to discover, a relatively high proportion are employed in jobs which in the Netherlands are currently known by a war metaphor as 'the frontline of society', such as teaching, care provision and the police. Compared with other parties, self-employed people – shop keepers, owners of hotels and restaurants, consultants – are overrepresented, whereas civil servants, journalists and employees from the cultural sector are underrepresented. It might be suggested that this division of professions – many self-employed people, few in governmental and semi-governmental organisations – fits the image of the PVV as a right-wing party fighting against 'left-wing hobbies' and subsidy-guzzling semi-governmental institutions.

Around 40 candidates were already on the PVV payroll as policy advisors, press officers or other such roles when they became candidates. Various data sources show that the PVV mainly attracts young employees, in their twenties and early thirties, at the beginning of their careers. A Frisian PVV member says when he visited the PVV headquarters in The Hague he was impressed by 'all those young, pretty, dark-haired girls, often dressed in black. It put me rather in mind of that video "Addicted to Love" by Robert Palmer.'[38] Many of the young employees are at university or in professional training alongside their jobs at the PVV headquarters, while a number also sit for the PVV on the States Provincial or on a municipal council.

The PVV is often portrayed as a party for those less educated, which may be true among voters, but certainly not among its representatives. In the House of

Representatives and European Parliament those with an academic degree or higher professional diploma dominate. Of 15 MPs, 13 are highly educated (the only doubtful cases being Wilders and Dion Graus), as are 8 of the 10 senators, and all the MEPs have a university degree. The information available on other candidates confirms this picture: many are highly educated, a couple are students, a few have been educated to secondary level, but there is almost no one with a lower level of education. Even in the PVV, Robert Putnam's famed 'law of increasing disproportion' applies – the higher a person's social status, the higher they are likely to rise on the political ladder.

Remarkably for a party often accused of racism and xenophobia, a number of candidates do not have Dutch backgrounds. The member of the North Holland Provincial Council, Rana Saleem, is an Iraqi (Christian) refugee; Sheren Cheng conducted a campaign in the Chinese community in 2006; while various candidates have an Indo-Surinamese or Antillean background. Undercover intern, Karen Geurtsen, notes in her diary that there were also several party employees and interns of non-European ethnic origin working at the party office: a glance at the internal directory confirms this impression. Moreover, it is noteworthy that many prominent PVV members have non-Dutch spouses, including Wilders (Hungarian), Fritsma (Filipino), De Roon (Costa Rican), Madlener (Croatian), and Van Dijck (Antillean). Such information is certainly relevant in the case of the PVV, because it at least lends nuance to the frequent accusations of xenophobia and racism. The party's anti-immigration stance, as we saw before, is not inspired by feelings of racial superiority or a principled aversion to all things non-Dutch.

It is known that at least 69 people, or 18.8%, have also been members of one or more other parties. At least 24 candidates, like Wilders, have been members of the VVD, while 23 have been active for the LPF or Livable Netherlands. For a few, the PVV appears to be yet another party in a long series. One candidate in Groningen had gone through as many as four parties, while a PVV member elected in Gelderland had already acted as a member of the States Provincial for three parties. Unsurprisingly perhaps, he decided to proceed as an independent candidate soon after becoming installed as a Provincial Council member for the PVV.

The political background of the various candidates tells us a bit, but far from everything, about their political views. What do we know about political views within the PVV? Are there political differences within the party and if so, what about? Which of the four PVV pillars of nationalism, populism, anti-Islamic alarmism and law and order do candidates feel most attracted to? Of course an extensive questionnaire would be the obvious way to gain a good overview, but as mentioned, the PVV refuses to cooperate on such surveys. From the sources collected for this study, it nonetheless appears that considerable differences in insight and priorities exist within the PVV. Various interviews show that a good many candidates, particularly in the provinces, attach much less importance to the battle against Islam than Wilders and Bosma. The exact subtleties of anti-Islamic alarmism are far from familiar to every candidate: people 'haven't really looked into it in detail', might not 'put it in those words exactly' or see the battle against Islam as synonymous with stricter policy on integration and immigration. It does seem that faith in anti-Islamic alarmism increases the nearer people come to the centre of power. Nevertheless, according to various dissidents, views on the danger of Islam differ even within the group in the House of Representatives. Van Bemmel:

> We were more or less in agreement that many Muslims needed to adapt better. But lots of us thought that whole Eurabia story by Fallaci and Bat Ye'or was really rather woolly-minded. You were expected to have read those books, but in my view hardly any of them really believed in them. Even Wilders seemed to see the battle against Islam as a kind of private crusade. In any case he never made much effort to convince others of those ideas...[39]

There are political differences within the party on many other themes. Many dissidents, for example, feel there is a clear left and right wing within the party when it comes to socio-economic issues. The right wing consists of PVV members who agreed with the 2006 party programme in which the PVV identified itself strongly on a socio-economic level as a liberal party in favour of cuts. They are in favour of a small state, little regulation, flat-rate income tax but also a higher defence budget. Opposed to that is a left wing, with powerful figures such as Fleur Agema and Martin Bosma, who have argued for the preservation of many of the facilities of the welfare state. This classic left–right opposition is further traversed within the PVV by opposition between conservatives and progressives when it comes to more post-material subjects such as equal rights for homosexuals, abortion, euthanasia and animal welfare. In opposition to libertarian old-Fortuynists are conservative Christians such as Raymond de Roon or the Flemish party ideologist and orthodox Catholic, Paul Beliën, who disfavour homosexual marriage. On the matter of animal welfare, defended primarily by Dion Graus, there is a certain degree of internal irritation and incomprehension. At Graus's insistence, for example, the PVV decided to support a proposal to prohibit ritual slaughter, which would affect Jews as well as Muslims. In doing so, Wilders forfeited a great deal of goodwill among Jews at home and abroad. There is much wild speculation within the PVV and beyond as to why Wilders nevertheless continues to support Graus.

How does the PVV recruit its candidates? Recruitment takes place in part through advertisements in newspapers and on the website, but in the end most people come in through personal connections, according to Joram van Klaveren. 'Recruitment worked mainly on the basis of trust. Hard-core members nominated people they felt they could rely on. Often those were family members, well-disposed acquaintances or friends. This gradually expanded the circle, but all relationships were based on trust.'[40] The candidates deemed suitable for the House of Representatives or European Parliament after a first interview were permitted to participate in special classes. Every Saturday in The Hague they received lessons in meeting skills, debating skills and media training with none other than Wilders himself, who was happy to sacrifice his day off for the purpose. Their knowledge of political science, current affairs and political history was also tested.[41] Books by anti-Islamic alarmists such as Bat Ye'or, Hans Jansen and Oriana Fallaci were recommended reading, but not compulsory. The aspiring candidates received thick readers for homework.

As we have seen, this strict training left the first PVV parliamentary party well prepared for its task. The MPs who represented the PVV after 2010, however, made much less of a good impression. Even the workaholic Wilders was unable to select and train all the new candidates alongside his parliamentary work and international trips. Lack of money and organisation also led to the neglect of thorough screening for new candidates. That cost the PVV dearly, as described above. Journalists came up with all sorts of revelations about new PVV MPs' pasts. In the provinces as well as on municipal councils, unwholesome facts regarding elected candidates came to light. Stories of tax fraud, domestic or public violence and alcohol abuse damaged the party's image, making it ever harder to find good candidates. Joram van Klaveren remembers:

> In the beginning there were really talented, clever people with good jobs, but with all the negative publicity and lack of say in what went on, many of them resigned, to be replaced by all sorts of mediocre figures. The result was the gradual intellectual impoverishment of the party atmosphere.[42]

After 2010, the PVV also saw the formation of a series of splinter groups. In 2004, Wilders had left the VVD but kept his seat. Many of the elected PVV members followed his example. Of the 48 seats in the House of Representatives won between 2006 and 2015, seven were lost due to members splitting from the party, and of 69 seats won in the in the 2011 States Provincial elections, 17 went to splinter groups. In the European Parliament and on the municipal councils of The Hague and Almere, too, members split from the party. In The Hague, a member of the municipal council suddenly converted to Islam after his inauguration and subsequently founded an Islamic party. By September 2015, in total, 33 of the 170 seats the PVV had won were lost to splinter groups, or 19.4% of the total – an impressive number, with which Wilders surpassed the LPF. The number of dissidents is even greater if we take into account the PVV activists who were no longer willing to stand for office or otherwise take part in activities for the party.

The fact that so many people have split from the PVV of course cannot be seen in isolation from the party's chosen model. The lack of traditional membership structure means that activists are not really bound to the party. They have no internal responsibilities and no opportunity to have their say, so they barely form a connection with the party at all. Wilders and his entourage show little interest in the representatives in the States Provincial and on the municipal councils. 'Emails with questions often went completely unanswered. They just left you out in the cold. Is it any surprise that people leave at some point?' an old member of a provincial council remarks.[43] Johan Driessen adds:

On the one hand you're expected to work extremely hard and sacrifice a great deal. On the other you feel as if you're not taken seriously at all. At some point a great many people think, what am I doing it all for?[44]

This lack of responsiveness means it is hardly a big step for dissidents to distance themselves from the PVV. Many of the representatives in the provinces or municipalities found they were able to split from the party without any great pangs of conscience. The PVV's ever worsening image raised the temptation for many members to turn their backs on the party and thus restrict the damage to their own careers as much as possible. In interviews some of them claimed they had 'made a mistake' and that they 'no longer wanted anything to do with the party'. According to Johan Driessen, many more PVV members wanted to leave the party but were held back by a lack of external career prospects: 'People think of their mortgages, and in the end MPs do get a good salary.' He is not the only former PVV member to view the group around Wilders in hindsight as a sort of sect:

> My departure really felt like a liberation. I stayed at home for a year and that did me a lot of good. It makes you look at things differently and you see how absurdly the whole party functioned and how strangely Wilders behaved.[45]

A poverty-stricken party? PVV finances

A new party requires not only media attention and sufficient staff, but also a considerable sum of money. Anyone who wishes to stand for election in the Netherlands must be registered with the Electoral Council as an association with legal capacity, with all the associated administrative and legal costs. Each party must also pay a deposit of around 11,000 euros, which is only returned if they achieve 75% of the quota. The election campaign then begins, with all the costs for advertisements, posters, room hire and broadcasting airtime. The costs of an election campaign vary by party and by country. In comparison with the United States, where politicians throw around many millions of dollars to become mayor, senator or president, campaigns in the Netherlands are relatively cheap. In 2010, the parties are thought to have spent between seven and nine million euros on the campaign altogether, the lion's share coming from the relatively wealthy PvdA, VVD, CDA and SP.[46] The parties obtain the money for election campaigns from member contributions, government subsidies, donations from third parties and sometimes through contributions from state reimbursements for representatives of the people. For new parties who do not yet have the right to government subsidies and often still have few members, donations are all the more important. In 2006, for example, the PvdD managed to enter the House of Representatives for the first time after an extensive, costly campaign largely financed by an animal-loving businessman. It is also known that Pim Fortuyn organised various fundraising dinners in the months running up to the elections.

How does the PVV make ends meet? The party's financial housekeeping is shrouded in secrecy due to its complex legal structure. Formally speaking, it is the Wilders Group Association (since August 2007, the PVV Association) which is the political party participating in elections. The budget for this association is 50 euros per year due to administrative costs such as registration with chambers of commerce. Allied with the association is the Wilders Group Foundation, later renamed the Friends of the PVV Foundation, whose aim is to acquire financial support. In 2007, a new foundation was also set up, the Foundation for the Support of the PVV House of Representatives Group, for administrative tasks as well as management of the capital formed by financial support from the state to the parliamentary party.

Due to its organisational structure, however, the PVV does not receive a subsidy under the Political Parties Funding Act. All parties in the Netherlands opting to operate as associations with more than 1000 members have a right to this subsidy. The PVV, however, has declared itself against subsidies to political parties on principle. 'No party should be fed by a state drip and receive money from the taxpayer. Parties should stand on their own two feet, otherwise they become lazy, bloated, bureaucratic organisations', Wilders proclaimed in the House of Representatives.[47] Furthermore, as Bosma repeatedly stated, it is 'wrong on principle that the state should determine how a political party organises itself. Parties regulate the state. The demand that parties operate as official associations, however, means that the state regulates the parties.'[48]

These are undoubtedly powerful arguments, and it is not only PVV supporters who defend them, but they are also extremely expensive in their consequences. Party subsidies, after all, are substantial sums of money. In 2009, parties with many members and seats such as the CDA and PvdA received more than three million euros in government subsidies each, while smaller parties such as Green-Left and the Christian Union received almost one million euros in the same year. Based on the rules and sums involved in 2009, we can estimate the financial consequences of opting for a memberless party. Even if the PVV had limited itself to the minimum demand of 1000 members, while foregoing a think tank or youth organisation, between 2006 and 2015 it might have received around six million euros in subsidies.[49]

How does the party come by its money? Ultimately, some of it does come from the taxpayer. Like all parties, the PVV receives around 165,000 euros of government subsidy per seat in the House of Representatives to finance party employees and secretarial support. Between 2006 and 2015, this soon ran up to a sum of around 15 million euros. With that money, the PVV has meanwhile set up a proper support apparatus, which must have offered employment to 50 members of staff in 2012. Thanks to creative accounting, some of that money is also used for other ends, such as research by the British agency Lombard Street Research into the costs and benefits of leaving the EU. The PVV MPs in the House of Representatives are also expected to put a small proportion of their salaries (around 200 to 300 euros per month) into party funds on a voluntary basis.

Finally the PVV also receives donations from third parties. Those donations go to the Friends of the PVV Foundation, which, since it has foundation status, is not obliged to publicise its budget. That means we cannot speak with any certainty about the sums of money involved. Based on claims in the media by the members of the foundation's board, such as Wilders, Martin Bosma and Hero Brinkman, however, these appear to be small sums, donated by 'ordinary Dutch citizens'. 'I would rather miss out on a million euros than be associated with the wrong types of people', Wilders said plainly in *Kies voor Vrijheid* (Choose Freedom).[50] Here the LPF again provided an example of how not to go about things; there were lots of stories doing the rounds about property tycoons who had bought their way into the party.

The fact that the PVV, by missing out on subsidies to avoid 'the wrong types', is a relatively poor party, is something Wilders and Bosma put up with. In his autobiography, Bosma states rather tersely, 'You can make a political party as expensive as you want.'[51] He believes that in the Internet era, a party can function perfectly well without all the expensive frills of a think tank, youth organisation or costly Amsterdam real estate for party headquarters. By not opening the party to members and conducting their campaigns mainly on the Internet and through the media, the PVV avoids the need for membership administration, hiring conference centres or running up costs keeping the departments satisfied. Bosma therefore feels there is little to say about the PVV budget – the PVV is no more and no less than an impecunious party with low overheads which thinks twice before spending the cents donated by sympathisers.

Many PVV followers are unconvinced by Bosma's sketch of financial housekeeping. Doesn't the PVV, like all the other parties, spend thousands, if not millions, of euros on its election campaigns? There are plenty of rumours circulating in the media, the corridors of power and on the Internet regarding secret sponsors from the United States and Israel. The PVV itself has fed such stories by fiercely resisting a new bill which would oblige parties to publicise donations of more than 4500 euros. Hero Brinkman, who represented the party in debates on the proposal, even announced that the PVV would rather pay the 25,000 euro fine than make its donors known. 'If Tracy from next door wants to give us 5000 euros, it's none of your damn business', Brinkman told his fellow MPs.[52] After his departure, Brinkman would in fact declare that not only did Tracy from next door donate money, but that substantial sums came from the United States too.[53] We can make a guess at the circles from which the money originates: the extensive network of anti-Islamic alarmists which now includes famous names such as Daniel Pipes, Pamela Geller and David Horowitz. They have certainly organised several fundraising dinners for Wilders, while Geller and Robert Spencer have also tried to raise funds for Wilders through their blogs. Pipes even claims to have raised a six-figure sum through the Legal Project to pay Wilders' legal costs. An organisation named Children of Jewish Holocaust Survivors, based in Los Angeles, also carried out an active fundraising campaign for the Geert Wilders Legal Defense Fund. Wilders is on good terms with extremely rich American widows like Joyce Chernick and Nina Rosenwald, who support all sorts of organisations in favour of the state of Israel.[54] It is highly probable that Rosenwald and Chernick have supported Wilders, in some cases through intermediaries. Nevertheless, all attempts at following the flow of money remain highly speculative. When money is donated to Wilders by named individuals, the sums, channels and conditions involved are still unclear.

According to Johan Driessen, who managed PVV finances for a while, many of the stories are highly exaggerated:

> Most of the money, half a million or so, was raised when the PVV was just starting out, making use of the networks of Bart Jan Spruyt in the United States among other things. Afterwards, money came in from time to time, but never large sums. Since 2006, they have eaten into that 500,000 quite considerably. I know that in 2010 there were 200,000 left, and as far as I know the party is now completely broke.

Driessen believes the reason Wilders refuses to make the finances public is a matter of image: 'Wilders would prefer not to admit that his party is penniless because he is afraid that that will be interpreted as a sign of weakness. He would prefer people to speculate over secret sources of finance.'[55]

Most indications do indeed point to the PVV being destitute. All the dissidents interviewed for this book state that there was regularly too little money for even the most ordinary activities. As described, the party organisation is characterised by enormous amateurism. The party never spent more than 10,000 euros on the elections for the European Parliament, municipal council or States Provincial. The campaign leaders of the various provinces each received a couple of hundred euros for the provincial campaign: the candidates themselves had to meet the remaining costs. According to campaign leader Jelle Hiemstra, this meant the PVV in Friesland did not have even a fraction of the budgets of other parties.[56] The three campaigns for the House of Representatives – in 2006, 2010 and 2012 – did cost the party rather more, but still a fraction of what other parties spent. Louis Bontes, who was responsible for the 2012 campaign finances, for instance, remembers that around 45,000 euros were spent on party political broadcasts on a few local television stations: 'But that was by far our biggest outlay during the campaign. There just wasn't much more money.'[57] The consequence was that the PVV was conspicuously absent from the Dutch streets in election times. PVV posters hung here and there on the boards provided by municipal councils, there were a few TV and radio broadcasts, and Wilders, accompanied by a campaign team, invariably visited a couple of PVV strongholds for a photo. Three times the PVV also hired an upstairs room in the Ahoy Complex in Rotterdam for candidate list presentations, which received a fairly mediocre turnout. However, there were no separate PVV stalls at the political markets or at summer festivals, no party election merchandise, such as pens, mugs and T-shirts, was handed out, and there was barely an advertisement to be found in newspapers or magazines. Few PVV supporters dared to put a PVV poster in their window either, fearing vandalism or social exclusion. The party did make full use of the Internet, including the launch of several digital complaints centres, but not a lot of money was put into that.

The PVV campaign strategy is mainly targeted at gaining free publicity in the media. As we saw, the party did not just focus on the election period, but attempted to attract continual media attention. Many sensational actions (from *Fitna* to the 'Poles Complaints Centre') and proposals (from selling the Antilles on eBay to the tax on headscarves) served this purpose, as did the many questions, motions and provocative behaviour of the municipal council members. The party was thus able to draw attention to the PVV brand without financial strain. Bosma's sketch of a relatively poor party, in other words, seems not so improbable. If you do not run up high costs, you do not need much money. In the past, the PVV has proven itself capable of achieving electoral success with a limited budget and relatively cheap campaigns – not just those studying new parties find this remarkable. In this respect the PVV disproves of the often repeated prediction that democracy will be increasingly dominated by wealthy political entrepreneurs who buy their success. Seen in this light, the party's success can also be viewed as a hopeful sign.

The party model of the future?

'We are ordinary citizens who come to The Hague to reclaim the square kilometre that is the Binnenhof as part of the Netherlands', it states in *De Agenda van Hoop en Optimisme* (The Agenda of Hope and Optimism), the 2010 election programme.[58] That makes it sound as if the PVV is a party of local activists who have spent years in dingy meeting rooms in the provinces preparing to march on The Hague. Nothing could be further from the case. Unlike most parties, the PVV did not come into being outside parliament but on the inside, as the one-man splinter party, the Wilders Group. From his nicely sheltered little corner of the Binnenhof, aided by Martin Bosma, Bart Jan Spruyt, a few interns and a secretary, Wilders set to work getting the party up and running. Members were not admitted, volunteers recruited in moderation. Initially, there was no question of a principled choice for this party model: it was largely inspired by the fear of 'going down the LPF route' (i.e. internal squabbling, embezzlement and the onrush of 'the wrong sort'), as well as the security measures confronting Wilders. In the short term, however, the model appeared to work very well. At least until 2007, the PVV may have had to make do with relatively few staff and little money, but the media attention for Wilders more than compensated for this. With his fierce proclamations, thorny personal security situation and conspicuous appearance, he had grown to become a media personality. Thanks to the Internet and social media (mainly Twitter), the PVV was also able to run its campaign and maintain contact with supporters by alternative means. In subsequent years, the PVV expanded step by step, in a very controlled manner. New candidates were trained, volunteers and employees were recruited. Around Wilders and his aides Bosma and Agema, a small but apparently loyal group of activists formed and became bound to the party with double mandates and paid positions. These are the people who hold the most prominent political positions within the PVV. To judge by statements from departing PVV members, there is an awe for Wilders amongst this group, in part inspired by fear, as well as a great mistrust of the outside world and a rather ruthless attitude to deserters. Some compare the PVV with a sect, with Wilders as its dominant guru, others use terms such as *mafia* or *Stasi*. Outside the group, as a result of various elections, a new circle of PVV candidates and volunteers has come into being since 2010–2011. The inner circle generally has little interest in this outer circle: there was barely any communication between them either during or after the election campaigns. It seems Wilders has little interest in growing the PVV into a party with a permanent following beyond the barely 80 people who make up the hard core.

According to Bosma, this chosen organisational model makes the PVV 'the first modern party in the Netherlands'. With modern communication options, Bosma explains in his book, members and departments are no longer needed to maintain a sense of connection with what is happening in the country or a particular region. The Internet offers enough options for maintaining contacts, communicating and staying informed. Setting up a membership structure would also lead to high costs in the short term and far-reaching bureaucratisation, while in the longer term there is the danger of forming an oligarchy of out-of-touch long-standing members. In his view, the memberless virtual party model selected by the PVV is perfectly suited to the modern age, in which most communication takes place over the Internet. So instead of official members, the PVV has employees and volunteers; instead of a big party office, heavily guarded, inaccessible headquarters in the Binnenhof; instead of a regularly issued party newspaper, a website and some virtual complaints centres. 'Our model is the model of the future. Many others will adopt it too', Bosma predicts.[59]

Of course the reverse also holds: without the Internet, a party like the PVV could never have existed at all. The Internet offers the PVV the opportunity to present itself to possible supporters without spending much money or energy. Thanks to the Internet they can hide anonymously and safely behind their computers, an advantage not to be underestimated in the case of a controversial party like the PVV. However, it is unlikely that the organisational model of the PVV will become the norm. In the short and medium term the memberless party with a strong leader certainly offers advantages, such as strong control from the centre, a high level of flexibility and relatively low costs. In the long term, however, this structure can cause problems less common in a democratic membership party: it lacks a good breeding ground from which members can work their way up; many activists will eventually be bothered by their lack of say, which will also scare off potentially capable candidates; volunteers will feel increasingly 'used' and fall away in the absence of any reward from the PVV. The party is also barely visible in society. Party members act as 'ambassadors' for their parties in their own social environments and also have a symbolic function, keeping the party rooted in society.[60] All those thousands of members are also needed to distribute flyers, put leaflets through letter boxes and mobilise voters to vote in the first place. This in part explains the fact that the PVV does not do well bringing its supporters to the polls for second-order elections. It lacks shock absorbers to soften feelings of dissatisfaction or frustration over party organisation. The only options for dissatisfied activists are to keep quiet or turn their backs on the party, a step made particularly tempting by the party's controversial image.

Another problem with this party model is that a high level of personal involvement and leadership is expected of the man in charge. In this chapter, we have seen plenty of indications that Wilders lacks these qualities. Perhaps a more socially involved, less solitary leader would do better with this model. Theoretically, after all, it is perfectly plausible that there should be space for a party functioning as a business with a fixed, uncontested director and employees hired on a temporary basis. The main problem ultimately facing such a party, however, is succession. In almost every party, succession from the founder is highly problematic, but in a memberless party such as the PVV these problems will reach the core. Will the new leader become the only member of the PVV from then on? Will Wilders' faithful supporters be as loyal to a new leader? It seems hard to imagine the PVV functioning without Wilders. The future of the party probably depends on its ambitions. If the PVV keeps this restricted to representation in a few institutions – with the emphasis on the House of Representatives – it may survive for a while as a small, close-knit party organisation. The advantages of this cheap, flexible party model then weigh against the disadvantages of the lack of breeding ground and control. Were they to decide to participate in municipal council elections in most municipalities, then this would inevitably lead to further loss of control, with all the associated risks, threatening Wilders' kingdom with collapse due to imperial overstretch. The chance of the succession issue leading to complete disintegration of the PVV then becomes as large as life.

Notes

1 D. Art, *Inside the Radical Right. The Development of Anti-Immigrant Parties in Western Europe*, 179–185, Cambridge: Cambridge University Press, 2011. Art and de Lange, 'Fortuyn versus Wilders'.
2 K. Haegens, 'Ik wil echt niet de Kim Il Sung uithangen', *De Groene Amsterdammer*, 4 May 2007.
3 R. Koole, 'Dilemmas of Regulating Political Finance, with Special Reference to the Dutch Case', in *Regulating Political Parties. European Democracies in Comparative Perspective*, I. van Biezen and H.M. ten Napel, eds, 45–69, Leiden: Leiden University Press, 2014.
4 *Spits*, 10 May 2010.
5 Interview, Jhim van Bemmel. Also his book: *Wilders' Ring van Discipelen. Angst en wantrouwen als bouwstenen van een politieke partij*, 45, Zoetermeer: Free Musketeers, 2012; and Hernandez, *Geert Wilders ontmaskerd*, 109–115.
6 Interview, Oege Bakker.
7 Interview, Oege Bakker.
8 Press report VvPVV, 12 December 2011.
9 Van Bemmel, *Wilders' Ring van Discipelen*; and Hernandez, *Geert Wilders ontmaskerd*.

108   The PVV as a party organisation

10 K. Geurtsen and B. Geels, *Undercover bij de PVV. Achter de schermen bij de politieke partij van Geert Wilders*, Amsterdam: Rainbow, 2010.
11 K. Haegens, 'Ik wil echt niet de Kim Il Sung uithangen', *De Groene Amsterdammer*, 4 May 2007.
12 Interview, Louis Bontes.
13 Interview, Joram van Klaveren.
14 Interview, anonymous III.
15 Interview, Jhim van Bemmel. Hernandez, *Geert Wilders ontmaskerd*, 80; Geurtsen and Geels, *Undercover bij de PVV*.
16 Interview, Johan Driessen.
17 Interview, Jhim van Bemmel.
18 Interview, Geert Tomlow. Also told by Bart Jan Spruyt.
19 Hernandez, *Geert Wilders ontmaskerd*, 86; also T.J. Meeus and H. Modderkolk, 'De gemaskeerde vergissingen van Geert Wilders', *NRC Handelsblad*, 3 July 2012.
20 Interview, Johan Driessen.
21 Geurtsen and Geels, *Undercover bij de PVV*, 36–37.
22 Interview, Bart Jan Spruyt.
23 Interview, anonymous III.
24 Interview, Louis Bontes.
25 Interview, Jhim van Bemmel.
26 Geurtsen and Geels, *Undercover bij de PVV*, 38.
27 Interview, Joram van Klaveren.
28 Interview, Geert Tomlow. Same stories by Martijn Kap, Frans van Rhee and anonymous I.
29 Interview, Jelle Hiemstra. Also interviews Frans van Rhee, Cor Bosman and Arie-Wim Boer.
30 Geurtsen and Geels, *Undercover bij de PVV*, 58.
31 Hernandez, *Wilders ontmaskerd*, 62.
32 Ibid., 59.
33 Interview, Jelle Hiemstra.
34 Interviews, Geert Tomlow, Jelle Hiemstra, Arie-Wim Boer, Harm Uringa.
35 'De onmogelijke missie van Geert Wilders', *HP De Tijd*, 5 February 2005.
36 *HP De Tijd*, 5 February 2005.
37 Interviews, Joram van Klaveren, Johan Driessen, Jelle Hiemstra, Arie-Wim Boer, Cor Bosman.
38 Interview, Jelle Hiemstra.
39 Interview, Jhim van Bemmel; also anonymous IV.
40 Interview, Joram van Klaveren.
41 Interviews, Cor Bosman, Harm Uringa, Martijn Kap. Also Hotze de Jong, *Duel in Debat. Hoe kom je bij de PVV?* (Leeuwarden, 2012.)
42 Interview, Joram van Klaveren.
43 Interview, anonymous III.
44 Interview, Johan Driessen.
45 Interview, Johan Driessen.
46 Report Sira Consulting for KRO Network *De Rekenkamer*. www.siraconsulting.nl.
47 *NRC Handelsblad*, 24 March 2011.
48 Bosma, *Schijnélite*, 217.
49 Based on governmental report *Overzicht subsidiëring politieke partijen 2009*.
50 Wilders, *Kies voor vrijheid*, 58.
51 Bosma, *Schijnélite*, 27.
52 Speech, Hero Brinkman, House of Representatives, 26 November 2009.
53 Meeus and Modderkolk, *NRC Handelsblad*, 3 July 2012.
54 American journalist Max Blumenthal has done some research on the financial sources of the counter-jihad movement: 'The Great Islamophobic Crusade', *CBS News*, 20

December 2012; 'The Sugar Mama of Anti-Muslim Hate', *The Nation*, 13 July 2012. Also A. Deutsch and M. Hosenball, 'US Groups Helped Fund Dutch Anti-Islam Politician', *Reuters*, 10 September 2012; R. de Wever, 'Wilders' joodse, christelijke en anti-islamitische geldschieters', *Trouw*, 3 July 2012; F. Vuijst, 'Op zoek naar dollars'. *Vrij Nederland*, 13 June 2009; H.E. Botje, 'Wie betalen Wilders?' *Vrij Nederland*, 14 November 2009; T.J. Meeus and G. Valk, 'De buitenlandse vrienden van Geert Wilders', *NRC Handelsblad*, 15 May 2010.
55 Interview, Johan Driessen. Confirmed by Louis Bontes and anonymous IV.
56 Interview, Jelle Hiemstra. Also interviews Harm Uringa, Cor Bosman and Frans van Rhee.
57 Interview, Louis Bontes.
58 *De Agenda van Hoop en Optimisme.*
59 Bosma, *Schijnélite*, 213.
60 M. Gallagher, M. Laver and P. Mair, *Representative Government in Modern Europe. Institutions, Parties and Governments*, 4th ed. and 5th revised ed., 329–340, New York: McGraw Hill Higher Education, 2011.

5 The many guises of Henk and Ingrid
On PVV voters

Who are the people who vote for the PVV? What are their reasons for supporting the party? There is no shortage of generalisation about PVV voters in the Netherlands. 'People with a grudge', was how Frits Bolkestein described his former pupil's supporters. 'They're unemployed, their daughter's on drugs and their son has run away.'[1] The Indonesian ambassador to the Netherlands diagnosed PVV voters as suffering from an anxiety disorder, a view supported by psychotherapist Joost Bosland, who saw a connection between the support for the PVV and psychiatric phenomena such as regressive behaviour and borderline personality disorder.[2] In Wilders' own view, his supporters were 'completely normal'. They are 'Mr and Mrs Average with their own houses, one nice holiday a year and an active social life'.[3] In 2009, he christened these 'average people' Henk and Ingrid, a couple who have since become part of Dutch political parlance.

All these generalisations are remarkable because the first thing that springs to mind about this group is its substantial size. Since 2006, at least 1.5 million Dutch citizens, probably more, have voted PVV at least once. In an absolute sense, this makes the PVV one of the largest national populist parties in Europe. Nevertheless, certain generalisations can indeed be made about this group without descending into oversimplification and cliché. This chapter describes a few characteristics of PVV voters, based mainly on electoral surveys. I will also offer several explanations for their voting choice.

Elections and polls

Of course, election results are the most reliable figures. At the time of writing (January 2016), the PVV had participated in nine elections in total. In the municipal council elections of 2010 and 2014, the party only participated in The Hague and Almere; in the other five elections the party was an option for voters throughout the country. This led to the results as presented in Table 5.1.

Interpreting election results remains a tricky business. Both the type of elections and the turnout percentages play a role. In 'second-order elections', such as those for the European Parliament and the States Provincial, far fewer voters go to the polls, while those who do go more often vote 'with their hearts'. This does

Table 5.1 Electoral analysis, 2006–2015

Type of election	Number of votes	Percentage of votes	Number of seats	Turnout percentage
Second Chamber 2006	579,490	5.9	9	80.4
European Parliament 2009	772,746	17.0	4	36.7
Second Chamber 2010	1,454,493	15.5	24	75.4
States Provincial 2011	869,626	12.4	69	56.0
Second Chamber 2012	950,263	10.1	15	74.6
European Parliament 2014	626,060	13.3	4	37.3
States Provincial 2015	711,176	11.7	66	47.8

not make the interpretation of the table above any easier. Was the PVV's enormous 2009 victory in part thanks to the low turnout, or would they have won far more if more people had voted? Was the 2011 States Provincial election a tad disappointing due to low turnout, or was that the beginning of the electoral decline of 2012?

We might seek answers to these questions in regular polls such as Peil.nl, IPSOS Synovate and TNS Nipo. In the case of the PVV, however, these have turned out to be notoriously unreliable. In the House of Representatives elections of 2006 and 2010, the PVV scored far higher than was predicted in the various polls. In 2010, the PVV achieved six or seven more seats than expected; in 2006, four or five. Soon it became accepted that the PVV was benefiting from what Martin Bosma termed the 'voting booth bonus': many voters would not dare to tell the opinion polls that they intended to vote PVV. Clearly the phenomenon of *taqiyya* appears not only among Muslims but also among Wilders' supporters. Remarkably, the situation was reversed in 2012, 2014 and 2015, when the PVV scored lower than the polls had predicted. Perhaps the polls had secretly responded by beginning to take the voting booth bonus into account?

Should we take these inaccuracies to mean that we can write off the polls altogether? Certainly not – for all their faults, they still reflect certain trends. Moreover, polls affect actual voting behaviour, as well as the behaviour of politicians, who feel supported or threatened. Polls can also lead journalists to pay particular attention to a party or politician. Over a long period, they clearly show that the PVV initially had little stable support. Wilders had already peaked significantly in the polls (around 25 seats) shortly after the murder of Theo van Gogh, but in 2005 and 2006, his party slumped to around four seats, even apparently dipping below the electoral threshold in summer 2006. Even within the party, no one had seriously expected the nine seats the party won in the elections for the House of Representatives in 2006, which were an important step forward.

At the end of 2007, however, the PVV gained a formidable new competitor in the form of Proud of the Netherlands, a party founded by Rita Verdonk, former Minister for Immigration and Integration, who had left the VVD in autumn 2007 after a series of conflicts. At that point she enjoyed enormous popularity due to the unbending determination with which she had approached her ministerial role. To the growing numbers of voters calling for stricter immigration and integration policy, 'Iron Rita', as she was called, initially appeared to be the perfect candidate. Her image as one of the common people made her an outsider, but one judged capable of being a minister. She was strict and resolute, lacked Wilders' rage and obsession with Islam, and also had the support of *De Telegraaf*, the Netherlands' number one newspaper. Despite the lack of any notable vision or organisation, Verdonk's new movement soon gained more than 20 seats in the polls.

The party disappeared as fast as it had emerged. First, Verdonk's ingenious plan of having the people set her programme over the Internet turned out to be a mistake. Jokers came up with all kinds of ludicrous proposals (such as free haemorrhoid cream and runways for UFOs), while Verdonk's supporters complained that she was too indecisive. Verdonk's image of resolution and sincerity was also undermined by several conflicts within her movement, along with revelations regarding her left-wing student days. In parliament Verdonk, in contrast to Wilders, came across as extremely weak. From summer 2008, her potential voters abandoned her in droves: from close to 30 virtual seats in March 2008, only one remained a year on. In the end Verdonk even lost this seat and left the Binnenhof under a cloud.[4]

By all appearances, Verdonk's failed solo career indirectly helped the PVV, as many of her supporters, rather than returning to the VVD, crossed over to the PVV. The swift decline of Proud of the Netherlands in the polls, after all, ran parallel to the equally fast rise of the PVV in late 2008 and early 2009. From around ten virtual seats at the end of December 2008, the party broke through to almost 30 in April–May 2009. After Verdonk's fall, the PVV became the natural meeting point for voters hoping for stricter policies in areas such as immigration, integration and fighting crime, domains in which studies indicate that it had become the *issue owner*, as it is aptly termed in political science, speaking to a large group of voters.

In other words, Wilders was extremely lucky that this dangerous competitor had fallen flat on her face. Where would Verdonk's career have ended if she had taken more time to structure her organisation and programme? Would she have succeeded with a sound organisation behind her? And if so, would the PVV have remained a relatively small, isolated party? Of course such what-ifs are unanswerable, but they rather suggest that the role of coincidence and luck should not be underestimated in Wilders' rise.

From left and right: PVV voters' parties of origin

The Dutch market research agency IPSOS Synovate traditionally presents profit and loss accounts after elections for the House of Representatives, indicating where each party's new seats come from and which parties have lost seats. This tells us that the PVV won their nine debut seats largely from right-wing parties such as the VVD, CDA and LPF; seven of the nine came from these parties. One seat was down to voters who had not voted (or were not yet able to vote) in 2003, and one came from the left, specifically the PvdA and SP.

Four years on, the picture was rather different because in addition to stealing votes from other parties, the PVV also lost votes. Almost a third of the PVV voters won over in 2006 were lost. There was busy two-way traffic between the PVV and VVD, with the PVV on balance winning more votes from liberals than they lost. In 2010, many new votes in particular came from Prime Minister Balkenende's CDA, while the PVV also attracted many voters who had not voted or had been unable to vote in 2006. A substantial proportion of the gain in 2010, however – 5 of 15 seats won – were down to voters coming from left-wing parties such as the PvdA and SP.[5] The more left-leaning welfare chauvinism the PVV had propagated in 2010 appears to have borne fruit.

In 2012, the PVV lost almost a third of its voters: of the 24 seats gained, 15 remained. A variety of reasons have been suggested for the loss. The most commonly heard and most likely is that the election campaigns of 2012 turned on the question of which out of the VVD and PvdA would become the bigger party. Many PVV voters were induced to vote for VVD leader Rutte in this race to prevent the PvdA from becoming the larger party.[6] This lost the PVV a minimum of three seats. Almost another three seats went because some 2010 supporters did not vote this time, probably those who felt that a vote for Wilders was now pointless because the PVV would almost certainly have no further influence. The PvdA and SP, too, profited from the PVV losses. The PVV's poor performance on socio-economic issues may have been a contributing factor. Their fierce opposition to a rise in pension age turned out to be worth little: not a day after the elections, Wilders indicated that he was willing to compromise on this point.

All in all, it seems we are justified in concluding that the PVV won its votes off various different parties, both from the right, such as the VVD and CDA, and to a lesser extent from the left, such as the PvdA and SP. Only the progressive GreenLeft and D66, with their strongly post-materialist orientation, barely represented competition. The PVV also has to deal with supporters who have a tendency to stay at home on election day. This is evident in elections for the House of Representatives, and even more so in the second-order elections.

On the periphery and in the major cities: where PVV voters live

It is currently quite easy to find out where most PVV voters live, based on results from the various municipalities. On the basis of this data, maps have been made showing at a glance the parts of the country in which the PVV attained the highest percentages.

At first glance, these maps seem to indicate that PVV support largely comes from the more remote regions. The high percentages in the south-eastern province of Limburg of course stand out the most. In elections in Wilders' birth province, the PVV attained a percentage almost twice as high as that in the rest of the Netherlands. An accepted explanation for this is that Limburgers have always liked to

Percentage of the votes for the PVV in parliamentary elections, 2010

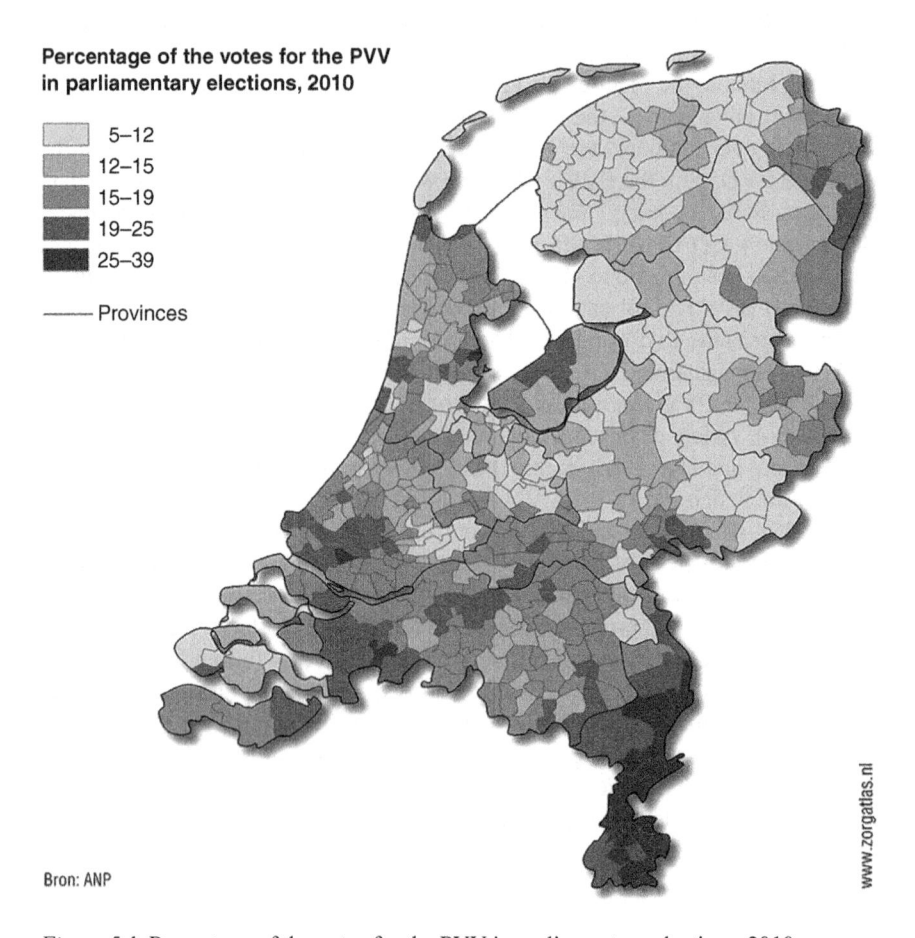

- 5–12
- 12–15
- 15–19
- 19–25
- 25–39

——— Provinces

Bron: ANP

Figure 5.1 Percentage of the votes for the PVV in parliamentary elections, 2010.

vote for their own, someone who understands the traditions, speaks the dialect and is prepared to promote Limburg's interests, but since most other parties exploit the same sentiment by also putting forward Limburg candidates, that cannot be a sufficient explanation.[7] With Wilders' rage against the establishment in The Hague it may well be that he has more to gain from the Limburgers' vibrant feeling of discrimination and inferiority. The changes which have taken place throughout the Netherlands have probably hit harder in Limburg due to the disappearance of the Catholic pillar as a shock absorber, a subject I will return to later.

What Limburg has in common with other peripheral regions where the PVV did well is its relatively poor socio-economic situation. South Limburg, East Groningen and Zeelandic Flanders are known as shrinking regions in the Netherlands, areas with negative economic growth and a declining and ageing population. These regions attempt to attract young families through advertising campaigns and promotions of various kinds, but without much success. The fact that the shrinking regions voted PVV in large numbers has provided journalists with material for stirring reports with atmospheric descriptions of dilapidated villages, empty shops, a prevalence of walking frames in the streets and increasingly poorly attended village associations. These journalists barely encountered immigrants, let alone Muslims. Journalist Irene van der Linde of news magazine *De Groene Amsterdammer* wrote an imaginative description of a game of cards one evening in a true PVV pub in the Limburg village of Bemelen:

> 'I simply disagreed with everything', Fon growled, throwing the jack of diamonds down on the table. It's dark outside; inside, four men sit at the round pub wooden table at the window, two others around them. They're all over fifty, some closer to seventy. There's a full glass of beer in front of each (...) The landlord pulls up a chair too; his pub is otherwise empty anyway. There's no music, just the heavy voices of the village men and the click of the cards on the table.[8]

Such grumbling elderly men in the provinces are not altogether representative of PVV voters in general, however, as percentages are different from absolute figures. Regions such as Zeelandic Flanders, Southeast Drenthe or East Groningen may stand out brightly on the map, but relatively few people live there, making their share of the total PVV vote small. Amsterdam, in fact, still provides many more PVV votes than the entire northern province of Groningen. When it comes to elections, even Limburg is less of a PVV heartland than often assumed. Converted into seats, only two of the 24 which the PVV carried off in 2010 came from Limburg.

When it comes down to it, the electoral heart of the PVV beats not in Limburg, but in densely populated South Holland. Around a fifth of all PVV voters live in the urban region of Rotterdam and The Hague. Many also live in the industrial area to the north of Amsterdam. In absolute figures, the PVV is therefore more a party of the cities and surrounding 'dormitory towns' than the countryside.

A closer examination of the situation in the cities and surrounding commuter towns reveals big differences. In 2010, PVV support could vary within one municipality from more than 35% at one polling station to less than 2% at another, sometimes less than a kilometre away. Crossing Amsterdam's River IJ takes us into a completely different electoral world: in the centre of Amsterdam, PVV voters are rare, whereas the largest groups are to be found in parts of Amsterdam North. In Rotterdam, the same effect can be observed when crossing the Erasmus Bridge: PVV support at most polling stations in central Rotterdam is small to very small, whereas in parts of Rotterdam South, the party sometimes takes 40% of the vote.[9] The commuter towns around the cities also exhibit big differences in polling station results. Electoral geographer Josse de Voogd has described these remarkable variations between the trendy neighbourhoods with the designer carrier bicycles, little shops and pavement gardens on the one hand,

and the neighbourhoods with the roll-down shutters, big dogs and pimped-up cars and vans on the other. The former areas are dominated by more highly educated, progressive voters, while the PVV voters live in the latter.[10] Statisticians will rightly caution against falling into the notorious 'ecological fallacy' of making simple connections between taste and voting behaviour, but the difference in atmosphere, appearance and taste between the neighbourhoods dominated by D66 and GreenLeft voters and those with many PVV voters is evident.

How can all these differences be explained? Since the party has built its image on views on immigration, Islam and integration, suggesting a connection with the presence of Muslim immigrants in certain neighbourhoods seems an obvious starting point. This is an all-too-familiar story of 'old city districts' which have changed significantly in character since the arrival of immigrants: many elderly residents have left; the local pub has closed; what used to be a bike shop is now a halal butcher's; and the new neighbour's wife doesn't speak a word of Dutch. Research by social geographers Wouter van Gent and Sako Musterd after the PVV's success in the 2010 municipal elections in The Hague shows that this 'social isolation thesis' remains relevant.[11] In neighbourhoods with many non-Western immigrants living alongside older native Dutch people, the numbers of PVV voters are 40% higher than in other areas. Cultural differences mean that the remaining elderly Dutch citizens have less contact with neighbours and no longer feel at home in their own neighbourhoods, despite relying on them more than ever. The PVV voters often only stand out when the percentage of immigrants in a neighbourhood is subtracted from the total. The districts where the high percentage of PVV voters is immediately clear are working class districts that remain largely white, but where there is an increasing influx of other ethnicities. These areas are often hit hard by the reduction or complete disappearance of jobs in the nearby factories or harbours, and fear they will meet the same fate as other nearby districts which have large concentrations of immigrants. People feel threatened on an economic level by labour market competition and on a cultural level by change in their own neighbourhoods.

Nevertheless, most PVV supporters live in a variety of post-war districts on the edge of the city, or in overflow towns such as Spijkenisse (near Rotterdam), Zoetermeer (The Hague) or Almere (Amsterdam). In the 70s and 80s, many working-class families moved from the cities to these more spacious, less busy commuter towns. Typically, these neighbourhoods and towns have neither large concentrations of non-Western immigrants nor a traditional link with certain – often vanishing – occupations, as is the case in old harbour and factory districts. In short, electoral geography alone does not tell the whole story.

Socio-cultural characteristics: non-religious, a 'troubled past', low level of education

In the Netherlands, countless studies have looked into the social and cultural characteristics of PVV support. In 2009 in particular, when the PVV rose like a comet in the polls, many market research agencies, often working for the media, showed an interest. In April 2009, the television programme *Netwerk* presented an exhaustive profile of the values of PVV voters based on a study by Motivaction. PVV voters emerged as a group of materialistically oriented people very much focused on their own lives, with an above average preference for technology, car racing, paintballing, Dutch music and home improvement. They are less negative than average about physical violence, show little interest in what motivates others or themselves and engage in 'activities that are against the rules for the thrill of it' more often than average. Both male and female PVV voters are oriented towards 'male values', Motivaction concluded.[12]

That is a surprisingly sharp image of a substantial group. Note, though, that the conclusions are based on a survey of 127 respondents, which cannot be seen as a particularly large population. Nevertheless, the results tally quite well with those from other surveys with more respondents. A survey presented in collaboration between the newspaper *NRC Handelsblad* and Synovate revealed the PVV voter as someone with an above average interest in computers, DIY and pets, but with very little interest in art, religion and books. On an 'election atlas', a graphical representation of characteristics, the research agency places PVV voters in the province of 'Worries' near the villages of 'Troubled Past' and 'Motoring and Commercial Channels', and miles from the villages of 'Good Health', 'Volunteer Work' and 'Fairtrade'.[13] The University of Groningen's Institute for Integration and Social Efficacy concluded on the basis of a study of 636 people that PVV voters scored poorly on personal qualities such as open-mindedness, cultural empathy and social initiative. They also struggled to combine multiple identities such as Frisian, Dutch and European.[14]

The trouble with these surveys is that the number of respondents is often very small, and many PVV voters are probably not prepared to participate. As we have already seen, the polling agencies often had difficulties predicting the number of PVV votes. It is also important to take into account that even the use of terminology can conceal a certain prejudice consistent with the researchers' world view. A lack of 'cultural empathy' is not just the preserve of PVV voters, who score 'poorly' on qualities, skills and behaviour which are implicitly seen as positive and desirable, such as open-mindedness, empathy, self-reflection and 'the ability to combine multiple identities'. On this basis, PVV voters are then often placed 'completely objectively' on a certain value spectrum with 'completely objective' opposing poles such as authoritarian vs free-thinking, traditional vs progressive, or nationalist vs cosmopolitan.

The data presented by the Dutch Parliamentary Electoral Studies may be somewhat less exciting, but ultimately offers greater certainty.[15] When it comes to gender, the PVV does indeed appear to attract more male than female voters, but the difference of 56% vs 44% is not particularly spectacular. With 59% male voters, the VVD, for example, turns out to be more of a 'men's party' than the PVV. The PVV does have to go to greater efforts to find female candidates, as we saw in the previous chapter.

When it comes to age, PVV supporters are fairly evenly distributed across the various categories. The party scores somewhat lower with those 65 and over, while faring better among young voters in the 18 to 25 category. Wilders' popularity among young people was in any case already clear from school mock elections in 2006 and 2010: in 2006, he already had 16 seats and in 2010, the PVV even became the largest party with 30 seats.

When it comes to education, there is quite a clear difference with other parties. The PVV has an above average proportion of voters with a much lower level of education (a lower level secondary school vocational diploma at most) and very few voters with academic degrees. 'Compared to the higher educated, those with only elementary or lower vocational schooling are almost four and even eleven times more likely to support the PVV', political scientist Teun Pauwels claims on the basis of an exhaustive analysis of PVV voters.[16] According to researchers Mark Bovens and Anchrit Wille, the rise of the PVV (and the SP, which is also supported by less educated voters) can also be understood as 'political emancipation of those less educated'. 'The SP and PVV have made the politics of those with low and medium levels of education visible in the political landscape and given them a voice', Bovens and Wille state in their widely discussed book *Diplomademocratie* (Diploma Democracy).[17] The established political parties were thus forced to pay for the fact that their supporters were more or less all highly educated people, who have been shown by various studies to hold different world views from those with less education. Since level of education often, but not always, determines level of income, it is not surprising that the PVV voters are also slightly overrepresented in the middle and lower income categories. By contrast, those with higher incomes are less well represented, as are those with the very lowest incomes. Pauwels' analysis also clearly shows that the PVV had greater success reaching lower income categories in 2010 than in 2006.

The PVV emerges as primarily a party for non-religious voters. According to the Dutch Parliamentary Electoral Studies (DPES), two-thirds of the voters are non-religious, a figure which more or less corresponds with that of the VVD, PvdA and SP. Nevertheless, the rise of the PVV was viewed with great concern, particularly in Protestant circles. The national chair of the General Synod of the Protestant Church of the Netherlands called the enormous PVV gain 'utterly shocking'. In November 2009, the Synod issued a memorandum taking a strong stance against advancing populism in the Netherlands.[18] Although the PVV had become the largest party in the traditionally Catholic south, the Roman Catholic Church took no clear public position on the matter. According to Bishop Gerard de Korte, the PVV's wins were mainly due to those known as 'cultural Catholics', people who are only Catholic in name and no longer attend church.[19] The lack of good data makes it difficult to establish whether he is right.

Why PVV voters vote PVV

Neutral information such as place of residence, religion and age is much easier to find out than information regarding voting motivation. Are people even aware of their reasons for making certain decisions? Are the motives they cite not retrospective rationalisations? Fortunately, such objections are not enough to prevent researchers from inquiring as to voters' motives and views. We therefore have access to a great deal of data relating to the opinions of PVV voters on a variety of issues. Examining the results of the different studies, they all appear to point in a remarkably clear direction. First, most of those who vote for the PVV apparently do so due to the party's views. Contrary to what is sometimes thought, few voters support the PVV out of a vague need to lash out at politics in general. As an outsider, the PVV naturally attracts more protest votes than the established parties, but they remain a clear minority. For most PVV voters, it is clearly about the party's views. What are the key points of the PVV programme in this respect? The 2010 DPES put a number of political issues to voters for various different parties.

Table 5.2 Political views by party choice, DPES 2010 (as presented in CBS report) (%)

Income differences	Total	CDA	PvdA	VVD	SP	D66	PVV
Higher	13	12	7	30	6	12	11
Neutral	24	35	16	38	13	33	18
Lower	63	53	77	32	81	55	71
Admission of asylum seekers							
More	19	19	36	11	26	27	3
Neutral	32	38	33	31	30	44	13
Less	49	43	31	58	44	28	84
Integration of immigrants							
No	17	10	31	10	22	28	3
Neutral	19	21	22	17	20	22	7
Yes	64	69	46	73	58	50	90
Fighting crime							
Too strict	5	3	9	2	5	8	2
Neutral	10	6	17	8	15	14	2
Stricter	85	91	74	90	79	77	95
Euthanasia							
Prohibit	10	17	14	3	5	3	3
Neutral	6	14	4	4	8	3	2
Allow	84	69	82	93	87	94	95
Nuclear power stations							
Build	34	45	26	58	26	33	33
Neutral	19	21	20	16	19	26	19
Don't build	47	34	55	26	54	41	48
European unification							
More	31	38	41	32	25	53	13
Neutral	22	26	25	26	21	23	11
Too much	47	37	35	42	54	24	76
International missions							
Never	23	13	27	17	31	13	25
Neutral	25	16	32	22	31	24	24
Always	52	71	41	61	38	63	51

What stands out first and foremost is that the views of PVV voters on many themes differ little from those of the rest of the electorate. There is a clear difference on three issues: asylum seekers, integration policy, and European unification. Most PVV supporters want fewer asylum seekers admitted and better assimilation of immigrants. A good proportion of supporters of other parties share these views, with 64% of Dutch citizens feeling that immigrants should assimilate and 49% in favour of stricter asylum policy, but for the PVV, these figures are 90% and 84% respectively. Similarly, PVV supporters' views on European unification differ, with a good three quarters feeling that this has gone too far, compared with 47% on average.

These figures appear obvious at first glance. After all, when it comes to European unification, integration and asylum policy, the PVV has the most extreme views. PVV voters are clearly capable of finding the stall on the voting market that sells what they are looking for. However, not all voters who feel that immigrants should assimilate more or that European unification is moving too quickly, vote PVV. Their behaviour is influenced by a number of factors, such as negative impressions of the PVV, confidence that other parties might be more effective in these areas, or the importance people attach to specific issues. An Ipsos Synovate study in 2009 shows that very few PVV voters – just 3% – consider the Europe issue a deciding factor.[20] Research by De Koster, Achterberg et al. points to culturally progressive issues such as euthanasia, equal rights for homosexuals and freedom of speech hardly playing any role in voting choice.[21] Their study, like all others on the motives of PVV voters, shows that the PVV's views on integration and immigration are the deciding factors, followed by law and order. A stricter stand against crime and imposition of tougher punishments, as desired by the PVV, emerge as very important for 90% and 84% of PVV voters questioned respectively. More than one-fifth of PVV voters saw a tougher stand on crime as the most important issue in deciding to vote for the party. The DPES 2010 tables above also show that almost all PVV supporters – 95% – are in favour of a tougher stand on crime, which in fact barely distinguishes PVV supporters from other Dutch citizens, 85% of whom are in favour. On this specific subject the PVV also encounters a good deal of competition, particularly from the VVD, which has increasingly cultivated an image as a party of law and order.

The tables above do not tell us much about whether PVV supporters also endorse the party's alarmist stance on Islam. The extent to which voters are attracted, deterred or uninterested in this position is unclear. In their study of feelings of unease in Limburg, journalists Johan van de Beek and Paul van Gageldonk come to the conclusion that there is not much to the 'Islam story', at least in their province. 'If there are tensions between "natives" of Limburg and migrants, that has little to do with Islamisation and more with fear of crime and harassment that is partly caused by migrants', they claim.[22] Peter Kanne of research agency TNS Nipo takes a different view. In his book *Gedoogdemocratie* (Tolerance Democracy), he states rather that 'the PVV has won and continues to win voters mainly thanks to their anti-Islamic standpoint'.[23] Might there be a difference between Limburg and the rest of the country? Various data point to anti-Islamic feeling throughout the Dutch electorate. The DPES 2010 study, for example, shows that 36% of those questioned – and 67% of PVV voters – agreed with the statement that all Muslims should be barred from entering the Netherlands. In 2009, TNS Nipo found that Wilders' views on Islam could count on plenty of support, based on a survey of 800 Dutch citizens, with 38% agreeing with Wilders' statement that there were 'Muslim colonialists' in the Netherlands, who had come 'to take over, to subjugate us'. Of the PVV voters, 86% agreed with this statement.[24] In short, Kanne appears to be correct: Islam is an important issue.

Certain points should nevertheless be taken into account to gain a proper perspective on this. It is unlikely that a substantial minority of Dutch people really fear Bat Ye'or's Eurabia scenario, to which Wilders' statement about Muslim colonists clearly refers. As we have seen, this theory is controversial even within Wilders' own party. Various surveys, however, show that around half of Dutch citizens hold predominantly negative views of Muslims and Islam. A study by The Netherlands Institute for Social Research from 2012–2013, for example, shows that 44% considered Islam to be incompatible with Western life.[25] That figure is more likely to have increased than to have dropped since the rise of the Islamic State, the terrorist attacks in Paris and Copenhagen and the refugee crisis.

Some vague fear of Islam and Islamic terrorism is one thing, but the view of Islam put forward by Wilders as a totalitarian ideology working towards world domination through a strategy of immigration is another matter altogether. What is more, questionnaires have shown that contrary to these surveys, a large proportion of PVV supporters believe Wilders goes too far in his rhetoric on Islam. Many, for example, disapproved of Wilders' proposed tax on headscarves and his call for 'fewer Moroccans'. The difficulty here is that the themes of integration, immigration and Islam have formed a knot of opinions which is difficult to unravel. It is hard to see where one stops and another begins. Are many Dutch citizens in favour of closing the borders to Muslims because of their religion or because they are in favour of a strict immigration policy in general? In questionnaires such as those sent out by the various polling agencies and the DPES, such nuances are difficult to distinguish.

Another problem with surveys is that many people questioned give their opinions on issues which they may never have considered before, or which they do not consider particularly important. When it comes to research into PVV voters, this risk is even greater because various surveys show that a substantial proportion of this group has little interest in politics or political issues, and does not really follow politics in general. This problem can be overcome by interviewing voters personally and allowing them to say in their own words what they really consider important. In recent years, journalists for various newspapers and magazines have set to work with that aim; this book alone draws on 40 reports (for an overview see Appendix 2). A more systematic study was conducted by political scientist Chris Aalberts. Together with a team of students, Aalberts thoroughly interviewed 87 people considered to be representative of PVV voters on their views and experiences.[26]

All these interviews similarly show that integration and immigration are the issues which most concern PVV voters, who tend to speak of 'the foreigners' as the cause of all kinds of problems. However, who 'the foreigners' includes exactly, varies substantially. 'Anyone who is not white or has no Dutch passport can fall into this category. Only white Dutch people can be sure of not counting as "foreigners"', Aalberts concludes.[27] Does this mean that many PVV voters are racist? Most of them strenuously deny this, but this may of course be due to the emotionally charged nature of the term *racism*. Thinking in terms of superior and inferior races or drawing a strict distinction between people on the basis of skin colour is, after all, seen as extremely inappropriate and even a criminal offence in the Netherlands. Interviews from Aalberts' book, as well as various media reports on PVV voters, show that most of them primarily apply cultural criteria to determine the line between foreigners and the Dutch, distinguishing between groups who, despite skin colour and background, have effectively assimilated into the national community, and groups who stubbornly refuse to do so and thus cause 'trouble', and judging the latter group much more harshly. As one voter states quite directly, 'Here in the Netherlands we are all the same. They should adapt, or they should get out. That's the Netherlands, that's tolerance. It's that simple. And that's precisely what Wilders says.'[28]

Variations on this line of thought, some more elegantly worded than others, can be found in pretty much all the interviews. Sometimes a distinction is drawn – as it is by the party – between different minorities based on a collectively ascribed capacity and will to assimilate and not to cause trouble. Indonesian and Hindu-Surinamese Dutch citizens are frequently distinguished from Muslims and Antilleans. Nevertheless, in many interviews the lack of assimilation of many foreigners is highlighted by contrast with examples of individual foreigners who exhibit model behaviour and do not cause trouble. 'I have a Surinamese colleague who eats *boerenkool* [a typical Dutch dish of kale and mashed potato]: he's assimilated.' Or, 'I've given my Turkish neighbour my spare key.'[29]

The concept of trouble so often mentioned is as vague as the term *foreigners*. Trouble can mean crime, intimidation or violence, but it can also point to degeneration of neighbourhoods, irritating cultural prominence, excessive use of social facilities, or economic competition. Most PVV supporters are in no doubt as to what should be done about crime and violence. 'Track those guys down and get them. Throw repeat offenders with two passports out of the country. Put the rest under house arrest, probation or parole, an injunction; pursue them and make their lives hell', as one commenter is quoted in the newspaper *NRC Handelsblad*.[30] Not everyone will come up with the same package of measures, but the various interviews and surveys show that as far as many PVV voters are concerned, there is no denying that 'everything could do with toughening up in the Netherlands'.

When it comes to a second kind of trouble, there is less agreement as to the complaint or the cure. Aalberts describes it as the undermining of specific fundamental values, in part due to the influx of immigrants.[31] These are values such as taking responsibility for one's own life and for fellow human beings, a certain degree of solidarity, honesty and justice. There is a consensus that it is reasonable to expect foreigners in particular to observe these values: after all, they are 'guests'. That is not to say that PVV voters think the Dutch entirely embrace these values. What is noticeable in the many interviews are the countless complaints about the general decline of society and the deterioration of values and standards. Many PVV voters analyse society, more or less as the party does, as having lost a certain 'natural order' over recent decades. Standards and values considered important in the past have disappeared without anything to replace them. When it comes to care for the elderly, raising children, keeping public places clean, using social facilities or spending taxpayers' money, we continually encounter the idea that society has hardened, that people have become egotistical and that no one is setting a good example anymore. People see their own rage at this decline of old values reflected in that of Geert Wilders. His clear language and far-reaching solutions at least give him the appearance of awareness of the problems. They remain unaware that politics in fact does discuss many of the themes on their agenda, according to Aalberts, because they generally 'fail to follow politics sufficiently to notice'. They show little interest in politics and feel emotionally attracted to the PVV due to a handful of issues (immigration and fighting crime) without having a detailed view on everything the party does or thinks.

To what extent does the specifically populist part of the PVV programme strike a chord with voters? It is not easy to say. Plenty of interviews indicate that PVV voters do not think much of politicians or politics. They tend to depict them as incompetent 'profiteers' and 'boasters' who never dare to put their money where their mouths are and are only interested in their own careers. This kind of political cynicism has been a widespread phenomenon in almost all democratic countries for donkey's years.[32] Complaints about politics are certainly not only the preserve of those with a limited interest in the subject. In the 90s, the opinion pages of Dutch newspapers constantly featured articles by intellectuals with roughly the same message, albeit rather more elegantly worded. Democracy did not mean much anymore due to the lack of real choices and the political parties had become useless instruments of power which mainly served as employment agencies for political jobs, they complained. Many politicians also turned to castigating themselves by distancing themselves, albeit in word rather than in deed, from the 'fuss in The Hague'.[33] Perhaps something of this sense of decline seeped through to the rest of society.

The main point which stands out from the criticism of many PVV supporters is the accusation that politicians beat about the bush rather than communicating clearly. 'Decisions should be better substantiated for the people to understand them. As it is, we don't understand, and it's all one-way traffic. Someone should take the time to sort this out', D66 leader Alexander Pechtold was told at a visit to a PVV voter.[34] At the same time, a common complaint is that politicians 'talk too much and do too little'. As in the line from the famous Feyenoord football club song, 'Actions, not words', talk and action are seen here as opposing activities. In the case of politics and policy formation, that is not a particularly practical starting point.

Many of these complaints are so trite that they appear to have become a knee-jerk reaction which is not really taken seriously. For many people, complaining about politics is like complaining about the weather: it's miserable, or it's on the turn. However, these complaints may not simply be ignored as they imply particular expectations of politics. There is no room for shades of grey on the palette of political opinions; they are required to be explicit and understandable to everyone. In this respect, PVV voters resemble the image Seymour Martin Lipset sketches in his famous book *Political Man*, of a mass of voters with a low level of education who have

> a tendency to view politics and personal relationships in black-and-white terms, a desire for immediate action, an impatience with talk and discussion, a lack of interest in organizations which have a long-range perspective, and a readiness to follow leaders who offer a demonological interpretation of the evil forces (either religious or political) which are conspiring against him.[35]

We could also state that the Dutch political system, with its many parties and necessary coalitions and compromises, is not particularly well suited to voters who think more in terms of conflict, and it appears from a recent study by Bram Spruyt that those people are indeed those with a lower level of education.[36] Where political insiders are fascinated by searching for consensus and balance of power, these voters predominantly see interminable debates, broken promises and postponed decisions. The much-praised Dutch consensus culture appears to reinforce mistrust and further feeds the idea that politicians are mainly out for themselves.

What solution do PVV supporters see for this flaw? Are they, like the party, in favour of introducing forms of direct democracy such as referenda? Do they perhaps want to see more 'common people' in politics? None of the voter surveys even begin to answer these questions. In the interviews no PVV voters, whether invited to or not, plead for more direct democracy, nor does the fact that many of the party's supporters fail to turn up to less important elections (for the States Provincial, for example) suggest they feel much need for involvement. A Synovate study did show that many PVV voters (83%) would like a stronger leader with more authority to exercise power.[37] Is the 'Actions, not words' slogan perhaps simply a veiled longing for an authoritarian leader who can get things in order? An anti-democratic view such as this, like racist ideas, is currently taboo and will thus not be readily vented in public. Besides, a preference for a more decisive, strong leader need not necessarily indicate an anti-democratic disposition. If that were the case, according to the Synovate study, a majority of the Dutch population would be seen as undemocratic: 61% were for a stronger leader with more authority to exercise power. It is reasonable to doubt whether there is really a significant sense of need for greater involvement among

PVV supporters, who rather appear to long for a leader who instinctively knows which policy voters want, without having to bother them too much for their opinions. In short, they probably do not so much want more involvement, but rather policies that better meet their wishes.

Is Wilders seen as the strong leader who instinctively perceives what the people want? For most PVV voters, that seems not to be the case. Wilders as a person is less important to most voters than the PVV's views. The 2010 DPES survey shows that few voters would follow Geert Wilders if he went over to another party with different views. 'Many PVV voters vote PVV without having a positive view of its leader', Gijs Schumacher and Matthijs Rooduijn conclude in their study. Their finding is:

> that Wilders succeeded in convincing voters that he is the one who represents the right-wing, anti-immigrant voters and the one who fights elites for the sake of the common people, but that he has not succeeded in getting the voter's sympathy.[38]

To judge by the many interviews, he does not invoke as strong an affection among his supporters as Pim Fortuyn, who took most of the potential voters with him when he left Liveable Netherlands. Wilders is admired, though, as someone who dares to tell the unvarnished truth and is prepared to pay a high price for this. Surrounded by bodyguards, prosecuted by the judiciary and beleaguered by other politicians, he makes politics tangible while other politicians seem to conceal it behind smokescreens. At the same time Wilders, unlike Verdonk, is seen as capable of putting his message across in The Hague. From his interviews, Aalberts concludes that most PVV supporters primarily view their vote for Wilders as a signal to politicians to wake up and listen to their problems. A vote for the PVV is more of an alarm bell than a statement of support for the solutions proposed by the party, as it seems that most people surveyed, when questioned further, considered many of the PVV's proposals extremely radical and did not expect Wilders to make a good prime minister. 'PVV voters primarily hope that other parties will pick up their signal and adjust their course a little in the direction of the PVV', Aalberts concludes.[39]

A distinction should also be drawn between this large group of occasional voters and a smaller group of loyal PVV supporters, for whom Wilders is a 'historic figure who will have an enormous impact on politics and society'.[40] In the media, these supporters are heard the most because they are often less afraid of showing their political colours and easier for journalists to find, since they are frequently active on PVV-affiliated websites. They are often people in their thirties and forties with a higher level of education and a much stronger interest in politics and social issues. Unlike many occasional voters, this group shares Wilders' concern about the rise of 'fascist' Islam, and exhibits a clear aversion to anything that smells of 'political correctness' or the 'Left Church'. It includes the PVV's Facebook fans, loyal visitors to its popular website and a few anti-Islamic alarmist web communities, although it is difficult to say how extensive the group is.[41] In the 2010 DPES survey, one in five PVV voters called themselves 'confirmed supporters', while the Synovate study shows that 11% regularly visit the PVV website. A cautious estimation suggests three to five of the PVV's seats are down to this group of loyal voters.

We can quickly conclude from surveys and interviews that most PVV voters decided on Wilders due to his position on immigration, integration and fighting crime. They want to see stricter policy on these themes and hope to get this message across via the PVV. The party might be too radical, for instance with respect to Islam, but that is not seen as a reason not to vote for them. An idea which often comes to the fore in interviews is that the PVV's radical nature might ensure that the message is at least heard loud and clear, and other parties are forced to listen. They see Wilders' ferocious rage as the sledgehammer they need to make their own wishes known. The question is whether the strategy is recognised as such. Are votes for Wilders really seen as a cry for attention? In other words, how is the rise of the PVV interpreted?

Driven by fear and resentment? Henk and Ingrid's rationality or lack thereof

If many PVV voters want their vote for Wilders to function as a wake-up call, they seem to have succeeded. The rise of the PVV is widely seen as a symptom of unease, sometimes even of deep crisis. The line taken by many commentators is that if someone with such radical and despicable views receives so much support, there must be something fundamentally wrong in the Netherlands. Opinions differ, however, as to what exactly that is. It all comes down to the following question: does the PVV's popularity point to real problems or is there in fact something wrong with PVV voters?

We encounter the latter judgement in various publications, where the authors tend to view PVV voters as irrational. In this respect they embody what has traditionally been seen as one of the great dangers of democracy, namely that voters, sometimes whipped up by an agitator, vote not with their heads but based on their gut feeling. In the 30s, Dutch writer Menno ter Braak described this danger very aptly in his essay 'Het nationaal-socialisme als rancuneleer' (National Socialism as a Doctrine of Resentment).[42] According to Ter Braak, national socialism was successful because it found inspiration in resentment, in his eyes one of the 'most essential phenomena in our culture'. The ideal of equality on which democratic culture is based, in Ter Braak's view, naturally clashes with a reality in which people are completely unequal for biological and sociological reasons. For many people, this leads to permanent dissatisfaction and envy, which they feel are also theoretically justified by the ideal of equality. In the polling booth, aggrieved and resentful citizens can vent their rage by voting for a party that encourages their sentiments. The resentful voter 'bears a grudge because in doing so, he at least experiences the passion of permanent dissatisfaction', while fascist and national-socialist parties who exploit this resentment are only after power for the sake of power.

After the rise of Fortuyn, Ter Braak's famous essay was regularly brought out to explain the advance of the LPF and PVV. The modern populism represented by the two movements is a typical doctrine of resentment, entirely tailored to the preferences and obsessions of the modern enraged citizen, an individualist who demands boundless freedom of expression, overestimates his own political judgement and sees the government as a takeaway window where he should be served whenever he clicks his fingers. According to cultural anthropologist Ton Zwaan, the PVV fulfils the 'gnawing need' of such aggrieved people to avenge themselves and 'briefly to express their own discontent'.[43]

Besides resentment, an emotion often found in analyses of PVV voters is fear. Fear of immigrants, fear of the changing economy, fear of criminality, fear of terrorist attacks, fear of Europe, fear of Islam. Essentially, fear of all kinds of phenomena which on inspection are barely worth fearing. Many fears, it appears from much of the data, are grossly exaggerated, such as fear of crime and immigration (which at least until 2015 have been dropping for years) or Islam (which is every bit as complex as Christianity, its rise in numbers vastly exaggerated). To many people, Europe and the changing economy are issues that will even ultimately make life more pleasant. With all his exaggerated and even irrational fears, the frightened citizen is a victim of what sociologist Willem Schinkel has termed 'social hypochondria', the contemporary tendency towards pessimism over non-existent or negligible problems.[44] Even politicians and the media indulge to their heart's content, stirring up all kinds of irrational fears to enormous proportions rather than reducing them or putting them in perspective.

In this respect, a politician such as Geert Wilders is first and foremost a shrewd businessman trading in fear, who talks society into a crisis in order to take the political stage as a great saviour. For those who exploit fear in this way, Ter Braak's 1937 statement about the politics of resentment essentially still applies: there is nothing to be learnt from it, so it should be countered with alternative arguments or, if all else fails, ignored. Historian Geert Mak also warned against failure to take seriously the sentiments inflamed by those who exploit fear, since 'even we, level-headed Dutch citizens as we are, will then end up in a closed, xenophobic fantasy world', in which 'discrimination and racism are elevated to new fundamental values'.[45]

PVV supporters did not really anticipate such responses when they cast their 'alarm vote' in Wilders' favour. Instead of the problems they wanted to draw attention to being addressed, they themselves were now seen as the problem. Interviews show that many PVV voters feel outraged at being characterised as frightened, angry victims of a sly villain. 'If I'm to believe the television, there is something fundamentally wrong with me but my mother says I'm a lovely boy', says one of them cynically.[46] Few will have found the scales falling from their eyes after hearing the diagnosis of resentment and fear. In fact, such criticism probably left them all the more convinced of Wilders' story of the elite looking down on hardworking people such as themselves. Some Dutch intellectuals have therefore warned against belittling PVV voters by dismissing them as thugs.[47] From a strategic point of view, that warning might be sensible, but not from a scientific point of view. Just because the diagnosis is unpleasant for the patient does not necessarily mean that it is not correct. The issue requires closer investigation. Do PVV voters really vote more based on gut feeling than other voters? Are they more driven by resentment and fear than others?

The answer to these questions depends on the essential matter of what motivates voters. If we are to believe the American Drew Westen's currently popular book *The Political Brain*, all voters are driven by gut feeling.[48] Brain scans show that they do not make a reasoned choice, but rather seek identification and affirmation. Assuming that the Dutch electorate has roughly the same brain as the American electorate, then it is not only PVV voters but rather *all* Dutch voters who decide based on gut feeling. At the other end of the spectrum we find researchers who believe that voters are generally rationally motivated. The same applies to PVV voters who, as various political scientists have shown, vote for the party closest to their policy preferences. In other words, they vote for the PVV because, like the PVV, they think immigrants should assimilate, crime should be better tackled and the borders should be closed to Muslims. There is nothing irrational about such voting behaviour per se: people simply buy the product they want. The preference for a strict immigration policy and harsher measures for tackling crime was in fact high on the agenda for much of the electorate from the early 90s, so this cannot be seen as sentiment whipped up by politicians such as Fortuyn and Wilders. The demand was already there; it was simply very meagrely supplied by just one politician, Hans Janmaat and his Centre Democrats.[49]

Of course it is a different matter if one sees certain policy preferences as irrational in the first place, for instance because higher penalties for criminals turn out not to work at all, or because fear of Muslims and Islamisation turn out to be wildly exaggerated. *Fact-free politics* is currently the term for such irrational beliefs free of a foundation in objective information. Whether or not he is rationally motivated, the PVV voter ultimately opts for an irrational form of politics. The anti-Islamic alarmist section of the PVV programme certainly warrants this judgement. There is not a single serious scholar in the Netherlands or elsewhere who foresees an Islamic takeover or demographic explosion in the coming decades. The scenario Bosma fears of the white Dutch citizen becoming a minority in the country in the foreseeable future is highly unlikely. Nevertheless, a term such as fact-free politics can also degenerate into a cheap form of resistance against unwelcome proposals. The question remains whether there are objective criteria for establishing the rationality of policy preferences, and if so who has access to them. We do not need to descend into a postmodern anything-goes scenario to realise that the facts tend to leave a good deal of room for interpretation – that is for politics to determine. What we can in any case conclude from the above is that the PVV voters are probably not fundamentally different from the rest of the electorate. That is to say, there is little reason to assume that they are driven by much more or less emotion or reason than other voters.

Signal received? The established parties and the PVV

Besides being a symptom of lack of political judgement, the PVV voters' 'signalling system' is also clearly taken as a sign of genuine problems and failing politics. The themes of immigration and integration in particular have found a prominent place on the political agenda since the rise of Fortuyn. Contrary to frequent claims, there was in fact no question of politically correct silence, or of problems surrounding immigration and integration being ignored. There was, however, a fear of these sensitive subjects becoming too coarsely politicised.[50] The rise of Fortuyn, followed by Wilders, appeared to have let the genie out of the bottle; 1.5 million voters saw immigration, integration and crime as extremely urgent problems not to be ignored, if only for the sake of keeping the peace. Most political parties – some more than others – also had electoral motives for receiving the signal: there were 1.5 million voters to win over.

Whether or not with the aim of regaining these voters, various parties advocated sharpening up immigration and integration policy. The clearest and furthest-reaching proposal came from the party which had suffered most from Wilders' rise and that of Fortuyn before him, the VVD. In 2007, the liberals had already argued for a substantial tightening of policy in the memorandum *Immigratie en Integratie* (Immigration and Integration). 'The immigration and integration problem is now so great that drastic measures are required. It is irresponsible not to take the necessary measures, blaming the Constitution, international treaties or privacy legislation.'[51] It was the kind of muscle-flexing language hitherto patented by Wilders. From 2006 the VVD, too, built a reputation as the party of law and order, making several firm proposals and placing resolute election slogans on its campaign posters ('Vandals will pay', 'More punishment and less understanding for criminals', 'Sympathise with victims, not offenders').

After many discussions and a year after the VVD, the PvdA published a new memorandum on integration following the line of left-wing publicist Paul Scheffer more than ever. In his article 'Het multiculturele drama' (The multicultural drama), published in 2000, and his later book *Het land van aankomst* (*Immigration Nations*), Scheffer argued for a healthy form of patriotism as a way of bringing together both immigrants and native Dutch citizens.[52] Following Scheffer's example, more social democrats criticised the progressive, highly educated party elite of the past, who were seen as having chased away much of the party's traditional support with their cosmopolitan values, Europhilia and multiculturalism. Others, however, felt that nationalist and populist sentiments were by definition at odds with social democratic principles. The PvdA had to stay true to itself without giving in to the 'limited world view' of the fearful, reactionary citizens they supposed PVV voters to be. The themes of integration and immigration were seen as very awkward in electoral terms as well as from an ideological perspective. Would too strict a tone not risk an exodus of the growing immigrant support? The integration memorandum seemed to further strengthen divisions within the party rather than reduce them.

The CDA was also presented with a dilemma. As the party advocating religious freedom and special schools, they could hardly turn against Islamic education or the construction of mosques, but as the party of the Catholic south they could not circumvent the growing popularity of the PVV in the provinces. Initially, the party seemed to solve the dilemma by giving the issue a wide berth. After its enormous losses in the 2010 House of Representatives election, however, the party was forced to show its colours. With great difficulty the temporary party leader, Maxime Verhagen, convinced the majority of the CDA that collaboration with the PVV could be a means of regaining the voters who had gone over to Wilders' side. The result was a parliamentary support agreement with the PVV, including very strict proposals on immigration and integration. In June 2011, Verhagen defended the decision to work with the PVV. In a speech at a CDA conference on populism, he humbly expressed understanding for the uncertainty people felt on immigration, the economy and Europe. 'We have to be there for the people for whom developments in Europe, the Internet and the world economy are moving too fast', said Verhagen.[53]

The response of the left-wing liberal D66 to the PVV's rise was also remarkable. This party, founded in 1966 as a strong advocate of democratisation and political reform, seemed as good as done for after yet another election defeat in 2006. Under the leadership of Alexander Pechtold, they opted for a new strategy, attacking the PVV and everything it stood for head-on. The more highly educated, progressive voters in particular valued this anti-PVV stance, which they saw as lacking in the PvdA, CDA and VVD, resulting in D66 winning two elections in a row and thereby benefiting indirectly from the rise of Wilders.

The established parties effectively pulled out all the stops to defeat the PVV. Can the loss of the PVV in the elections of 2012 be seen as a sign that many voters felt that their signal vote had been sufficiently received? Was the strategy of partial imitation and encapsulation successful? As we saw, the available data shows that the CDA in any case did not benefit from the loss of the PVV (the party in fact made some losses to the PVV). The VVD did benefit, but it is impossible to tell whether that was because of a sense that the earlier complaints had been adequately recognised. Similarly, the fact that many PVV voters stayed at home in 2012 is open to different interpretations: did they omit to vote because their message had been understood or because their mistrust of politics had grown?

A factor which may well have contributed to the PVV loss is the less prominent role of immigration and integration in the party's 2012 election campaign. Research on the phenomena of issue ownership and framing shows that the 'owner' of an issue always benefits the most if their issue is raised.[54] In other words, whenever immigration and integration were discussed, even within other parties, the discussion automatically turned to Wilders, indirectly proving him right for prioritising the issue and directly resulting in rising popularity. It made the signal given off in 2010 particularly awkward for the other parties: speaking about it was grist to Wilders' mill, but silence on the matter could equally be seen as arrogance. All they could really do was hope that the importance of the problems of integration and immigration would gradually decline. Sometimes in politics, important issues are not so much solved as gradually pushed into the background; formerly divisive themes or wedge issues such as abortion, squatting and the positioning of nuclear weapons have been almost forgotten in the Netherlands. With the continuing flow of immigration to Europe, however, immigration and integration do not look like they will disappear into the background for the time being. The same applies to Islam, which seems more topical than ever with the rise of the Islamic State and the new wave of Islamic terrorism.

A marriage crisis and the longing for a new cocoon

But what if the PVV's popularity now points to a completely different problem which the voters have not even identified as such? What if they are really suffering other, deeper wrongs? Many sociologists and cultural historians indeed suspect a 'crisis behind the crisis'.[55] The nature of the crisis they identify varies widely. Some authors see Wilders' success as a symptom of a psychological crisis in a large proportion of Dutch society, described largely in sociological terms such as *individualisation, fragmentation, secularisation* and *meritocratisation*. In the post-Christian and post-ideological era, people have primarily become individual, unattached consumers who are judged on their individual qualities and therefore embroiled in permanent competition with others. The losers have only themselves to blame: 'destiny' and 'the system', after all, have largely disappeared as excuses. In this hard, meritocratic society, many citizens feel 'uprooted' and 'deserted': they long for a clear, safe society in which they can feel secure, with a clear hierarchy. Unlike the established parties, who seem set in their ways, parties like the PVV and SP offer the prospect of a certain security. In the PVV's case, it comes in the form of the sovereign, mono-cultural nation in which law and order prevail, and pride and self-respect can be derived from membership of a close-knit community. It is the promised return to a romanticised past, often located in the 50s, when 'the Netherlands was the Netherlands', everyone knew their place in society and 'happiness was still a normal thing'. 'In search of the cocoon' is the way journalists Johan van de Beek and Paul van Gageldonk describe this sentiment in their analysis of the unease felt in Limburg, which is apparently also taking root across the Netherlands.[56]

Here again the PVV supporter is seen as a frightened citizen, but that fear is taken much more seriously. It is fed by the real costs of individualisation, secularisation and meritocratisation: the loss of former collective identities and bonds, the disappearance of a sense of purpose, of order and regularity and the lack of guidance from a committed leadership. These processes, moreover, coincide with worldwide changes to the economy, communication, mobility, technology and political hierarchy, which are often lumped together as globalisation. Changes which may benefit the 'mobile polyglots' (highly educated, internationally employable, open-minded individuals capable of combining multiple identities) are a bane to the 'monolingual population tied to particular locations' (those with less education, inwardly focused and less able to combine identities). Thus a growing gap opens up between what Hanspeter Kriesi has termed the *winners of globalisation*, who see the new developments as exciting challenges, and the *losers*, who primarily see globalisation as a threat to their own existence.[57] Bram Spruyt argues that in order to depersonalise their own negative experiences, many of these losers of globalisation tend to see the world in terms of conflicts and 'Us vs Them' relationships.[58]

This crisis also goes hand in hand with a crisis of representation, which coincides with what Mark Bovens and Anchrit Wille call 'diploma democracy': the dominance of the more highly educated in almost all political institutions and forums, from the House of Representatives to public participation at council meetings, from party leadership to interest groups. Of course that has always been the case, but Bovens and Wille show that there is a substantial difference in political values and preferences between those with lower levels of education and the more highly educated when it comes to issues such as crime, Europe and multicultural society.[59]

The suspicion that there was a widening socio-cultural gap in levels of education has in turn damaged the self-image of the Netherlands as an egalitarian society, free of fierce class warfare. The Netherlands Institute for Social Research and the Scientific Council for Government Policy were tasked with publishing an exhaustive report on the existence of the 'divided worlds' of higher and lower levels of education.[60] The reports concluded that, although there was not yet a sharp divide or 'culture war' in the Netherlands, as there is in the United States for example, two socio-cultural families were forming, comprising the highly educated universalists and the less educated particularists. The two groups name their children differently, have different hobbies and interests, consume different media, opt for different holiday destinations, laugh about completely different kinds of jokes and only marry within their own group. As electoral geographer Josse de Voogd put it, it comes down to an opposition between the neighbourhoods with the carrier bicycles and those with the roll-down shutters.

Of course we should be wary of rediscovering something which has long existed, namely the class difference between what would once have been termed the *upper* and *working* class. An analysis by Rotterdam sociologists Peter Achterberg and Dick Houtman, along with their Flemish colleague Anton Derks, however, shows the extent to which the social democratic parties in Europe in particular have suffered over recent decades due to this class difference.[61] The success of these parties was founded on a bond between voters of the middle class and the working class, rooted in socio-economic issues. It was a 'marriage of school masters and labourers' based on a consensus regarding the welfare state. Other socio-cultural issues that gained importance from the 60s and 70s, such as the environment, democratisation, crime prevention and individual freedom, put this marriage under pressure. The partners also turned out to have different opinions on many non-socio-economic issues. Simply put, the school master embraced modern progressive values of self-development, international solidarity and multiculturalism, whereas the

Henk and Ingrid: on PVV voters 133

labourer held onto more conservative values such as law and order and national and local solidarity. In the social democratic parties dominated by school masters, the less educated labourers began to feel alienated. What did they have to gain from all those open borders and European laws, shows of solidarity with Chile and Nicaragua, or development aid to Tanzania and Bangladesh? Where the labourer in the old social democratic party was glorified as the source of prosperity and symbol of righteousness, people now implicitly pointed to his shortcomings, such as lack of schooling, broadmindedness and cultural heritage. Such criticism, be it implicit or explicit, does not do a marriage any good. When new marriage candidates presented themselves in the form of the SP, LPF and PVV, singing the praises of 'ordinary people', it was a simple choice. The integration memorandum issued by the PvdA in 2008, with its emphasis on 'healthy patriotism' was effectively too little too late.

Is the PVV the new home for the lost PvdA voters? A substantial amount of data has already been reviewed which suggests that the PVV scored well among those who previously voted PvdA. The party had been popular in the old working class districts and average satellite towns, with people of lower and medium levels of education substantially overrepresented, lower and middle incomes lightly overrepresented, and a preponderance of non-religious voters. What stands out in Ipsos Synovate's calculations of losses and gains is a very limited interaction between the PVV and the PvdA: in 2010, the PVV won two seats off the PvdA, in 2006 not even half a seat. How can this be explained? First, the left-wing populist SP is of course a formidable competitor to the PVV in the battle for this sector of the electorate. Traditional connections between political parties and parts of the electorate based on belief and social class have been eroded ever since the 70s and 80s. If the PVV has benefited from the social democratic 'marriage crisis', then many voters will have been through one or more transient relationships on the way. The SP and LPF would be the usual suspects here. What is often missed, moreover, is that every election brings a whole new cohort of voters, who have only heard of devout socialist upbringings from tedious history lessons and grandparents' recollections. The electoral career of former PVV MP Richard de Mos, as he once sketched it in an interview, is illustrative here. De Mos himself came from a socialist milieu: 'We didn't talk much about politics at home. We really just voted PvdA out of tradition.' So when he was able to vote for the first time, he almost automatically voted for PvdA leader Wim Kok. Dissatisfied with the arrival of people of different races and rising poverty in many working class districts, he had no qualms about switching to the party which had once been the class enemy, the VVD. In his view, Bolkestein saw through the integration problem much better than the 'politically correct' PvdA. In 2002, De Mos then fell for Fortuyn because in his eyes, the VVD had become too left wing after Bolkestein's departure. In 2005 he ended up with Wilders, whom he saw as Fortuyn's successor.[62] This relationship was not to last either: De Mos left the party in 2012, after Wilders failed to put him on the candidate list. De Mos's next station remains to be seen, as in the case of so many PVV supporters. On the electoral market, long-term marriages have, after all, become rare. The old templates are much less applicable.

Many PVV voters in their twenties, thirties and forties will have heard stories from their grandparents, not about old-school socialism, but about the 'rich Roman Catholic life'. Has a similar marriage crisis taken place here, a break between the curate and the farmer? Unfortunately, there is a shortage of good research on the subject such as that of Achterberg, Houtman and Derks, who have studied social democracy and the working class. In any case, the changes which have taken place here in a short time period are certainly as dramatic: the Catholic pillar organisations collapsed; the crowds of Catholic children left, some of them for the universities of Nijmegen and Tilburg where many embraced modern progressive values; most farm businesses disappeared; the mines closed; and industry largely disappeared from cities such as Tilburg, Eindhoven and Enschede. The Catholic Church lost its function as a guide, due to a battle between progressive and conservative powers, followed by a series of sex scandals. While the Catholic People's Party still expected loyalty from its voters, the CDA found itself becoming one option among many. That meant that from the 90s, voters in the southern provinces in particular only entered into short-term relationships. Nowhere were the shifts in voting behaviour as great as in Limburg and North Brabant: winners won more, losers lost more and newcomers, such as the parties for the elderly, the SP and LPF, were slightly more successful than elsewhere in the country. That is quite significant when we consider that in the past hundred years in Western Europe, there were no elections in which voters changed party so often as in the Netherlands in 1994, 2002 and 2010. The Limburg and Brabant voters, once seen as the international paragon of dogged electoral devotion, are currently the most fickle voters in modern Western European history.[63] What lies beneath that electoral lack of commitment? Are the voters of Brabant and Limburg still celebrating their freedom after the collapse of the Catholic pillar, or does their fickleness point to a deep longing for a new shepherd? Do Fon and his grumbling card-playing friends from the pub in Bemelen really hanker after 'a new cocoon'? And if so, why has that search brought them to the PVV's door; a party without members, without departments, without a clear regional presence, led by someone who seldom leaves The Hague? These are questions which will not be answered here, but which are crying out for a thorough, empathic study.

In conclusion, anyone wanting to explain the success of the PVV has to deal with a whole series of trends and patterns which seem suddenly to have become more visible than ever in recent years. Many of those trends are not specifically Dutch, such as the modernisation and globalisation of the economy, the decline of traditional institutions such as the Church and political parties, increased assertiveness among citizens and the problems around the arrival and integration of large groups of immigrants since the 70s and 80s. Many of the explanations mentioned for the PVV's success therefore also apply to other national populist parties in Europe. Like the PVV, parties such as the Front National in France,

Lega Nord in Italy, UKIP in Britain or the FPÖ in Austria attract voters from different layers of the population, but as in the case of the PVV, people of lower levels of education, men, youths and non-religious people are overrepresented among their voters. Another thing the voters for all these parties have in common is dissatisfaction with the political situation in their countries and the belief that the arrival and integration of foreigners is an important problem that is insufficiently recognised by the established parties. Anyone talking about the popularity of the PVV is automatically talking about immigration and integration. The mass immigration of Turkish, Moroccan, Surinamese and Antillean people since the 70s has had far-reaching consequences in many areas. Within 50 years, Islam in the Netherlands has grown from a small religion with a couple of thousand believers to almost a million followers and the third religion in the country. It would be surprising if such changes had not had any effect on the Dutch political landscape.

But what layers you come across as you dig deeper depends very much on local context, age, background and social position. An obvious explanation for the popularity of the PVV (and SP) in Limburg and North Brabant is that it is a consequence of the decline of the Catholic pillar in a time of large-scale social and economic change. In the Randstad, the urban conglomeration in the west of the Netherlands, the social democratic 'marriage crisis' created a large reservoir of uprooted working-class voters, from which newcomers such as the SP, LPF and eventually the PVV have benefited. For other voters, the choice is less clearly explained by such historical sociological meta-analysis. Explanations which apply to one voter often turn out to be unusable for others. This is not surprising, as any right-minded person will understand that 1.5 million voters cannot be reduced to the imaginary couple Henk and Ingrid.

Henk is essentially an older policeman from Venlo, who is irritated by light punishments in the Netherlands and has not resonated with the CDA in years; or the young estate agent from Almere, who has had enough of all the Dutch rules and regulations and wavers between the PVV and VVD; the disaffected plumber from Amsterdam North, who has felt for years that politicians are not interested in people like him, and so often does not bother to vote. However, he is also the 18-year-old school student, who often gets into fights with Moroccan youths; the chemistry teacher with a Dutch Reformed upbringing, who started reading more about Islam after the death of Theo van Gogh; or the retired office worker, who is constantly shocked at the numbers of immigrants in the nearest city. Ingrid might be an older nurse from Spijkenisse, who fears for the position of women with the rise of Islam, or a hairdresser from Utrecht, whose salon has been broken into three times and who therefore votes for 'that man with the funny hair'; or a young student from Den Bosch, who increasingly has problems with immigrant men ogling her in the street. Of course we could go on without coming close to capturing all of the many guises of Henk and Ingrid. In fact, we could say the same about the average PVV voter as Princess Maxima once remarked, to Wilders' rage, of the average Dutch citizen: he does not exist.

Notes

1 *De Dagelijkse Standaard*, 17 February 2011.
2 J. Bosland, *De waanzin rond Wilders. Psychologie en polarisatie in Nederland*, Amsterdam: Balans, 2010.
3 *NRC Handelsblad*, 24 November 2006.
4 K. Vossen, 'Populism in the Netherlands After Fortuyn: Rita Verdonk and Geert Wilders Compared', *Perspectives on European Politics and Society*, 11 (2010): 22–39.
5 *Ipsos Nederland*, 11 June 2010 www.politiekebarometer.nl/pdf/winst%20en%20verlies.pdf
6 'De Tweede Kamerverkiezingen van 12 september 2012', *Peil.nl*. Maurice de Hond. Available at www.maurice.nl/beheer/wp-content/uploads/2012/09/De-analyse-van-de-verkiezingsuitslag-van-TK2012.pdf.
7 R. de Jong, H. van der Kolk and G. Voerman, *Verkiezingen op de kaart 1848–2010*, Utrecht, 2011; J. van de Beek and P. van Gageldonk, *Het onbehagen. Een zoektocht naar de Limburgse ziel*, Sittard: Media groep Limburg, 2012.
8 I. van der Linde, 'Wat maakt het uit wat ik stem', *Groene Amsterdammer*, 24 October 2012. Also coverage in *Vrij Nederland*: 'Het land van Wilders', 25 April 2009; 'Simpelveld: dan maar Wilders', 13 July 2007; 'Alles is niks na Geert en Camiel', 13 October 2012; *NRC Handelsblad*, 'Hoe God verdween uit het zuiden', 18 September 2010; *Trouw*, 'Alleen CPN kwam op voor ons soort mensen', 6 June 2009.
9 www.nrc.nl/verkiezingen/2012/10/03/wat-stemden-uw-buren (database with results per polling station).
10 J. de Voogd, *Bakfietsen en rolluiken. De electorale geografie van Nederland,*, Utrecht: Bureau de Helling, 2011; J. de Voogd, 'Redrawing Europe's Map', *World Policy Journal*, 8 December 2014.
11 W.P.C. van Gent and S. Musterd, 'The Unintended Effects of Urban and Housing Policies on Integration: "White Discontent" in the Dutch City', *Geography Research Forum* 33 (1) (2013): 64–90.
12 'De achterban van de PVV', *Motivaction*. Stand TV, Measurement 26, Amsterdam, 2009.
13 'Wie stemt wat: de atlas van de kiezers', *De Politieke Barometer*, Extra week 22, 2010.
14 A. Dotinga and K.I. van Oudenhoven-Van der Zee, *Identiteit en diversiteit. Wie is de PVV-stemmer?* Groningen: University of Groningen, 2010.
15 Data DPES from CBS report, *Verkiezingen: Participatie, Vertrouwen en Integratie*, Den Haag: Statistiek Den Haag, 2010.
16 Pauwels, *Populism in Western Europe*; van Kessel, 'Explaining the Electoral Performance'.
17 M. Bovens and A. Wille, *Diplomademocratie. Over de spanning tussen meritocratie en democratie*, 112–113, Amsterdam: Bert Bakker, 2011.
18 *Trouw*, 26 November 2009.
19 *Trouw*, 10 June 2009; *Trouw*, 30 June 2009.
20 K. Sanderse, 'Motivaties om op de PVV te stemmen', *Synovate*, August 2009. Also M. Hooghuis, M. Bank, 'De PVV-stemmer. Profiel, achtergrond en motieven', *Synovate*, 2009.
21 W. De Koster, P. Achterberg, J. van der Waal, S. van Bohemen and R. Kemmers, 'Progressiveness and the New Right: The Electoral Relevance of Culturally Progressive Values in the Netherlands', *West European Politics* 37 (3) (2014): 584–604.
22 Van de Beek and Van Gageldonk, *Het onbehagen*, 102.
23 P. Kanne, *Gedoogdemocratie. Heeft stemmen eigenlijk wel zin?*, 177, Amsterdam: Meulenhoff, 2011.
24 T. Broer and S. Derkzen, 'Veertig procent steunt opvattingen Wilders', *Vrij Nederland*, 21 April 2009.

25 I. van der Valk, *Monitor Moslim Discriminatie*, 19, Amsterdam: Institute for Migration and Ethnic Studies. Amsterdam University, 2015.
26 C. Aalberts, *Achter de PVV. Waarom burgers op Geert Wilders stemmen*, Delft: Eburon, 2012.
27 Aalberts, *Achter de PVV*, 123.
28 T. Broer and S. Derkzen, 'Het land van Wilders', *Vrij Nederland*, 25 April 2009.
29 S. Derix, W. Luyendijk and J. Mat, 'Waarom Wilders', *NRC Handelsblad*, 26 September 2009; E. van Outeren, 'In Ondiep ergeren ze zich ook aan luie Hollanders', *NRC Handelsblad*, 6 October 2010.
30 Derix, Luyendijka and Mat, 'Waarom Wilders'.
31 Aalberts, *Achter de PVV*, 74.
32 G. Stoker, *Why Politics Matters. Making Democracy Work*, New York: Palgrave Macmillan, 2006.
33 de Rooy, *A Tiny Spot on the Earth*, 265–280.
34 A. Pechtold, *Henk, Ingrid en Alexander*, Amsterdam: Bert Bakker, 2012.
35 S.M. Lipset, *Political Man*. London: Mercury Books, no. 43. 1964, 120–121.
36 B. Spruyt, 'Vlaanderen – conflictdenken als nieuwe scheidslijn', in *Gescheiden werelden? Een verkenning van sociaal-culturele tegenstellingen in Nederland*, M. Bovens, P. Dekker and W. Tiemeijer. Sociaal Cultureel Planbureau/Wetenschap pelijke Raad voor het Regeringsbeleid (Den Haag, 2014).
37 'Hoe populair is populisme?', *Synovate*, 2009.
38 G. Schumacher and M. Rooduijn, 'Sympathy for the "Devil"? Voting for Populists in the 2006 and 2010 Dutch General Elections', *Electoral Studies* 32 (1) (2013): 124–133.
39 Aalberts, *Achter de PVV*, 203.
40 Ibid., 67–68.
41 J. Bartlett, J. Birdwell and S. de Lange, *Populism in Europe: The Netherlands*. London: Demos, 2012.
42 M. ter Braak, *Het Nationaal-Socialisme als Rancuneleer*, Assen: Van Gorcum, 1937. On Ter Braak: Reinder P. Meijer, *Literature of the Low Countries. A Short History of Dutch Literature in the Netherlands and Belgium*, 322–326, The Hague; Boston: Martinus Nijhoff, 1978.
43 *NRC Handelsblad*, 10 July 2009.
44 W. Schinkel, *Denken in een tijd van sociale hypochondrie*, Kampen: Klement, 2007.
45 Mak, *Gedoemd tot kwetsbaarheid*.
46 *Vrij Nederland*, 25 August 2009.
47 Herman Vuijsje, 'Deugt wel, deugt niet...'., *NRC Handelsblad*, 16 January 2010, and Joost Zwagerman, 'Links helpt Wilders door PVV-kiezers te kleineren', *De Volkskrant*, 25 September 2010.
48 D. Westen, *The Political Brain. The Role of Emotion in Deciding the Fate of the Nation*, New York: Perseus Book Group, 2007.
49 P. Lucardie, 'The Netherlands: The Extremist Center Parties', in *The New Politics of the Right. Neo-Populist Parties and Movements in Established Democracies*, H.G. Betz and S. Immerfall, eds, 111–124, New York: St. Martin's Press, 1998.
50 Lucassen and Lucassen, 'The Strange Death of Dutch Tolerance'.
51 H. Kamp, *Immigratie en integratie*, VVD, 12 November 2007.
52 P. Scheffer, *Immigrant Nations*, London: Wiley, 2011.
53 Speech, Maxime Verhagen in *NRC Handelsblad*, 28 June 2011.
54 H. de Bruijn, *Geert Wilders Speaks Out*.
55 F.i. Tj. Swierstra and E. Tonkens, 'PVV is antwoord op zinverlies', *Trouw*, 27 September 2009; J.A.A. van Doorn, 'Herfsttij der democratie. Over de huidige malaise in de Nederlandse politiek', in *Nederlandse Democratie. Historische en sociologische waarnemingen*, 475–517, Amsterdam: Mets & Schilt, 2009; B. Heijne, *Moeten wij van elkaar houden? Het populisme ontleed*, Amsterdam: De Bezige Bij, 2011.

56 Van de Beek and Van Gageldonk, *Het onbehagen*.
57 Hanspeter Kriesi, Edgar Grande, Martin Dolezal, Marc Helbling, Dominic Höglinger and Bruno Wuest, eds, *Political Conflict in Western Europe*. Cambridge; New York: Cambridge University Press, 2012; R. Cuperus, 'Populism Against Globalisation. A New European Revolt', in *Immigration and Integration: A New Centre-Left Agenda*, O. Cramme and C. Motte, eds, 1010–1120, London: Policy Network, 2007; R. Cuperus, 'The Vulnerability of the European Project', in *Global Europe, Social Europe*, A. Giddens ed., 91–105, London: Wiley, 2006.
58 Spruyt, 'Vlaanderen – conflictdenken als nieuwe scheidslijn'.
59 Bovens and Wille, *Diplomademocratie*.
60 M. Bovens, P. Dekker and W. Tiemeijer, *Gescheiden werelden? Een verkenning van sociaal-culturele tegenstellingen in Nederland*. Sociaal Cultureel Planbureau/Wetenschappelijke Raad voor het Regeringsbeleid (Den Haag, 2014).
61 D. Houtman, P. Achterberg and A. Derks, *Farewell to the Leftist Working Class*, New Brunswick: Transaction Publishers, 2007.
62 *Trouw*, 16 May 2011.
63 P. Mair, 'Electoral Volatility and the Dutch Party System: A Comparative Perspective'. *Acta Politica* 7 (2008), 43 (2–3): 235–253; de Jong, van der Kolk and Voerman, *Verkiezingen op de kaart 1848–2010*.

Conclusion

The Danish political scientist Mogens Pedersen has described the life cycle of political parties: a party is born, catches various childhood illnesses (to which many young parties succumb), reaches adulthood and eventually, sometimes after prolonged illness, dies.[1] What phase has the PVV reached? Do they still have a long future ahead of them or are they past their peak and has the decline begun? It is tempting to assume the latter, if only because it would allow me to present a more rounded story in this book. The end could then be described as follows: by dropping the coalition in 2012 Wilders overplayed his hand, thereby forfeiting his position of influence. The PVV's loss in the September 2012 House of Representatives elections shows that many voters are tired of a party with whom they felt little connection in the first place. Wilders' attempt to force a breakthrough at the European level has ended in failure. Conditions in his party are worsening, as witnessed by internal conflicts and the departure of dissidents. Seen in this light, the PVV appears doomed.

The reality, however, is that this account of the PVV will have to manage without any such ending. On completing this book in January 2016, the party's future remains entirely open. The PVV continues to score quite well in the opinion polls with 20–25%. In most polls, such as Peil.nl and Ipsos for example, it even emerges as the largest party, although the extremely fragmented nature of Dutch politics is more conducive to this state of affairs than would be the case in most other countries. These high polls made the final results in European elections in 2014 and provincial elections in 2015 somewhat disappointing. The results at these elections, however, could also be interpreted as a sign that the PVV is gradually acquiring a fixed position in the Dutch political landscape.

It remains difficult for many Dutch citizens to understand how a party like the PVV with a leader like Wilders can become a lasting political presence in the Netherlands. In many respects, the PVV differs substantially from what has long been seen as normal in Dutch politics. For a party which presents itself as the representative of 'our country' and 'our people', it is remarkable how little the PVV fits into Dutch political culture and tradition, how very un-Dutch it actually is. The PVV's ideology, for example, contains ingredients which are quite unusual in the Netherlands. Nationalism and populism have never been powerful political movements here, as they have in many other countries. The two currents are at odds with the pillarization which split the nation into different parts, and subsequently with the self-image, cherished since the 60s, of a model progressive country in which what was seen as primitive chauvinism and popular sentiment had no chance. Neither is there a big tradition in the Netherlands of the conservatism towards which Wilders was so strongly oriented in the early days in particular, which continues to manifest itself in his thinking on law and order. The anti-Islamic alarmism propagated by Wilders is completely new, although it builds on historic tensions between Christian Europe and the Islamic Middle East. This alarmism is undoubtedly the most mysterious part of the PVV's ideology. On the one hand there is much to indicate that this specific vision of Islam does not really resonate with many PVV voters or activists. Few PVV voters will be aware of the meaning of concepts such as *taqiyya* or *dhimmis*, or know the names Bat Ye'or or Oriana Fallaci. On the other hand, for Wilders the battle against Islam is essential, as he persists in stating: 'That's what I wake up to in the morning and what I take to bed at night, it's what I think about every second.'[2] For several years now, he has been travelling the world like an anti-Islamic Al Gore, warning everyone of the danger.

The PVV is a case apart, not only in its ideology but also in its chosen structure: to my knowledge it is the only memberless party. By opting for this structure, Wilders challenges political theories on the necessity of party formation. Theoretically, there are plenty of reasons why the PVV in its current form might be doomed; how can a party function in the long term without members, departments, participation, not to mention subsidies? How can they recruit and train new talent without proper organisation? Can they pick up on signals from society without having departments? Does the concentration of all power in the hands of one leader not lead irrevocably to disintegration the moment the leader disappears? Where does the party obtain the money to finance campaigns? Nevertheless, for ten years now Wilders has succeeded in keeping the party alive, albeit with increasing problems and tensions arising as a result of his chosen party structure. Although it is unlikely that the PVV will become the model party of the future as predicted by Martin Bosma, it does get party researchers thinking. Is it not conceivable that in the strongly media-dominated spectator democracy there will continue to be space for a new type of party, in which members are replaced by a few professional employees? Does the success of the PVV not show that a clever publicity policy can more than compensate for the lack of full campaign coffers and a large army of volunteers? Having said that, the many splits with which the PVV has dealt at provincial and local levels suggest that such a party would do well to restrict itself to select bodies such as the House of Representatives or the European Parliament.

What is also unusual in the Dutch context is the way in which the PVV behaves. Since the start, the party has followed a strategy of confrontation and conflict in a political culture traditionally characterised by consensus and negotiation. It is remarkable that the PVV particularly courts confrontation in parliament. Inspired by the SP, the PVV seeks out the boundaries of formal and informal parliamentary rules, and greedily exploits its powers in the various forums where it is represented. To the PVV, parliament is first and foremost a forum in which it is set up as a representative of the needs of the people, making it largely dependent on the willingness of the media to achieve this by reporting on the party's performance; the fate of the PVV in the European Parliament shows the effect of the absence of this willingness. The rise of such a strongly parliament-oriented party as the PVV is intrinsically connected with increased interest in the House of Representatives as the foremost national forum. Anyone effectively wanting to ignore the PVV has to ignore the House of Representatives and the European Parliament. As long as the cameras are trained on the House of Representatives, the PVV will always remain in the picture. Its unusual views and aberrant behaviour make the party perfectly suited to the new media era which has arisen since the 90s. In the battle for viewers and readers, many journalists increasingly go in search of the unusual, the spectacular and the unorthodox. Fortuyn's rise and murder has reinforced their willingness to report on issues such as immigration, political dissatisfaction and new parties. Wilders effectively met with a very favourable media climate and has succeeded in exploiting it to the full.

This mutual dependency between the media and the PVV nevertheless does not explain why demand was so strong among voters. Has the Netherlands changed so much in recent years? In order to answer this question, we must focus on the views of the electorate. Studies show that many voters, even as far back as the 90s, were seriously concerned about issues such as immigration, integration and crime. VVD leader Frits Bolkestein was already expressing some criticism of multicultural society, but after his departure the demand for a party pushing for stricter policy remained unfulfilled. The prevailing consensus among the established political parties was that honouring this demand would endanger the peace of society and the tone of political debate, distracting attention from socio-economic issues. This mismatch between supply and demand made the established parties vulnerable to the populist accusation that none of them were listening to the citizens, leaving important problems unsolved as a result.

In retrospect, Pim Fortuyn was the final missing piece of the puzzle. His formula for success was a combination of sharp attacks on the political elite, direct emotional appeal to the ordinary people in the country and criticism of multicultural society in the name of the free-thinking Dutch values he embraced as a homosexual. This put him in a unique position to break through the taboo on nationalism and populism, supplying what historian Hans Wansink called the 'strange normalisation of Dutch politics'.[3]

As in other European countries, issues such as immigration and crime made it onto the agenda in the Netherlands and the political elite could no longer afford to ignore the views of so many voters. The balance of power in politics has, in Wansink's view, swung from the supply side (political parties) to the demand side (voters). From that perspective it should have been child's play for the established parties to win back the voters who had abandoned them by listening more and sharing their fears about immigration and crime. The success of the PVV, however, shows that this is not as simple as it appears. Some of the electorate (10–20%) do not trust the established parties and have a low opinion of the abilities of politicians to solve problems. They continue to see the need for a politician who at least keeps other parties on their toes with his powerful language and radical proposals. It is difficult to predict how long this need will remain. In countries such as Belgium, France, Austria, Denmark and Italy, ideologically comparable parties have become a fixture of the political landscape, although they – like other parties – encounter the fluctuating favour of the electorate.

Viewed from a distance, a party like the PVV is therefore an ordinary phenomenon in a democracy with several parties. Wansink is right, however, to speak of a 'strange normalisation'. The swing in the long and difficult year 2002 was, after all, abrupt and radical. The rapid rise of the flamboyant Fortuyn, and especially his dramatic end at Hilversum Media Park, have given that 'normalisation' in the Netherlands an unsettling edge; a feeling that was reinforced by the murder of Theo Van Gogh 18 months later. For a small country like the Netherlands with its peaceful, almost boring history, the two murders can be viewed as cultural trauma, as argued by Ron Eyerman.[4] Many Dutch citizens interpreted this double event as a rift in the national self-image. Without taking these two murders into account, however, the nature of the PVV's popularity is barely comprehensible. The possibility of violence has been inextricably bound up with Dutch politics ever since the two murders, symbolised by Wilders' bodyguards. The events of 2002 and 2004 have blurred the boundaries between typical Dutch level-headedness and naïvety, between vigilance and scaremongering. For one thing, Wilders' fear of falling victim to violence is no longer merely an exaggerated, fearful fantasy, while the strict security simultaneously lends his ideas and behaviour a certain status and urgency, forming a permanent affirmation of his rightness in the eyes of many. It is also very likely that the constant presence of bodyguards around him has contributed to his anti-Islamic alarmist convictions.

What would have become of Geert Wilders if Fortuyn and Van Gogh had not been murdered? This is an unanswerable question, but it does lead us to the conclusion that there have been a number of people around Wilders who, in their own ways, have contributed to his status: from the murderers of Van Gogh and Fortuyn to teachers such as Frits Bolkestein and Ayaan Hirsi Ali, from the strategist Martin Bosma to his fallen competitor Rita Verdonk, and of course Henk and Ingrid, in all their guises.

Notes

1 M.N. Pedersen, 'Towards a New Typology of Party Lifespans and Minor Parties', *Scandinavian Political Studies* 5 (1982): 1–16.
2 *De Telegraaf*, 28 February 2015.
3 H. Wansink, *De erfenis van Fortuyn. De Nederlandse democratie na de opstand van de kiezers*, Amsterdam: Meulenhoff, 2004.
4 Eyerman, *Cultural Sociology*.

Appendix

Election results

Table A1.1 Second Chamber election results, 1989–2012: percentage (and number of seats)

	1989	1994	1998	2002	2003	2006	2010	2012
CDA	35.3 (54)	22.2 (34)	18.4 (29)	27.9 (43)	28.6 (44)	26.5 (41)	13.6 (21)	8.5 (13)
PvdA	31.9 (49)	24.0 (37)	29.0 (45)	15.1 (23)	27.3 (42)	21.2 (33)	19.6 (30)	24.8 (38)
VVD	14.6 (22)	20.0 (31)	24.7 (38)	15.4 (24)	17.9 (28)	14.7 (22)	20.5 (31)	26.6 (41)
D66	7.9 (12)	15.5 (24)	9.0 (14)	5.1 (7)	4.1 (6)	2.0 (3)	6.9 (10)	8.0 (12)
GL	4.1 (6)	3.5 (5)	7.3 (11)	7.0 (10)	5.1 (8)	4.6 (7)	6.7 (10)	2.3 (4)
SP	0.4 (–)	1.3 (2)	3.5 (5)	5.9 (9)	6.3 (9)	16.6 (25)	9.8 (15)	9.6 (15)
CU	2.2 (3)	3.1 (5)	3.3 (5)	2.5 (4)	2.1 (3)	4.0 (6)	3.2 (5)	3.1 (5)
SGP	1.9 (3)	1.7 (2)	1.8 (3)	1.7 (2)	1.6 (2)	1.6 (2)	1.7 (2)	2.1 (3)
PvdD					0.4 (–)	1.8 (2)	1.3 (2)	1.9 (2)
CD	0.9 (1)	2.5 (3)	0.6 (–)					
LPF			17.0 (26)	5.7 (8)				
PVV						5.9 (9)	15.4 (24)	10.1 (15)
	100 (150)	100 (150)	100 (150)	100 (150)	100 (150)	100 (150)	100 (150)	100 (150)

Main personae

Agema, Fleur, *Member of Parliament PVV 2006–present. Parliamentary Group Secretary.*
Balkenende, Jan Peter, *Prime Minister Netherlands CDA 2002–2010.*
Bat Ye'or (née Giselle Litmann), *Swiss British author 'Eurabia'.*
Beliën, Paul, *Personal assistant to Geert Wilders. Editor weblog Brussels Journal.*
Bolkestein, Frits, *Leader VVD 1990–1998, EU Commissioner 1999–2004.*
Bontes, Louis, *Member European Parliament/Member Parliament PVV 2009–2013. Dissident since 2013.*
Bos, Wouter, *Leader PvdA 2002–2010.*
Bosma, Martin, *Personal assistant to Geert Wilders 2004–2006. Member of Parliament PVV 2006–present.*
Brinkman, Hero, *Member of Parliament PVV 2006–2012. Dissident since 2012.*
Cohen, Job, *Mayor Amsterdam 2003–2010 Leader PvdA 2010–2012.*
Dijkstal, Hans, *Leader VVD 1998–2002.*
Drees, Willem, *Prime Minister Netherlands PvdA 1948–1959.*
Driessen, Johan, *Personal assistant to Geert Wilders 2006–2010. Member of Parliament PVV 2010–2012. Dissident since 2012.*
Fallaci, Oriana, *Italian journalist and writer.*
Fortuyn, Pim, *Founder and leader Pim Fortuyn List 2002.*
Geurtsen, Karen, *Undercover journalist.*
Graus, Dion, *Member of Parliament PVV 2006–present.*
Hernandez, Marcial, *Member of Parliament PVV 2010–2012. Dissident since 2012.*
Hirsi Ali, Ayaan, *Member of Parliament VVD 2003–2006. Author.*
Janmaat, Hans, *Leader CentrumPartij en CentrumDemocraten 1980–1998.*
Jansen, Hans, *Author and Arabist. Member European Parliament PVV 2014–1015.*
Kok, Wim, *Prime Minister Netherlands. PvdA 1994–2002.*
Leers, Gerd, *Minister for Immigraton and Integration CDA 2010–2012.*
Lubbers, Ruud, *Prime Minister Netherlands CDA 1982–1994.*
Marijnissen, Jan, *Leader Socialistische Partij 1989–2010.*
Pechtold, Alexander, *Leader D66 2006–present.*
Rutte, Mark, *Prime Minister Netherlands VVD 2010–present. Parliamentary leader VVD 2006–2010.*
Spruyt, Bart Jan, *Director Edmund Burke Stichting 2000–2005. Co-founder PVV 2004–2006.*
Van Bemmel, Jhim, *Member of Parliament PVV 2010–2012. Dissident.*
Van Gogh, Theo, *Controversial columnist and filmmaker.*
Van Klaveren, Joram, *Member of Parliament PVV 2010–2014. Dissident.*
Verdonk, Rita, *Popular Minister for Integration and Immigration VVD 2003–2006. Leader Proud of the Netherlands/Trots op Nederland 2007–2010.*
Verhagen, Maxime, *Leader CDA 2010–2012.*

Dutch political parties/media/institutions

Binnenhof. *A complex of buildings in The Hague, which houses both the First and Second Chambers as well as the office of the Prime Minister of the Netherlands. Most ministries are located within walking distance of the Binnenhof. In the Netherlands, the Binnenhof is synonymous with national politics.*

Catholic People's Party (Katholieke Volkspartij/KVP). *Between 1918 and 1967 the biggest party in the Netherlands with around 30–35% of the vote. After dramatic electoral losses in 1980 merged with two protestant parties in the CDA.*

CD (CentrumDemocraten). *National-populist Party in the 1980s and 1990s, led by Hans Janmaat. Electoral peak in 1994 (2.4%).*

CDA (Christen-Democratisch Appèl). *Christian Democratic party, merger of the Catholic People's Party and two protestant parties. Biggest party in the Netherlands 1977–1994 and 2002–2010. Prime ministers Dries van Agt (1977–1982), Ruud Lubbers (1982–1994) and Jan Peter Balkenende (2002–2010). Scores between 35% (1989) and 8.5% (2012).*

Christian Union (CU/ChristenUnie). *Small Christian party. Scores between 2% (2003) and 4% (2006).*

D66 (Democrats '66/Democraten '66). *Left-liberal party, founded in 1966. Between 1994 and 2002 coalition partner in Purple Coalition. Since 2006 led by Alexander Pechtold. Scores between 2% (2006) and 15% (1994).*

De Telegraaf. *Conservative newspaper.*

De Volkskrant. *Progressive newspaper.*

DPES (Dutch Parliamentary Election Studies). *Main electoral research body in the Netherlands.*

Edmund Burke Foundation. *Conservative think tank founded by Bart Jan Spruyt in 2000.*

Elsevier. *Conservative magazine.*

First Chamber (Eerste Kamer). *Dutch Senate, 75 seats are elected once every four years by members of States Provincial. Less important than the Second Chamber.*

GeenStijl. *Popular, politically incorrect shock blog in the Netherlands. Runs the slogan 'Tendentious, unfounded and needlessly offensive'.*

GreenLeft (GL/GroenLinks). *Founded in 1990 from the merger of four small left-wing parties. Scores between 2% (2012) and 7% (1998 and 2002) of the vote.*

House of Representatives. *Aka the Second Chamber and the (more important) lower house of the bicameral parliament. It has 150 seats which are filled through elections using proportional representation.*

HP/de Tijd. *Dutch weekly magazine.*

Ipsos Synovate. *Bureau for electoral research and market research.*

Liveable Netherlands (Leefbaar Nederland). *Political party, founded in 1999 as a platform for local parties. In 2001 Pim Fortuyn became the leader, but in February 2002 he left the party after controversial remarks in a newspaper.*

Liveable Rotterdam (Leefbaar Rotterdam). *Local party in Rotterdam, led by Pim Fortuyn.*

LPF (Pim Fortuyn List/Lijst Pim Fortuyn). *Party founded in 2002 by Pim Fortuyn. After the death of its leader, the LPF took part in a coalition but due to internal conflicts in the LPF this coalition was short-lived. In 2003 the LPF lost most of its seats; in 2007 the party was disbanded.*

NRC Handelsblad. *Left-liberal newspaper.*

NSB (National Socialist Movement/Nationaal-Socialistische Beweging). *Main national-socialist party in the Netherlands, peaked in 1935 with 8% of the vote. Between 1940 and 1945 a Nazi collaborator party, prohibited after 1945. Led by Anton Mussert.*

NVU (Dutch People's Union/Nederlandse Volksunie). *Marginal extreme right party in the Netherlands.*

Party for Animals (Partij voor de Dieren). *Small political party, founded in 2002 in order to promote animal rights and animal welfare. In parliament since 2006. Around 1.5% of the vote.*

Peil.nl. *Bureau for electoral and opinion research.*

Proud of the Netherlands (Trots Op Nederland). *Political party founded by Rita Verdonk in 2008. In 2008 very popular in the polls, but in 2010 the party failed to pass the electoral threshold.*

Purple Coalition. *Coalition of social-democratic PvdA, conservative-liberal VVD and social-liberal D66, led by Wim Kok. Ruled 1994–2002. First coalition without Christian Democrats since 1918. In 2012 a new purple coalition was formed without D66.*

PvdA (Labour Party/Partij van de Arbeid). *Social Democratic party. Founded in 1946. Electoral heydays in 1970s and 1980s with around 30% of the vote. Led by Wim Kok, Wouter Bos, Job Cohen and Diederik Samsom. Since the 1990s scores between 15% (2002) and 29% (1998).*

Second Chamber. *Aka House of Representatives. The (more important) lower house of the bicameral parliament. It has 150 seats which are filled through elections using proportional representation.*

SGP (Reformed Political Party/Staatkundig Gereformeerde Partij). *Small orthodox protestant party, founded in 1918. Around 2% of the vote.*

SP (Socialist Party/Socialistische Partij). *In 1972 founded as a Maoist party. Until 1994 the party failed to enter parliament. With a left-wing populist campaign the SP was eventually elected in the Second Chamber. Its leader, former factory worker Jan Marijnissen, became the fiercest critic of the Purple Coalition. Electoral peak in 2006 (16.6%). With Emil Roemer as its leader the SP fared worse (around 10% of the vote).*

States Provincial (Provinciale Staten). *The provincial parliament and legislative assembly in each of the 12 provinces of the Netherlands. It is elected in each province simultaneously once every four years. Members of the States Provincial elect the First Chamber.*

TNS Nipo. *Bureau for electoral research and market research.*

Trouw. *Christian newspaper.*

Vrij Nederland. *Progressive weekly magazine.*

VVD (People's Party for Freedom and Democracy. Volkspartij voor Vrijheid en Democratie). *Conservative liberal party. Since 2010 the biggest party in the Netherlands. Scores between 15.4% (2002) and 26.6% (2012). Main leaders: Frits Bolkestein, Hans Dijkstal, Gerrit Zalm, Mark Rutte.*

VvPVV (Association for the PVV/Vereniging voor de PVV). *Organisation founded in 2011 by Oege Bakker and Geert Tomlow to democratise the PVV. Disbanded in 2012.*

Bibliography

Literature

Aalberts, C. *Achter de PVV. Waarom burgers op Geert Wilders stemmen* (Behind the PVV. Why Citizens Choose Geert Wilders). Delft: Eburon, 2012.

Akkerman, T. 'Anti-Immigration Parties and the Defence of Liberal Values: The Exceptional Case of the Pim Fortuyn List'. *Journal of Political Ideologies* 10 (2005): 337–354.

Albertazzi, D. and D. McDonnell. *Twenty-First Century Populism. The Spectre of Western European Democracy*. New York: Palgrave Macmillan, 2008.

Alter, P. *Nationalism*. London: Oxford University Press, 1994.

Ali, W., Eli Clifton. *Fear, Inc. The Roots of the Islamophobia Network in America*. [n.p.] Center for American Progress, 2011.

Andeweg, R.B. and Galen A. Irwin. *Governance and Politics of the Netherlands*. 4th ed. New York: Palgrave Macmillan, 2014.

Art, D. *Inside the Radical Right. The Development of Anti-Immigrant Parties in Western Europe* 179–185. New York: Cambridge University Press, 2011.

Art, D. and S.L. de Lange. 'Fortuyn versus Wilders. An Agency-Based Approach to Radical Right Party Building'.*West European Politics* 34.6 (2011): 1229–1249.

Bakvis, H. *Catholic Power in the Netherlands*. Kingston, Ontario: McGill-Queen's University Press, 1981.

Bangstad, S. *Anders Breivik and the Rise of Islamophobia*. London: Zed Books, 2014.

Bartlett, J., J. Birdwell and S. de Lange. *Populism in Europe: The Netherlands*. London: Demos, 2012.

Bat Ye'or. *Islam and Dhimmitude: Where Civilizations Collide*. New York: Fairleigh Dickinson, 2001.

Bat Ye'or. *Eurabia. The Euro–Arab Axis*. New York: Fairleigh Dickinson, 2005.

Bawer, B. *While Europe Slept. How Radical Islam is Destroying the West From Within*. New York: Broadway Books, 2006.

Betz, H.G. 'Against the "Green Totalitarianism": Anti-Islamic Nativism in Contemporary Radical Right-Wing Populism in Western Europe'. In *Europe for the Europeans. The Foreign and Security Policy of the Populist Radical Right*, edited by C. Schori Liang, 34–54. Aldershot; Burlington: Ashgate Publishing House, 2009.

Beyen, M. and H. Te Velde. 'Passion and Reason. Modern Parliaments in the Low Countries'. In *Parliament and Parliamentarism. A Comparative History of a European Concept*, edited by P. Ihalainen, C. Ilie and K. Palonen, 81–96. New York: Berghahn Books, 2016.

Bibliography

Blaas, P. 'Gerretson en Geyl: de doolhof der Grootnederlandse gedachte'. *Tijdschrift voor geschiedenis*, 97 (1984): 37–51. ('Gerretson and Geyl: The Labyrinth of the Greater Netherlands Ideology', *Journal of History*).

Blok, A. and J. van Melle. *Veel gekker kan het niet worden. Het eerste boek over Geert Wilders.* (It Cannot Get Any Worse. The First Book on Geert Wilders). Hilversum: Aspekt, 2008.

Bosland, J. *De waanzin rond Wilders. Psychologie en polarisatie in Nederland.* (The Madness around Wilders. Psychology and Polarisation in the Netherlands). Amsterdam: Balans, 2010.

Bosma, M. *De schijnélite van de valse munters. Drees, extreem rechts, de sixties, nuttige idioten, Groep Wilders en ik.* (The Sham Elite of Counterfeiters. Drees, Extreme Right, the Sixties, Useful Idiots, the Wilders Group and Me). Amsterdam: Bert Bakker, 2010.

Bosma M. *Minderheid in eigen land. Hoe progressieve strijd ontaardt in genocide en ANC-apartheid.* (Minority in Their Own Country. How Progressive Struggle has Degenerated into Genocide and ANC Apartheid.) [n.p.] Uitgeverij Van Praag, 2015.

Bosma, Tj. 'Het parlement van binnenuit onderuit halen. Een onderzoek naar het gedrag van de Partij voor de Vrijheid in het Europees Parlement'. (Tackling Parliament from Inside. Research on the Behaviour of the PVV in the European Parliament). Master's thesis, Leiden University, 2012.

Bovens, M. and A. Wille. *Diplomademocratie. Over de spanning tussen meritocratie en democratie.* (Diploma Democracy. On the Tension Between Meritocracy and Democracy). Amsterdam: Bert Bakker, 2011.

Braak, M. ter. *Het nationaal-socialisme als rancuneleer.* (National Socialism as a Doctrine of Resentment). [n.p.]: 1937.

Bruijn, H. de. *Geert Wilders Speaks Out. The Rhetorical Frames of a European Populist.* The Hague: Boom Lemma, 2011.

Bukman, B. *Het slagveld. De lange weg naar het kabinet Rutte.* (The Battlefield. The Long Road to the Rutte Cabinet). Amsterdam: Meulenhoff, 2011.

Buruma, I. *Murder in Amsterdam. Liberal Europe, Islam and the Limits of Tolerance.* London: Penguin, 2007.

Caldwell, C. *Reflections on the Revolution in Europe. Immigration, Islam and the West.* New York: Knopf Double Day, 2009.

Carr, M. 'You Are Now Entering Eurabia'. *Race & Class* 48.1 (2006): 1–23.

Cuperus, R. 'The Vulnerability of the European Project'. In *Global Europe, Social Europe*, edited by A. Giddens, 91–105. London: Wiley, 2006.

Cuperus, R. 'Populism Against Globalisation. A New European Revolt'. In *Immigration and Integration: A New Centre-Left Agenda*, edited by Olaf Cramme and Constance Motte, 1010–1120. London: Policy Network, 2007.

Davidovic, J. van Donselaar, P.R. Rodrigues and W. Wagenaar. 'Het extreemrechtse en discriminatoire gehalte van de PVV'. (The Extreme Right and Discriminating Content of the PVV). Monitor Racisme. Anne Frank-Stichting (Monitor Racism. Anne Frank Foundation): Amsterdam, 2008.

De Beus, J. 'Audience Democracy. An Emerging Pattern in Postmodern Political Communication'. In *Political Communication in Postmodern Democracy*, edited by Kees Brants and Katrin Volmer, 19–36. New York: Palgrave Macmillan, 2011.

De Koster, W., P. Achterberg, J. Van der Waal, S. Van Bohemen and R. Kemmers. 'Progressiveness and the New Right: The Electoral Relevance of Culturally Progressive Values in the Netherlands'. *West European Politics* 37.3 (2014): 584–604.

De Rooy, P. *A Tiny Spot on the Earth: The Political Culture of the Netherlands in the Nineteenth and Twentieth Century*. Amsterdam: Amsterdam University Press, 2015.

De Voogd, J. *Bakfietsen en rolluiken. De electorale geografie van Nederland.* (Designer Carrier Bycycles and Roll-Down Shutters. The Electoral Geography of the Netherlands). Utrecht: Bureau de Helling, 2011.

Dotinga, K. and K.I. van Oudenhoven-Van der Zee. *Identiteit en diversiteit. Wie is de PVV-stemmer?* (Identity and Diversity. Who is the PVV Voter?'). Groningen: University of Groningen, 2010.

Duyvendak, J.W. *Een eensgezinde, vooruitstrevende natie. Over de mythe van dé individualisering en de toekomst van de sociologie.* (A United, Progressive Nation: On the Myth of the Individualization and the Future of Sociology). Amsterdam: Vossius Press, 2004.

Duyvendak, J.W. *The Politics of Home. Belonging and Nostalgia in Western Europe and the United States*. New York: Palgrave Macmillan, 2011.

Ekman, M. 'Online Islamophobia and the Politics of Fear: Manufacturing the Green Scare'. *Ethnic and Racial Studies* 38.11 (2015): 1986–2002.

Eyerman, R. *The Cultural Sociology of Political Assassination. From MLK and RFK to Fortuyn and Van Gogh*. New York: Palgrave Macmillan, 2011.

Fallaci, O. *The Rage and the Pride*. New York: Rizzoli, 2002.

Fallaci, O. *The Force of Reason.* New York: Rizzoli, 2004.

Fennema, M. *Geert Wilders. Tovenaarsleerling.* (Geert Wilders. Sorcerer's Apprentice). Amsterdam: Prometheus, 2010.

Gallagher, M., M. Laver and P. Mair. *Representative Government in Modern Europe. Institutions, Parties and Governments*. 5th ed. New York: McGraw Hill Higher Education, 2011.

Gellner, E. *Nationalism*. London: Orion Publishing, 1997.

Genga, N. 'The Front National and the National-Populist Right in France'. In *The Changing Faces of Populism. Systemic Challengers in Europe and the US*, edited by H. Giusto, D. Kitching and S. Rizzo, 69–86. Brussels; Rome: Foundation for European Progressive Studies, 2014.

Geurtsen, K. and B. Geels. *Undercover bij de PVV. Achter de schermen bij de politieke partij van Geert Wilders.* (Undercover at the PVV. Behind the Scenes of Geert Wilders' Political Party). Amsterdam: Rainbow, 2010.

Gottschalk, P. and G. Greenberg. *Islamophobia. Making Muslims the Enemy.* Plymouth: Rowman & Littlefield, 2008.

Heilbrunn, J. *They Knew They Were Right. The Rise of the Neocons.* New York: Anchor, 2009.

Heinisch, R. 'Success in Opposition – Failure in Government: Explaining the Performance of Rightwing Populist Parties in Public Office', *West European Politics* 26.3 (2003): 91–130.

Heymans, J. *Over Rechts. De formatie.* Amsterdam: Bertram & De Leeuw, 2010.

Heijne, B. *Moeten wij van elkaar houden? Het populisme ontleed.* (Do We Have to Love Each Other? The Anatomy of Populism). Amsterdam: De Bezige Bij, 2011.

Hernandez, M. *Geert Wilders ontmaskerd. Van messias tot politieke klaploper*. (Geert Wilders Unmasked. From Messiah to Political Freerider). Soesterberg: Aspekt, 2012.

Hooghuis, M. and M. Bank. 'De PVV-stemmer. Profiel, achtergrond en motieven'. (The PVV Voter. Profile, Background and Motives). Antwerp; Amsterdam: *Synovate*, 2009.

Houtman, D., P. Achterberg and A. Derks. *Farewell to the Leftist Working Class*. New Brunswick: Transaction Publishers, 2007.

Bibliography

Jansen, H. *Islam voor varkens, apen, ezels en andere beesten.* (Islam for Pigs, Monkeys and other Beasts.) Amsterdam: Van Praag, 2008.

Jansen, H. and B. Snel. *Eindstrijd. De finale clash tussen het liberale Westen en een traditionele islam.* (Endgame. The Final Clash Between the Liberal West and Traditional Islam). Amsterdam: Van Praag, 2009.

Jong, H. de. *Duel in debat. Hoe kom je bij de PVV?* (Duel in Debate. How do You Get into the PVV?). Leeuwarden: self-publish, 2012.

Kanne, P. *Gedoogdemocratie. Heeft stemmen eigenlijk wel zin?* (Tolerated Democracy. Does it Make Sense to Vote?). Amsterdam: Meulenhoff, 2011.

Kennedy, J.C. *Building New Babylon: Cultural Change in the Netherlands During the 1960s.* Iowa City, IA: University of Iowa, 1995.

Knippenberg, H. 'The Incorporation of Limburg in the Dutch State'. In *Nationalising and Denationalising European Border Regions, 1800–2000. Views from Geography and 1999*, J.D. Markusse and H. Knippenberg, 153–172. Dordrecht: Kluwer Academic Publishers, 2001.

Komrij, G. *Morgen heten we allemaal Ali* (Tomorrow We Will All Be Named Ali). Amsterdam: De Bezige Bi, 2010.

Koole, R. 'Dilemmas of Regulating Political Finance, with Special Reference to the Dutch Case'. In *Regulating Political Parties. European Democracies in Comparative Perspective*, edited by I. van Biezen H.M. and Ten Napel, 45–69. Leiden: Leiden University Press, 2014.

Kriesi, H., E. Grande, M. Dolezal, M. Helbling and D. Höglinger, eds. *Political Conflict in Western Europe.* Cambridge; New York: Cambridge University Press, 2012.

Kuitenbrouwer, J. *De woorden van Wilders & hoe ze werken.* (Wilders' Words and What They Do). Amsterdam: De Bezige Bij, 2010.

Laclau, E. *On Populist Reason.* New York: Verso, 2005.

Lechner, F.J. *The Netherlands. Globalization and National Identity.* New York: Routledge, 2007.

Lipset, S.M. *Political Man.* London: Mercury Books, 1964.

Louwerse, T. and S. Otjes. *Kiezen voor confrontatie. Hoe stelt de PVV zich op in de Tweede Kamer.* (Choosing Confrontation. How the PVV Behaves in the Second Chamber). [n.p.] Report, Argos Radio, 2010.

Louwerse T. and S. Otjes. *Loyaal met een scherpe rand. Stemgedrag PVV 2010–2011 in kaart gebracht.* (Loyal with a Sharp Edge. PVV Voting Behaviour, 2010–2011). [n.p.] Report, Argos Radio, 2011.

Lucardie, P. 'Prophets, Purifiers and Prolocutors. Towards a Theory on the Emergence of New Parties'. *Party Politics* 6 (2000): 175–185.

Lucardie, P. 'The Netherlands: The Extremist Center Parties'. In *The New Politics of the Right. Neo-Populist Parties and Movements in Established Democracies*, edited by H.G. Betz and S. Immerfall, 111–124. New York: St. Martin's Press, 2002.

Lucardie, P. and G. Voerman. 'Geert Wilders and the Party for Freedom. A Political Entrepreneur in the Polder'. In *Exposing the Demogogues: Right-Wing and National Populist Parties in Europe*, edited by K. Grabouw and F. Hartleb, 187–204. Brussels; Berlin: Centre for European Studies and Konrad-Adenauer-Stiftung, 2013.

Lucardie, P. and G. Voerman. 'Rootless Populists? The Dutch Pim Fortuyn List, the Freedom Party and Others'. In *Rural Protest Groups and Populist Political Parties*, edited by D. Strijker, G. Voerman and I. Terluin, 265–290. Wageningen: Wageningen Academic Publishers, 2015.

Bibliography 151

Lucassen, L. and J. Lucassen. *Winnaars en verliezers. Een nuchtere balans van vijfhonderd jaar immigratie.* (Winners and Losers. A Plan Balance of Five Hundred Years of Immigration). Amsterdam: Bert Bakker, 2011.

Lucassen, L. and J. Lucassen. 'The Strange Death of Dutch Tolerance: The Timing and Nature of the Pessimist Turn in the Dutch Migration Debate'. *The Journal of Modern History* 87.1 (2015): 72–101.

Maas, A., G. Marlet and R. Zwart. *Het brein van Bolkestein.* (Bolkestein's Brain). Nijmegen: SUN, 1997.

Mair, P. 'Electoral Volatility and the Dutch Party System: A Comparative Perspective'. *Acta Politica* 7 (2008), 43 (2–3): 235–253.

Mak, G. *Gedoemd tot kwetsbaarheid* (Doomed to Vulnerability). Amsterdam: Atlas, 2005.

Manin, B. *The Principles of Representative Government.* Cambridge: Cambridge University Press, 1997.

Margry, P.J. 'The Murder of Pim Fortuyn and Collective Emotions. Hype, Hysteria and Holiness in the Netherlands?' *Etnofoor* (2003): 16, 102–127.

Mearsheimer, J.J. and S. Walt. *The Israel Lobby and US Foreign Policy.* Chicago: Farrar, Straus and Giroux, 2008.

Mény, Y. and Y. Surel, eds. *Democracies and the Populist Challenge.* New York: Palgrave Macmillan, 2002.

Meijer, R.P. *Literature of the Low Countries. A Short History of Dutch Literature in the Netherlands and Belgium.* The Hague; Boston: Martinus Nijhoff, 1978.

Mudde, C. 'The Populist Zeitgeist'. *Government and Opposition* 39.4 (2004): 542–563.

Mudde, C. *Populist Radical-Right Parties in Europe.* Cambridge: Cambridge University Press, 2007.

Müller, W.C. and K. Strøm. *Policy, Office or Votes. How Political Parties in West Europe Make Hard Choices.* Cambridge: Cambridge University Press, 1999.

Niemantsverdriet Th. *De vechtpartij. De PvdA van Kok tot Samsom.* (The Fighting Party. The PvdA from Kok to Samsom). Amsterdam: Atlas Contact, 2014.

Otjes, S. and T. Louwerse. 'Populists in Parliament: Comparing Left-Wing and Right-Wing Populism in the Netherlands'. *Political Studies* 63.1 (2015): 60–79.

Pauwels, T. *Populism in Western Europe. Comparing Belgium, Germany and the Netherlands.* London: Routledge, 2014.

Pechtold, A. *Henk, Ingrid en Alexander.* (Henk, Ingrid and Alexander). Amsterdam: Bert Bakker, 2012.

Pedersen, M.N. 'Towards a New Typology of Party Lifespans and Minor Parties'. *Scandinavian Political Studies* 5 (1982): 1–16.

Pels, D. *De geest van Pim. Het gedachtegoed van een politieke dandy.* (The Ghost of Pim. The Ideology of a Political Dandy). Amsterdam: Ambo, 2003.

Prins, B. 'The Nerve to Break Taboos: New Realism in the Dutch Discourse on Multiculturalism'. *Journal of International Migration and Integration* 3 (2007): 363–379.

Psychosociale gevolgen van dreiging en beveiliging. Rapport Nationale Coördinator Terrorismebestrijding, March 2008. ('Psycho-Social Consequences of Threats and Security'. Report, National Coordinator for Counterterrorism, March 2008).

Sanderse, K. 'Motivaties om op de PVV te stemmen'. (Motivations to vote for the PVV). Amsterdam: *Synovate* report, August 2009.

Scheffer, P. *Immigrant Nations.* London: Wiley, 2011.

Schinkel, W. *Denken in een tijd van sociale hypochondrie* (Thinking in Times of Social Hypochondria.) Kampen: Klement, 2007.

Scholten, N., A. Ruigrok eds. *Stemmen krijgen of stemming maken?* (Getting Votes or Spreading Fear?). Amsterdam: Nieuwsmonitor Vrije Universiteit Amsterdam, 2009.

Schumacher, G. and M. Rooduijn, 'Sympathy for the "Devil"? Voting for Populists in the 2006 and 2010 Dutch General Elections'. *Electoral Studies* 32.1 (2013): 124–133.

Scroggins, D. *Wanted Women. Faith, Lies and the War on Terror: The Lives of Ayaan Hirsi Ali and Aafia Siddiqui.* London: Harper Collins Publishing, 2012.

Solomon, S. and E. Al Maqdisi. *Modern Day Trojan Horse: Al Hijra, the Islamic Doctrine of Migration.* Charlottesville, VA: Advancing Native Missions, 2009.

Spruyt, B. 'Vlaanderen – conflictdenken als nieuwe scheidslijn'. En *Gescheiden werelden? Een verkenning van sociaal-culturele tegenstellingen in Nederland*, M. Bovens, P. Dekker and W. Tiemeijer. ('Flanders – Conflict thinking as a New Cleavage'. In *Separated Worlds. An Exploration of the Social–Cultural Contrasts in the Netherlands.*) The Hague: Sociaal Cultureel Planbureau/Wetenschappelijke Raad voor het Regeringsbeleid, 2014.

Spruyt, M. *Wat het Vlaams Blok verzwijgt.* (What the Vlaams Blok Conceals). Berchem: Van Haldewyck, 2000.

Stanley, B. 'The Thin Ideology of Populism'. *Journal of Political Ideologies* 13.1 (2008): 95–110.

Steyn, M. *America Alone. The End of the World as We Know It.* Washington, DC: Regnery Publishing, 2006.

Stolk, R. 'New Words for an Old Fear? Opposition to Catholicism and Islam'. Master's thesis. University of Leiden, 2010 via openacces.leidenuniv.nl.

Taggart, P. *Populism.* Buckingham: Open University Press, 2000.

Te Slaa, R. *Is Wilders een fascist?* (Is Wilders a Fascist?). Amsterdam: Boom, 2012.

Te Velde, H. *Van regentenmentaliteit tot populisme. Politieke tradities in Nederland.* (From Regent Mentality to Populism. Political Traditions in the Netherlands). Amsterdam: Bert Bakker, 2010.

Van Bemmel, J. *Wilders' Ring van Discipelen. Angst en wantrouwen als bouwstenen van een politieke partij.* (Wilders' Group of Disciples. Fear and Distrust as Building Blocks of a Political Party.) Zoetermeer: Free Musketeers, 2012.

Van de Beek, J. and P. van Gageldonk. *Het onbehagen. Een zoektocht naar de Limburgse ziel.* (The Unease. A Quest for the Limburg Soul). Sittard: Mediagroep Limburg, 2012.

Van der Brug, W. 'How the LPF Fuelled Discontent. Empirical Tests of Explanations of LPF support'. *Acta Politica* 38.1 (2006): 89–106.

Van der Brug, W., M. Fennema and J. Tillie. 'Anti-Immigrant Parties in Europe: Ideological or Protest Vote?' *European Journal of Political Research* 37 (2000): 77–102.

Van der Valk, I. *Monitor Moslim Discriminatie*, 19. (Monitor Muslim Discrimination). Amsterdam: Institute for Migration and Ethnic Studies, University of Amsterdam, 2015.

Van Doorn, J.A.A. *Nederlandse Democratie. Historische en sociologische waarnemingen.* (Dutch Democracy. Historical and Sociological Perceptions). Amsterdam: Mets & Schilt, 2009.

Van Gent, W.P.C. and S. Musterd, 'The Unintended Effects of Urban and Housing Policies on Integration: "White Discontent" in the Dutch City', *Geography Research Forum* 33.1 (2013): 64–90.

Van Kessel, S. 'Explaining the Electoral Performance of Populist Parties: The Netherlands as a Case Study', *Perspectives on European Politics and Society* 12.1 (2013): 68–88.

Van Praag, Ph. 'Winners and Losers in a Turbulent Political Year'. *Acta Politica* 38 (2003): 5–22.

Van Schoonhoven, G.J. *De nieuwe kaaskop. Nederland en de Nederlanders in de jaren negentig*. (The New Cheesehead. The Netherlands and the Dutch in the 1990s). Amsterdam: Promotheus, 1999.

Vellenga, S.J. 'Huntington in Holland. The Public Debate on Muslim Immigrants in the Netherlands'. *Nordic Journal of Religion and Society* 21.1 (2008): 21–41.

Verkiezingen: Participatie, Vertrouwen en Integratie, Rapport Centraal Bureau voor de Statistiek Den Haag, 2010. ('Elections: Participation, Trust and Integration'. Report, Central Bureau for Statistics).

Von der Dunk, H. 'Conservatism in the Netherlands'. *Journal of Contemporary History* 13.4 (2008): 741–763.

Vossen, K. *Vrij vissen in het Vondelpark. Kleine politieke partijen in Nederland, 1918–1940.* (Free Fishing in the Vondelpark. Small Political Parties in the Netherlands, 1918–1940). Amsterdam: Wereldbibliotheek, 2003.

Vossen, K. 'Populism in the Netherlands after Fortuyn: Rita Verdonk and Geert Wilders Compared'. *Perspectives on European Politics and Society* 11 (2010): 22–39.

Vossen, K. 'Classifying Wilders. The Ideological Development of Geert Wilders and his Party for Freedom'. *Politics* 31.3 (2011): 179–190.

Vossen, K. 'The Different Flavours of Populism in the Netherlands'. In *The Changing Faces of Populism. Systemic Challengers in Europe and the US*, edited by Hedwig Giusto, David Kitching and Stefano Rizzo. Brussels; Rome: Foundation for European Progressive Studies, University of Rome, 2013.

Wansink, H. *De erfenis van Fortuyn. De Nederlandse democratie na de opstand van de kiezers.* (The Legacy of Fortuyn. Dutch Democracy after the Revolt of the Voters). Amsterdam; Meulenhoff, 2004.

Wansink, H. *Het land van Beatrix. De eerste geschiedenis van hedendaags Nederland, 1980–2015.* (The Country of Beatrix. The First History of Contemporary Netherlands, 1980–2015). Amsterdam: Bert Bakker, 2013.

Weezel, M. van and L. Ornstein. *Frits Bolkestein. Portret van een liberale vrijbuiter.* (Frits Bolkestein. Portrait of a Liberal Freebooter). Amsterdam: Prometheus, 1999.

Westen, D. *The Political Brain. The Role of Emotion in Deciding the Fate of the Nation.* New York: Perseus Book Group, 2007.

Zalm, G. *De romantische boekhouder.* (The Romantic Accountant). Utrecht: Balans, 2009.

Zaslove, A. *The Re-Invention of the European Radical Right. Populism, Regionalism and the Italian Lega Nord.* Montreal: McGill-Queen's University Press, 2011.

Zúquete, J.P. 'The European Extreme-Right and Islam. New Directions'. *Journal of Political Ideologies* 10, 2008: 321–344.

Geert Wilders publications

Hirsi Ali, A. and G. Wilders. 'Steniging laat moslims koud' (Stoning Leaves Muslims Indifferent). *Trouw*, 20 March 2003.

Hirsi Ali, A. and G. Wilders. 'Het is tijd voor een liberale jihad' (It is Time for a Liberal Jihad'). *NRC Handelsblad*, 12 April 2003.

Hirsi Ali, A. and G. Wilders. 'Democratiseer het Midden Oosten' (Democratize the Middle East). *Trouw*, 27 April 2004.

Wilders, G. 'Stop de vakbondsmacht' (Curb the Unions' Power). *De Volkskrant*, 15 February 2001.

Wilders, G. *Kies Vrijheid. Een eerlijk antwoord. Inclusief Onafhankelijkheidsverklaring* (Choose Freedom. An Honest Answer. Including Declaration of Independence). [n.p.] Groep Wilders, 2005.

Wilders, G. *Marked for Death. Islam's War against the West and Me.* Washington, DC: Regnery Publishing, 2012.

Wilders, G. 'Islamification of Western Societies Threatens Everyone's Freedoms'. *The Australian*, 18 February 2013.

Wilders, G. and M. Bosma. 'Nederland en Vlaanderen horen bij elkaar' (The Netherlands and Flanders Belong Together). *NRC Handelsblad*, 31 July 2008.

Wilders, G. and M. Bosma. 'WC-eend adviseert Ter Horst' (untranslatable advertisement slogan, meaning 'Ter Horst advises herself'). *De Volkskrant*, 30 January 2010.

Party documents

Een Nieuw Realistische Visie (A New Realistic Vison). March 2006.

Klare Wijn (Clear Wine). April 2006.

Een Nieuwe Gouden Eeuw (A New Golden Century). April 2006.

Verkiezingspamflet Partij voor de Vrijheid (Election Pamphlet Party for Freedom). August 2006.

Verkiezingsprogramma Europees Parlement (Election Manifesto, European Parliament). 2009.

De Agenda van Hoop en Optimisme 2010–2015 (The Agenda of Hope and Optimism 2010–2015).

Hún Brussel, óns Nederland (Their Brussels, Our Netherlands). 2012.

Interviews

Oege Bakker, North Holland candidate. Chairman VvPVV.
Interview, 3 April, 2012.
Jhim van Bemmel, Member of Parliament 2010–2012
Interview, 20 November, 2012.
Arie-Wim Boer, States Provincial North Holland candidate, 2011
Interview, 3 February, 2012.
Louis Bontes, Member European Parliament 2009–2010, Member of Parliament 2010–2013
Interview, 26 March, 2015.
Cor Bosman, Member States Provincial Limburg 2011–2012
Interview, 27 August, 2012.
Johan Driessen, Member of Parliament 2010–2012; Geert Wilders' personal assistant 2008–2010
Interview, 21 May, 2015.
Jelle Hiemstra, Member States Provincial Friesland 2011
Interview, 1 February, 2012.
Martijn Kap, Member States Provincial North Brabant 2011
Interview, 18 January, 2012.
Joram van Klaveren, Member of Parliament 2010–2014
Interview, 21 May, 2015.
Frans van Rhee, Member of Parliament Drenthe 2011–2012

Interview, 14 June, 2012.
Gijs Schaap, Press Officer PVV 2008–2009
Interview, 21 May, 2015.
Bart Jan Spruyt, Director Edmund Burke Foundation, co-founder PVV 2004–2006
Interview, 13 August, 2012.
Geert Tomlow, Parliamentary elections candidate 2006. Member board VvPVV
Interview, 24 February, 2012.
Harm Uringa, Member States Provincial Limburg 2011
Interview, 2 February, 2012.
Anonymous I, 19 January 2012.
Anonymous II, 22 November 2012.
Anonymous III, 5 March 2015.
Anonymous IV, 2 April 2015.

Media coverage

Albers, J. 'Hoe Wilders over zijn eigen grens ging' (How Wilders Pushed Past his Own Limits). *Vrij Nederland*, 21 May 2014.
Blumenthal, M. 'The Sugar Mama of Anti-Muslim Hate'. *The Nation*, 13 July 2012.
Botje, H.E. and Th. Niemantsverdriet. 'De draai van Geert' (Wilders' U-turn). *Vrij Nederland*, 10 April 2010.
Chavannes, M. 'Wilders snuift in de Verenigde Staten conservatieve thema's op' (Wilders is Sniffing Conservative Themes in the United States). *NRC Handelsblad*, 15 January 2005.
Botje, H.E. 'Wie betalen Wilders?' (Who Pays Wilders?). *Vrij Nederland*, 14 November 2009.
De Boer, E. and J. Hoedeman. 'Hard blaffen en niet bijten' (Barking, no Biting). *De Volkskrant*, 22 October 1999.
De Boer, E. and T. Koele. 'Een rechtse directe' (A Right Jab). *De Volkskrant*, 20 November 2003.
De Hoog, T. 'De sterke wil van Wilders' (The Strong Will of Wilders). *Nieuw Israelitisch Weekblad*, 3 October 2005.
De Jong, A. 'De blonde engel kiest de aanval' ('The Blonde Angel Chooses to Attack'). *De Telegraaf*, 13 March, 1999.
'De onmogelijke missie van Geert Wilders' (The Impossible Mission of Geert Wilders). *HP De Tijd*, 5 February 2005.
'De vakantieplek van Geert Wilders' (The Holiday Destination of Geert Wilders). *Elsevier*, 6 July 2005.
De Vries, M. 'De wilde haren en jonge jaren van Geert Wilders' (The Wild Years of the Young Geert Wilders). *HP De Tijd*, 2 September 2009.
De Wever, R. 'Wilders' joodse, christelijke en anti-islamitische geldschieters' (Wilders' Jewish, Christian and Anti-Islamic Financiers). *Trouw*, 3 July 2012.
Derkzen, S. 'Jekyll & Hide'. *Vrij Nederland*, 27 June 2009.
Deutsch A. and M. Hosenball. 'US Groups Helped Fund Dutch Anti-Islam Politician'. *Reuters*, 10 September 2012.
Donkers, S. 'Alles is niks na Geert en Camiel' (After Geert and Camiel, There's Nothing Left). *Vrij Nederland*, 13 October 2012.
Hoedeman, J. and R. Meijer 'Alles voor Geerts gerief' (Everything to Please Geert). *De Volkskrant*, 22 February 2014.

156 Bibliography

Jansen, P. 'Geert Wilders: Mijn focus is altijd op Islam gericht' (Geert Wilders: My Focus Will Always Be on Islam). *De Telegraaf*, 28 February 2015.

Koelé, T. and M. Kruyt. 'Verliefd op Israel' (In Love With Israel). *De Volkskrant*, 10 April 2007.

Lammers, E. 'Het is leuk, die heftige reacties' (It is Fun, All These Fierce Reactions). *Trouw*, 17 December 1999.

Marbe, N., 'Ik ben van nature recalcitrant' (I Am Recalcitrant by Nature). *Vrij Nederland*, 31 July 2004.

Mat, J. 'Éen man, zeven gezichten' (One Man, Seven Faces). *NRC Handelsblad*, 19 June 2010.

Meeus, T.J. and H. Modderkolk. 'De gemaskeerde vergissingen van Geert Wilders' (The Concealed Mistakes of Geert Wilders). *NRC Handelsblad*, 3 July 2012.

Meeus, T.J. and G. Valk. 'De buitenlandse vrienden van Geert Wilders' (The Foreign Friends of Geert Wilders). *NRC Handelsblad*, 15 May 2010.

Meijer, R. 'Gedreven door ideeën en complotten' (Driven by Ideas and Conspiracies). *De Volkskrant*, 16 June 2008.

Niemöller, J. 'Geert Wilders: ik capituleer niet' (Geert Wilders: I Will Not Capitulate). *HP De Tijd*, 12 December 2007.

Soetenhorst, B. 'Geert Wilders: Ik ben geen extremist' (Geert Wilders: I am Not an Extremist). *Het Parool*, 31 December 2004.

Soetenhorst, B. 'Een roepende in de woestijn op het Binnenhof' (An Isolated Voice at the Binnenhof). *Het Parool*, 22 September 2001.

Van Deijl, F. 'Ik lust ze rauw' (I'll Eat Them Alive). *HP De Tijd*, 6 February 2004.

Van Leeuwen, L. 'Wreker van zijn Indische grootouders. De politieke roots van Geert Wilders' (Revenger of his Indonesian Grandparents. The Political Roots of Geert Wilders). *Groene Amsterdammer*, 2 September 2009.

Van Soest, H. 'VVD'er Wilders schopt iedereen naar zich toe'. *Rotterdams Dagblad*, 21 June 2001.

Visser, A. 'De tien geboden van Geert Wilders' (The Ten Commandments of Geert Wilders). *Trouw*, 16 October 2004.

Vrijsen, E. 'Wij worden de grootste' (We Will be the Biggest). *Elsevier*, 2 October 1999.

Vuijst, F. 'Op zoek naar dollars' (Searching for Dollars). *Vrij Nederland*, 13 June 2009.

Vuijsje, H. 'Deugt wel, deugt niet..'. (Right, Wrong). *NRC Handelsblad*, 16 January 2010.

Zwagerman, J. 'Links helpt Wilders door PVV kiezers te kleineren' (By Belittling PVV Voters the Left Helps Wilders'). *De Volkskrant*, 25 September, 2010.

Specific coverage on voters

'Amsterdam ontdekt PVV' (Amsterdam discovers PVV). *Het Parool*, 17 May 2009.

'Berghemse kiezers laten Wilders nu links liggen' (Voters in Berghem Are Now Ignoring Wilders). *Brabants Dagblad*, 12 September 2012.

Berkhout, K. and D. Pinedo. 'Israel-liefde Wilders verdeelt de sjoel ' (Wilders' Love for Israel Divides the Synagogue). *NRC Handelsblad*, 27 April 2010.

Broer, T. and S. Derkzen. 'Simpelveld: dan maar Wilders' (Simpelveld: in that Case Wilders). *Vrij Nederland*, 13 July 2007.

Broer, T. and S. Derkzen. 'Het land van Wilders' (The Country of Wilders). *Vrij Nederland*, 25 April 2009.

Broer, T. and S. Derkzen. 'Veertig procent steunt opvattingen Wilders' (Forty Percent Supports Wilders' Opinions). *Vrij Nederland*, 21 April 2009.

'Boze witte mannen' (Angry White Men). *De Limburger*, May 22 2010.

Derix, S., W. Luyendijk and J. Mat. 'Waarom Wilders' (Why Wilders). *NRC Handelsblad*, 26 September 2009.
Donkers, S. 'Alles is niks na Geert en Camiel' (After Geert and Camiel, There's Nothing Left). *Vrij Nederland*, October 13 2012.
Ellenbroek, E. 'Alleen CPN kwam op voor ons soort mensen' (Only the CPN Stood For Our Kind of People). *Trouw*, 6 June 2009.
Groen, J. and A. Kranenberg. 'Wilders heeft een angstige achterban' (Wilders has Anxious Followers). *De Volkskrant*, 20 February 2009.
Haegens, K. 'De martelaar van Venlo' (The Martyr of Venlo). *De Groene Amsterdammer*, 8 December 2006.
Jungmann, B. 'Wilders held van de familie Doorsnee' (Wilders: Hero of Family Average). *De Volkskrant*, 27 November 2004.
Kamerman, S. and G. Valk. 'Op zoek naar een politicus met lef' (Searching For a Courageous Politician). *NRC Handelsblad*, 13 December 2004.
Logtenberg, H. 'De stemmen van nieuw-rechts' (The Votes of the New Right). *Intermediair*, 8 April 2008.
Mat J. and L. Starink. 'Hoe God verdween uit het zuiden' (How God Disappeared From the South). *NRC Handelsblad*, 18 September 2010.
Nicolasen, L. 'In Volendam hebben ze wel wat anders aan hun hoofd' (In Volendam They Have Something Else on Their Minds). *De Volkskrant*, 21 March 2012.
'Nog altijd het volste vertrouwen in Wilders' (Still Absolute Confidence in Wilders). *NRC Handelsblad*, 16 November, 2010.
Penning, W. 'Wilders-kiezer is 'n blijvertje' (Wilders Voter is here to stay). *Algemeen Dagblad*, 30 March 2009.
'Pim sorry, Geert is er klaar voor' (Sorry Pim, Geert is ready now). *De Pers*, 14 April 2009.
'Stemmen zonder Wilders' (Voting without Wilders). *Elsevier*, 14 November 2009.
Ten Hove, J.M. 'Wild van Wilders' ('Wild of Wilders). *Reformatorisch Dagblad*, 11 July 2009.
Van der Bol, B. 'Ook het Haagse zand steunt de PVV' (The Hague Sand Also Supports the PVV). *NRC Handelsblad*, 26 February 2010.
Van der Linde, I. 'Wat maakt het uit wat ik stem' (What Does it Matter What I Vote). *Groene Amsterdammer*, 24 October 2012.
Van Houten, M. 'De kerkelijk aanhang van Wilders' (The Church-Going Supporters of Wilders). *Trouw*, 15 February 2010.
Van Houten, M. 'Zodra Geert wat zegt, liggen ze overhoop' (As Soon as Wilders Says Something, They are at Loggerheads). *Trouw*, 3 September 2010.
'Vuile was laat PVV-kiezer koud' (Dirty Laundry leaves PVV voter Indifferent). *Algemeen Dagblad*, 5 July 2012.
Walters, D. 'Alleen voor Wilders gaat Volendam naar de stembus' (Volendam Only Votes Because of Wilders). *NRC Handelsblad*, 6 June 2009.
'Wat bent u lief de laatste tijd' (You're So Sweet Lately). *De Limburger*, 25 February 2011.
'Wilders is onze man' (Wilders is Our Man). *De Volkskrant*, 4 June 2005.

Television

Wilders' wereld (Wilders' World). NPO, 5 July 2014.
'Profiel PVV stemmer' (PVV Voter Profile). *Een Vandaag*, 18 August 2007.

Bibliography

'De PVV in Urk' (The PVV in Urk). *Netwerk*, 9 June 2009.

'De zegetocht van de PVV' (The Triumphal March of the PVV). *Netwerk*, 5 June 2009.

'PVV en de Hofstad' (The PVV and the Residence). *Netwerk*, 29 January 2010.

'Almere in de ban van de PVV' (Almere Under the Spell of the PVV). *Netwerk*, 19 February 2010.

'Gemeenteraadsverkiezingen Venlo' (Venlo Municipal Elections). *Netwerk*, 16 September 2009.

'Wie wil Wilders' (Who Wants Wilders). *Netwerk*, 20 April 2009.

'Alexander Pechtold versus Henk en Ingrid' (Alexander Pechtold versus Henk and Ingrid). *Nieuwsuur*, 31 August 2012.

'De mening van de PVV'ers' (The Opinion of the PVV voters). *Nieuwsuur*, 30 April 2012.

'Henk en Ingrid in Spijk' (Henk and Ingrid in Spijk). *Zembla*, 23 October 2010.

Index

Aalberts, Chris 121–3, 125, 137
Aboutaleb, Ahmed 66
Achterberg, Peter 120, 132, 134, 136
AfD (Alternative für Deutschland) 79
Agema, Fleur xii, 60, 65, 69, 91, 94, 95, 99, 105, 144
Åkesson, Jimmie 79
Al Qaeida 11, 17, 30
Albayrak, Nebahat 66
American Enterprise Institute 21
Anne Frank Foundation 53
Annemans, Gerolf 55, 78
Anti-Fascist Action 95
anti-Islamic alarmism 14–18, 24–5, 29–38, 46, 52–8, 77–84, 98–100, 103–4, 120–1, 128, 140
Ariel Center for Policy Research 81
Arpaio, Joe 50
asylum seekers; *see also* refugees 4, 13, 45, 50, 54, 74, 84, 119–20
Ataka 77
Atkinson, Janice 79
Atlas Shrugs 81
Atwater, Lee 21
Australia Liberty Alliance 82
authoritarianism 48–51; *see also* Law and Order

Bachman, Michelle 82
Bakker, Oege 89, 90, 107, 146
Balkenende, Jan Peter 13, 14, 65, 69, 71, 85, 113, 144
Ban Ki-moon 80
Bat Ye'or (a.k.a. Giselle Littman) 34–8, 55, 59, 99, 100, 121, 140, 144
Bawer, Bruc 35–6
Beatrix, Queen 39, 74
Beliën, Paul 35, 81, 99, 144
Berlusconi, Silvio 1

Bloom, Alan 21
Blumenthal, Max 108
Boer, Arie Wim 108
Bolkestein, Frits 7–11, 16, 33, 37, 110, 133, 141, 142, 144
Bontes, Louis 71, 74, 75, 77, 83, 85, 86, 91, 93, 104, 108, 108, 144
Bos, Wouter 14, 85, 144
Bosland, Joost 110
Bosma, Martin xii, 20, 21, 24, 25, 28–44, 53, 55, 59, 60, 64, 67, 91–4, 98, 99, 102–9, 111, 128, 140, 142, 144
Bosman, Cor 108–9
Bovens, Mark 118, 132
Brandt, Willy 34
Breivik, Anders Behring 83, 86
Brinkman, Hero 24, 61, 66–9, 73, 75, 89, 90, 103, 108, 144
Brussels Journal 81, 144
Buchanan, Pat 21
Buruma, Ian 14, 26, 27
Bush, George W. 11, 16, 17, 24, 27, 69

Caldwell, Christopher 36, 59
Catholic People's Party (KVP) 2, 134, 145
CD (Centrum Democraten) 6, 67, 128, 144, 145
CDA 2, 5–10, 13, 14, 20, 37, 63, 71–176, 83, 85, 93, 101, 102, 112, 113, 119, 130, 134, 135, 144, 145
Centre Democrats *see* CD
Chávez, Hugo 44
Cheng, Sheren 60, 98
Chernick, Joyce 103, 104
Christian Union (ChristenUnie) 69, 102, 145
Churchill, Winston 80, 84
Clinton, Bill 10
Cohen, Job 144–6

Index

Condell, Pat 30, 58
consensus culture 5, 9, 12, 17, 124, 140
Counter Jihad Movement 81–108
cultural trauma 14–15, 142

D66 (Democraten 66) 6, 8, 9, 14, 25, 37, 68, 70, 85, 113, 116, 119–20, 123, 130, 145
Danish People's Party (DFP) 55, 71, 77–9, 87
De Gaulle, Charles 1
De Jong, Piet 71
De Korte, Gerard 118
De Koster, W. 120, 136
De Mos, Richard 133–4
De Roon, Raymond 93, 98, 99
De Ruyter, Michiel 45, 54
De Tocqueville, Alexis 24
De Voogd, Josse 115, 132, 136
Derks, Anton 134, 138
Dewinter, Filip. 55, 78, 79
dhimmi (-tude) 32–5, 69, 140
Die Freiheit 82
Dijkstal, Hans 16, 144, 145
diploma democracy 118, 132
direct democracy 23, 37, 39, 41, 44, 57, 124
DPES (Dutch Parliamentary Election Studies) 118–21, 125, 126, 136, 145
DPK (Democratic Political Turning Point) 89
Drees, Willem 47, 144
Driessen, Johan 70, 84, 86, 92, 100, 101, 104, 108, 109
Duyvendak, J.W. 19, 28

Edmund Burke Foundation 20–1, 144, 145
Eldad, Aryeh 56, 81
Emerson, Steve 22
English Defence League 83
eurabia-theory 29, 31–5, 99, 121, 144
Europe of Nations and Freedom 78–9
European Parliament 42, 43, 58, 63, 64, 77, 79, 98, 99, 100, 104, 110, 111, 140, 141, 144
European Union x, 18, 23, 32, 40–5, 54–7, 72–5, 80
Eyerman, Ron 15, 27, 142

Fallaci, Oriana 34, 36, 39, 99, 100, 140, 144
Farage, Nigel xi, 78
Farmers' Party 67
fascism xi, 6, 20, 30–3, 40, 44, 51–6, 87, 95, 126

Finns Party 77
First Chamber *see* Senate
Fitna (movie) 34, 66, 69, 79, 80, 82, 105
Fjordman (Peder Are Nøstvold Jensen) 35
Flemish Bloc/Flemish Interest *see* Vlaams Blok/Belang 46, 55–6, 65, 76–8, 82, 84
Fortuyn, Pim 11–20, 23–6, 30, 33, 38, 53–6, 67, 88, 99, 101, 125–9, 133, 141–5
Foreign Policy Research Institute 21
Forza Italia 1
FPÖ (Freiheitliche Partei Österreichs) 55–6, 76, 78, 82, 89, 135
Friends of the PVV Foundation 102, 103
Fritsma, Sietse 25, 98
Front National 56, 76–9, 82, 83, 86, 87

Gates of Vienna 81
Gatestone Institute 35, 81
GeenStijl 15, 66, 145
Geert Wilders Legal Defense Fund 103
Geller, Pamela 81, 82, 103
Geurtsen, Karen 91–4, 98, 108, 144
Geyl, Pieter 44
Giuliani, Rudolph 49
globalisation winners and losers 131–4
Gohmert, Louis 82
Gore, Al 140
Graus, Dion 24, 25, 51, 66, 69, 98, 99, 144
GreenLeft (GroenLinks) 6, 10, 25, 37, 69, 113, 116, 145
Gül, Abdullah 74

Haider, Jörg 55, 77, 81
Halsema, Femke 85
hate speech trial *see* trial on Geert Wilders
Hatikva Party 56, 82
Havel, Václav 77
Hedegaard, Lars 35, 81
Heinisch, Reinhard 73
Heritage Foundation 22
Hernandez, Marcial 80, 85, 86, 92–5, 107, 108, 144
Herre, Stefan 81
Heyn, Piet 43, 54
Hiemstra, Jelle 104, 108, 109
Hobbes, Thomas 21
Horowitz, David 103
House of Representatives (Second Chamber) x, xii, 5–10, 13, 16–19, 23, 25, 31, 35, 39–44, 50, 51, 58–60, 62–76, 79, 84–7, 89, 96–104, 107, 108, 111–13, 130, 132, 139–41, 145, 146
Houtman, Dick 132–4, 138
Huntington, Samuel 12

Identity, Sovereignty and Transparency 77
immigration 6–18, 22–5, 30–4, 38–49, 54, 55, 65–74, 77, 78, 98, 99, 111–12, 115–16, 119–31, 134–5, 141
International Free Press Society 35
International Socialists 95
Investigative Project for Terrorism 21–2
IPSOS Synovate 111, 112, 120, 133, 136, 140
Islamophobia *see* anti-Islamic alarmism
Israel 3–6, 9–10, 18, 20, 29, 34, 42, 45, 56–8, 61, 66, 79–83, 103–4

Janmaat, Hans 67, 128, 144, 145
Jansen, Hans 34–6, 53, 81, 100, 144
Jihad Watch 81

Kanne, Peter 120–1, 136
Kap, Martijn 108
Kerry, John 41
Kim Il-sung 91
King, Martin Luther 15
Kissinger, Henry 34
Kjaersgaard, Pia 55, 71
Klaus, Václav 78
Kok, Wim 7–10, 133, 144, 146
Komrij, Gerrit 36
Kriesi, Hanspeter 132, 138
Kristoll, Irving 21
KVP *see* Catholic People's Party
Kyle, Jon 82

Laclau, Ernesto 37
Laqueur, Walter 2
Law and Order 2, 22, 47–54, 57, 87, 98, 119–20, 129, 131, 133, 140
Le Pen, Jean Marie 55, 77, 81
Le Pen, Marine xi, 55, 56, 76–9
Leers, Gerd 74, 144
left church 11, 16, 38, 53, 67, 125
Lega Nord 76, 78, 82, 135
Lieberman, Avigdor 56, 57, 61
Likud 57
Limburg (province of) 1–4, 7, 24, 58, 73–5, 113–15, 120, 121, 134, 135
Lindh, Anna 15
Lipset, Seymour Martin 124
Littmann, Gisele (see Bat Ye'or)
LN (Liveable Netherlands) 12, 98, 125, 145
Lombard Street Research 102
LPF (Lijst Pim Fortuyn) 12–17, 20, 25, 35, 53, 54, 67, 71, 81, 87, 88, 98, 100, 103, 105, 112, 127, 133–5, 145

Lubbers, Ruud 7, 63, 144, 145

Madlener, Barry 24, 25, 71, 91, 98
Mak, Geert 57, 61, 127
Marfai, Krisztina 7
Marijnissen, Jan 10, 144, 146
Maroni, Roberto 78
May, Edward S. 81
media attention 12–17, 24, 25, 64, 67–70, 73–5, 77, 80, 82–4, 93–5, 101, 103, 105, 140–1
Meir, Golda 34
Merkel, Angela 69, 71
Messerschmidt, Morten 71
Middle East Forum 35
Moszkowicz, Bram 50
Motivaction 117
Mudde, Cas 54, 55, 59, 60
Müller, Wolfgang C. 62
Musterd, Sako 116

nationalism 7, 8, 29, 40–7, 140, 141
NATO 7, 40
neoconservatism 16–24, 38–9, 42, 55–6
Netherlands Antilles; *see also* Dutch Antilles 44–7, 66, 105, 122, 155
Noonan, Peggy 21
Norqvist, Grover 21
NSB (National Socialist Movement) 52, 145

Obama, Barack 69, 85

Palme, Olof 15
parliamentary support agreement 70–6
party finances 101–7
Party for Animals *see* PvdD
party organisation 1, 87–107, 140
Pauwels, Teun 127, 60, 118
Pearson, Malcolm 78, 82
Pechtold, Alexander 85, 123, 130, 137, 144, 145
Pedersen, Mogens 147
Pegida 82, 83
Peil.nl 111, 136, 140, 146
Perle, Richard 21
personal security protection Wilders xi, 15, 19–20, 22, 23, 58, 63, 67, 84, 89, 95, 96, 105, 142
Pi-news.net 81
Pim Fortuyn List *see* LPF
Pipes, Daniel 35, 103
Podhoretz, Norm 21
Poles Complaints Centre 74, 92, 105

populism 36–42, 40–58, 98, 99, 123–5, 140–2
Prins, Baukje 8
Proud of the Netherlands 111, 112, 144, 146
purple coalition 8–14, 53, 145, 146
Putin, Vladimir 69
Putnam, Robert 98
PvdA (Partij van de Arbeid) 6–14, 37, 63, 70, 75, 83, 85, 93, 101, 102, 113, 118, 119, 129, 130, 133, 144, 146
PvdD (Partij voor de Dieren) 51, 67, 101, 145

Q Society 82

racism xi, 20, 40, 43, 45, 46, 78, 95, 98, 122, 124, 127
Rassemblement du Peuple Francais 1
Reagan, Ronald 9, 21, 47
Reform Party 1
resentment 56, 126–8
Robinson, Peter 21
Roemer, Emil 146
Rooduijn, Matthijs 125, 137
Rosenwald, Nina 103, 104
Ross Perot, Henry 1
Rove, Karl 21
Rumsfeld, Donald 10
Rutte, Mark 25, 58, 71–6, 83, 85, 92, 113, 144, 146

Saleem, Rana 98
Sarkozy, Nicholas 69, 85
Second Chamber *see* House of Representatives
Senate (First Chamber) 39, 58, 70, 73, 87, 98, 101, 145, 146
Scheffer, Paul 129, 137
Schinkel, Willem 127, 137
Schinkelshoek, Jan 66–8
Schumacher, Gijs 125, 137
SGP (Staatkundig Gereformeerde Partij) 97, 146
Shrum, Bob 21
Sloterdijk, Peter 24
SP (Socialistische Partij) 10, 27, 65, 69, 88, 95, 101, 113, 118, 119, 131–5, 140, 144, 146
Spencer, Robert 35, 81, 82, 103
Spruyt, Bart Jan 20–5, 28–30, 39, 93, 96, 104, 105, 108, 144, 145
Spruyt, Bram 124, 132, 137, 138
Stadtkewitz, René 82

States Provincial 58, 63, 64, 73, 96–100, 104, 110, 111, 124, 145, 146
Steyn, Marc 36, 59
Strauss, Leo 21, 24
Strøm, Kaare 62
SVP (Schweizerische Volkspartei) 55
Swedish Democrats 76, 78, 82

taqqiya 32, 33, 111, 140
Ter Braak, Menno 126
Thatcher, Margaret 9
TNS Nipo 11, 120, 121, 146
Tomlow, Geert 25, 89, 90, 92, 94, 108
trial of Geert Wilders 50–1

UKIP (United Kingdom Independence Party) 77–9, 82, 135
Uringa, Harm 108–9

Van Agt, Dries 71, 145
Van Bemmel, Jhim 60, 86, 89, 92, 94, 99, 107, 108, 144
Van de Beek, Johan 120, 131, 136
Van der Linde, Irene 115, 136
Van Dijck, Teun 25, 98
Van Gageldonk, Paul 120, 131, 136
Van Gent, Wouter 116, 136
Van Gogh, Theo 14, 15, 19, 21, 33, 35, 54, 67, 111, 135, 142, 144
Van Klaveren, Joram 60, 91, 94, 95, 99, 100, 108, 144
Van Leeuwen, Lizzy 2, 26
Van Rhee, Frans 108, 109
Verdonk, Rita 25, 27, 85, 111, 112, 125, 136, 142, 144, 146
Verhagen, Maxime 71, 130, 137, 144
Vermeulen, Urbain 35
Vlaams Blok/Vlaams Belang *see* Flemish Bloc/Interest
VVD (People's Party for Freedom and Democracy) 5–27, 30, 37, 41, 47, 53, 63, 67, 70–6, 83, 85, 88–92, 98–101, 111–13, 117–20, 129–30, 133, 135, 137, 141, 144, 146
VvPVV (Association for the PVV) 90, 107, 146

Wansink, Hans 141–2
Warraq, Ibn 35
welfare state 5, 9, 11–12, 16, 19, 22, 23, 32, 41, 47, 53–7, 78, 99, 113, 132
Westen, Drew 128
Wilders Group 19–23, 87, 96, 97, 105
Wilders Group Association 87, 102

Wilders Group Foundation 87, 102
Wille, Anchrit 118, 132
Willem Alexander, Crown-Prince/King 10

YIsrael Beiteinu 56

Zalm, Gerrit 17, 146
Zorreguieta, Máxima (Queen) 10, 39, 135
Zwaan, Ton 127

Taylor & Francis eBooks

Helping you to choose the right eBooks for your Library

Add Routledge titles to your library's digital collection today. Taylor and Francis ebooks contains over 50,000 titles in the Humanities, Social Sciences, Behavioural Sciences, Built Environment and Law.

Choose from a range of subject packages or create your own!

Benefits for you

- Free MARC records
- COUNTER-compliant usage statistics
- Flexible purchase and pricing options
- All titles DRM-free.

REQUEST YOUR FREE INSTITUTIONAL TRIAL TODAY

Free Trials Available
We offer free trials to qualifying academic, corporate and government customers.

Benefits for your user

- Off-site, anytime access via Athens or referring URL
- Print or copy pages or chapters
- Full content search
- Bookmark, highlight and annotate text
- Access to thousands of pages of quality research at the click of a button.

eCollections – Choose from over 30 subject eCollections, including:

Archaeology	Language Learning
Architecture	Law
Asian Studies	Literature
Business & Management	Media & Communication
Classical Studies	Middle East Studies
Construction	Music
Creative & Media Arts	Philosophy
Criminology & Criminal Justice	Planning
Economics	Politics
Education	Psychology & Mental Health
Energy	Religion
Engineering	Security
English Language & Linguistics	Social Work
Environment & Sustainability	Sociology
Geography	Sport
Health Studies	Theatre & Performance
History	Tourism, Hospitality & Events

For more information, pricing enquiries or to order a free trial, please contact your local sales team:
www.tandfebooks.com/page/sales

Routledge
Taylor & Francis Group

The home of Routledge books

www.tandfebooks.com